Communications in Computer and Information Science 913

Commenced Publication in 2007
Founding and Former Series Editors:
Phoebe Chen, Alfredo Cuzzocrea, Xiaoyong Du, Orhun Kara, Ting Liu,
Krishna M. Sivalingam, Dominik Ślęzak, Takashi Washio, and Xiaokang Yang

More information about this series at http://www.springer.com/series/7899

Changjun Hu · Wen Yang ·
Congfeng Jiang · Dong Dai (Eds.)

High-Performance Computing Applications in Numerical Simulation and Edge Computing

ACM ICS 2018 International Workshops, HPCMS and HiDEC
Beijing, China, June 12, 2018
Revised Selected Papers

 Springer

Editors
Changjun Hu
University of Science and Technology
Beijing, China

Wen Yang
China Institute of Atomic Energy
Beijing, China

Congfeng Jiang
Hangzhou Dianzi University
Hangzhou, China

Dong Dai
Computer Science
Texas Tech University
Lubbock, USA

ISSN 1865-0929   ISSN 1865-0937 (electronic)
Communications in Computer and Information Science
ISBN 978-981-32-9986-3   ISBN 978-981-32-9987-0   (eBook)
https://doi.org/10.1007/978-981-32-9987-0

This Springer imprint is published by the registered company Springer Nature Singapore Pte Ltd.
The registered company address is: 152 Beach Road, #21-01/04 Gateway East, Singapore 189721, Singapore

Preface

This volume contains the papers presented at two different workshops, held in conjunction with the 32nd ACM International Conference on Supercomputing (ICS 2018) during June 12–15, in Beijing, China. ICS is the premier international forum in high-performance computing systems and has evolved into one of the leading forums for scientists and engineers to present their latest studies in this rapidly changing field, focusing on architecture, productivity, systems, and applications.

High-performance computing (HPC) is a paradigm which uses the parallel processing technologies for running advanced application programs efficiently, reliably, and quickly. The selected workshops present research results on facilitating compute- or data-intensive applications, especially in the fields of edge computing and numerical simulation. In addition to traditional techniques in HPC programming, new ideas are introduced from emerging research areas like big data and deep learning.

This volume focuses on two topics, covering the accepted papers of the two workshops HiDEC 2018 and HPCMS 2018. A description of each workshop is given below.

The International Workshop on HPC Supported Data Analytics for Edge Computing (HiDEC 2018) is a forum for both academics and industry practitioners to share their ideas and experiences, discuss challenges and recent advances, introduce developments and tools, identify open issues, present applications and enhancements for both edge computing and high-performance computing systems and report state-of-the-art and in-progress research, leverage each other's perspectives, and identify new/emerging trends in this important area. It was held for diverse constituency, including top researchers, engineers, students, entrepreneurs, and government officials, to discuss the opportunities and challenges that arise from rethinking HPC architectures and embracing edge computing.

Edge computing is a new computing paradigm, which is closer to the data source, fusing network, computing, storage, and application, to provide more real-time and intelligent services. These two computing paradigms are complementary; the edge computing can be more powerful and HPC can be more real-time after combination. We believe that high-performance computing and edge computing will benefit from close interaction between researchers and industry practitioners.

HiDEC 2018 was organized as a half-day workshop and received 22 full paper submissions. After a thorough reviewing process, only 8 submissions were accepted for publication in these proceedings, which represents a 36% acceptance rate.

The International Workshop on High Performance Computing for Advanced Modeling and Simulation (HPCMS) is a relatively new workshop series which aims to facilitate and speed up modeling and simulation on supercomputers. One of the key goals of HPCMS is to provide engineers and computer scientists with a dedicated place where they can share their research experience in interdisciplinary collaboration, especially in dealing with multi-physics and multi-scale simulations. HPCMS 2018 - The Second International Workshop on High Performance Computing for Advanced Modeling and Simulation in Nuclear Energy and Environmental Science - was the second edition of HPCMS. After a successful event in Texas, USA, in 2015, it was held on June 12, 2018, in Beijing, China, and was hosted by Computer Network Information Center of Chinese Academy of Sciences, University of Science and Technology Beijing, and China Institute of Atomic Energy. In conjunction with ICS 2018, HPCMS 2018 played a complementary role in the areas of computational models and optimization techniques, providing an opportunity to bring together experts in numerical simulation and high-performance computing.

HPCMS 2018 focused on efficient solution of multi-physical problems on high-performance computers. The challenges have been proposed in many different areas of engineering, such as virtual nuclear reactors, hydrology, and meteorology, due to their compute- or data-intensive nature. To leverage the power of supercomputers for faster simulations and new findings, innovative mathematical models, parallel algorithms, high-performance computing tools, and machine learning were discussed.

HPCMS 2018 was organized as a full-day workshop and received 40 full paper submissions. After a thorough reviewing process, 12 submissions were accepted for publication in these proceedings, which represents a 30% acceptance rate. Each paper received three independent reviews.

We would like to express our thanks to the many people who helped to make HiDEC 2018 and HPCMS 2018 such successful events. Firstly, thanks to all authors who submitted their contributions to HiDEC 2018 and HPCMS 2018. Many thanks also to the review work performed by the members of the Program Committee, as well as additional reviewers, and to webmasters Yeliang Qiu (Hangzhou Dianzi University, China) and Genshen Chu (University of Science and Technology Beijing, China).

We wish to thank Xiaolan Yao, Celine Chang, Jane Li, Leonie Kunz, etc. from Springer for their patience and support in finalizing the proceedings.

Finally, we would like to acknowledge EasyChair for facilitating all activities starting from the submission of the papers to the preparation of the proceedings.

July 2018

Congfeng Jiang
Dong Dai
Changjun Hu
Wen Yang

Organization

HiDEC General Chairs

Congfeng Jiang	Hangzhou Dianzi University, China
Dong Dai	Texas Tech University, USA

HiDEC Program Chairs

Jian Wan	Zhejiang University of Science and Technology, China
Jilin Zhang	Hangzhou Dianzi University, China

HiDEC Program Committee Members

Gangyong Jia	Hangzhou Dianzi University, China
Woosung Jung	Chungbuk National University, South Korea
Peng Di	University of New South Wales, Australia
Xiaofei Zhang	Hong Kong University of Science and Technology, SAR China
Jue Wang	Computer Network Information Center, CAS, China
Jian Zhao	Institute for Infocomm Research, Singapore
Youhuizi Li	Hangzhou Dianzi University, China
Tingwei Chen	Liaoning University, China
Hui Ma	Victoria University of Wellington, New Zealand
Zujie Ren	Hangzhou Dianzi University, China

HiDEC Publicity Chair

Yuyu Yin	Hangzhou Dianzi University, China

HiDEC Webmaster

Yeliang Qiu	Hangzhou Dianzi University, China

HPCMS Organizing Committee

Xuebin Chi	Computer Network Information Center, CAS, China
Linwang Wang	Lawrence Berkeley National Laboratory, USA
Andreas W. Goetz	San Diego Supercomputer Center, USA
Fei Gao	University of Michigan, USA
Wen Yang	China Institute of Atomic Energy, China
Jose Luis	Vazquez-Poletti Universidad Complutense de Madrid, Spain

Junchao Zhang	Argonne National Laboratory, USA
Changjun Hu	University of Science and Technology Beijing, China
Zhong Jin	Computer Network Information Center, CAS, China
Jue Wang	Computer Network Information Center, CAS, China

HPCMS Program Committee

Yang Wang	Pittsburgh Supercomputing Center, USA
Yunquan Zhang	Institute of Computing Technology, CAS, China
Zhonghua Lu	Computer Network Information Center, CAS, China
Dmitry Terentyev	SCK-CEN, Nuclear Materials Institute, Germany
Dongsheng Xu	Institute of Metal Research, CAS, China
Guangming Tan	Institute of Computing Technology, CAS, China
Guohui Li	Dalian Institute of Chemical Physics, CAS, China
Jian Zhang	Computer Network Information Center, CAS, China
Jianjiang Li	University of Science and Technology Beijing, China
Peng Di	University of New South Wales, Australia
Shigang Li	Institute of Computing Technology, CAS, China
Xiaofei Zhang	Hong Kong University of Science and Technology, SAR China
Xinfu He	China Institute of Atomic Energy, China
Yangang Wang	Computer Network Information Center, CAS, China
Zhi Zeng	Hefei Institutes of Physical Science, CAS, China

HPCMS Additional Reviewers

Cao, Qian
Chen, Wei
Cheng, Yongqiang
Deng, Huiqiu
Deng, Sungen
Feng, Yangde
Han, Zhijie
He, Xijun
He, Xinfu
Hu, Ying
Hu, Yun
Li, Jianjiang
Li, Shigang

Liu, Yuan
Nie, Ningming
Shi, Peng
Wang, Xuesong
Wu, Baodong
Wu, Mingyu
Wu, Shi
Yang, Hongwei
Zhang, Jilin
Zhang, Xiaoming
Zhao, Minfu
Zhou, Chunbao

Contents

HPC Supported Data Analytics for Edge Computing

Towards Computation Offloading in Edge Computing: A Survey

Xiaolan Cheng[1,2], Xin Zhou[1,2], Congfeng Jiang[1,2(✉)], and Jian Wan[3]

[1] Key Laboratory of Complex Systems Modeling and Simulation,
Hangzhou Dianzi University, Hangzhou 310018, China
cjiang@hdu.edu.cn
[2] School of Computer Science and Technology, Hangzhou Dianzi University,
Hangzhou 310018, China
[3] School of Information and Electronic Engineering,
Zhejiang University of Science and Technology, Hangzhou 310023, China

Abstract. The explosive growth of massive data generation from Internet of Things in industrial, agricultural and scientific communities has led to a rapid increase in cloud data centers for data analytics. The ubiquitous and pervasive demand for near-data processing urges the edge computing paradigm in recent years. Edge computing is promising for less network backbone bandwidth usage and thus less data center side processing, as well as enhanced service responsiveness and data privacy protection. Computation offloading plays a crucial role in network packets transmission and system responsiveness through dynamic task partitioning between cloud data centers and edge servers and edge devices. In this paper a thorough literature review is conduct to reveal the state-of-the-art of computation offloading in edge computing. Various aspects of computation offloading, including energy consumption minimization, Quality of Services (QoS), and Quality of Experiences (QoE) are surveyed. Resource scheduling approaches, gaming and tradeoffing among system performance and system overheads for offloading decision making are also reviewed.

Keywords: Edge computing · Computation offloading · Game theory ·
Resource scheduling · Task partitioning · Edge-Cloud collaboration

1 Introduction

The traditional cloud computing model is a service provisioning model that provides access to computing, network, and storage services in the cloud data centers for scalable distributed computing capabilities. From the beginning, cloud computing has changed the way of people's life and work, over the past few decades, from service offerings to infrastructure cloud computing has changed dramatically. Varghese *et al.* [1] introduced the development of cloud computing from cloudlet, ad hoc cloud, multi-cloud, heterogeneous cloud, micro-cloud, explore the development and advantages of four emerging cloud computing architectures which include fog and mobile edge computing, volunteer computing, serverless computing and software-defined computing. Besides, the author also predicts the impact of future cloud computing on the

© Springer Nature Singapore Pte Ltd. 2019
C. Hu et al. (Eds.): HPCMS 2018/HiDEC 2018, CCIS 913, pp. 3–15, 2019.
https://doi.org/10.1007/978-981-32-9987-0_1

Internet of Things, big data computing, service space, and autonomous learning systems and outlines the challenges of developing the next cloud computing system that include how to ensure the security and reliability of cloud systems, how to build a sustainable cloud infrastructure, and how to provide efficient resource management strategies.

With the explosion of data, relying on the traditional cloud computing model will generate huge network delays and can't meet real-time, privacy protection and the requirements of energy consumption for mobile data transmission and computing, so many emerging technologies have paved the way for big data. Fog computing is proposed as a new cloud computing model closing to edge device, migrating the tasks of cloud computing center to network edge device, and providing storage, computing, and networking services between end devices and cloud computing centers. Fog computing as a complement of traditional cloud computing models and the combination of fog-cloud has attracted lots of attention in mitigating the potential of IoT services and new resource sharing, so fog-cloud integration provides a foundation for creating a new highly heterogeneous computing and network architecture.

Ramirez *et al.* [2] evaluated the potential benefits of F2C (Fog-to-Cloud) architecture in dynamic service scenarios, including response time of service, power consumption, network bandwidth usage, and the probability of service outage. The results proved that compared to the traditional cloud, the combined fog-to-cloud architecture brings significant performance benefits. Masip-Bruin *et al.* [3] compared two existing hierarchical resource architecture models (OpenFog RA, F2C) and aiming at the problems of cloud computing and fog computing in resource continuity and collaborative management, a distributed management framework is proposed to guarantee resource continuity within a layered architecture effectively.

The rapid development of the Internet of Things (IoT), the demand for real-time data from business, and the expectations of users for high-quality services are important reasons for the rapid development of edge computing. More and more smart devices and sensors are connected to the Internet of Things, data generation and consumption are concentrated to the edge of the network gradually, which leads edge computing used in various fields widely. As we all know, the application of an information technology is the most direct and effective way to test whether the technology is valuable, therefore, only through the instantiation application of edge computing, can we find various problems and opportunities about it, while there are many research cases about edge computing, such as Internet of Things, smart home, smart city, smart home and so on. Computation offloading is an important part of edge computing which can specify different offloading strategies according to the actual application scenario, such as when to uninstall, where to uninstall, how to uninstall, which part to uninstall, etc. and get a balance between energy consumption and system performance finally. Computation offloading method is also a very important part of edge computing and existing computation offloading methods include game and cooperation between edge and cloud, heuristic offloading and so on.

The reminder of this paper is organized as follows. In Sect. 2, we introduce the edge computing concepts. Then we survey some work on Edge-Cloud collaboration in Sect. 3, and we evaluate the work on decision making of computation offloading in

Sect. 4. The computing offloading strategies are discussed in Sect. 5. Finally, we summarize the survey of state-of-the-art of computation offloading and identify future work in Sect. 6.

2   The Edge Computing Paradigm

2.1   Architecture

The data generated by various applications running in the edge computing environment is not only very large in scale, but also has obvious heterogeneity, so the traditional middleware software can't complete computing tasks effectively, it is especially important to develop new system architecture suitable for edge computing environments. Some researchers hope to implement dynamic management of resources and on-demand scheduling of computing tasks by introducing a new edge operating system. By studying the edge operating system architecture deployed in smart homes, Shi [4], an edge computing advocate, proposes the challenges of reliability, isolation, scalability, and differentiation that may be faced when designing new architectures and operating systems in edge computing environments and the corresponding solution.

The communication between edge devices and cloud data centers is affected by various factors such as transmission distance and network bandwidth. Therefore, ensuring the service quality of edge devices has always been the research focus in cloud computing, and it also is the important driving force promoting the generation and development of other computing models such as edge computing. Offloading the tasks compute-intensive and delay-sensitive to the edge or nearby cloud is an effective way to guarantee user service quality in edge computing mode. Liu *et al.* [5] attempt to find the correct trade-off relationship between fog energy calculation, energy consumption, execution delay and offloading cost, and proposed an optimization strategy for optimizing three indicators simultaneously. Simulation experiments proved that the joint optimization strategy can guarantee Edge devices provide better quality of service.

2.2   Computing Model

Figure 1 shows the traditional cloud computing model, the data producers transmit the generated source data to the cloud while the terminal devices such as computers, mobile phones, and tablets send requests to the cloud center to obtain data. However, with the rapid increase of IoT devices' number, lots of mobile devices and applications needs more stringent requirements on service quality and real-time about data processing. This cloud-edge service model generates high network communication negatives and service delays and the problems about privacy and energy consumption during data transmission are difficult to control.

The problems in the traditional cloud computing model promoting the generation of fog computing proposed in 2012 by Cisco who defined fog computing as a highly virtualized computing platform for migrating cloud computing center tasks to network edge devices. As shown in Fig. 2, fog computing centralizes data storage, processing, and applications into devices on the edge network, eliminates the need to save all of the

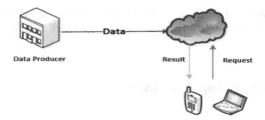

Fig. 1. Traditional cloud computing model

data to the cloud data center and adds an intermediate layer between the terminal device and the data center. The intermediate layer consists of fog servers deployed at the edge of the network to reduce the communication between cloud data centers and edge devices and reduce the bandwidth load and power consumption of the backbone links.

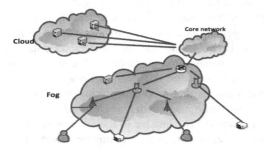

Fig. 2. Fog calculation model

Figure 3 shows another new computation model, edge computing, Unlike traditional cloud computing, that performs computations at the edge of the network and extends computing, networking, and storage capabilities from the cloud to the edge of the network, exploits the computing power of edge endpoints fully, converges computing, networking, storage, and caching capabilities close to end devices or data sources, and performs some or all of the computing tasks nearby, handles private data, reduces cloud center computing and transmission load, and achieves lower latency and power consumption. Shi *et al.* [6] believe that edge computing and fog computing have great similarities, but the difference is that fog computing focuses on the management of back-end distributed shared resources, while in addition to the infrastructure and edge devices, edge computing emphasizes the design and implementation of edge intelligence, further extends the processing power to the data end, and the real-time processing of data is done by devices in the edge network.

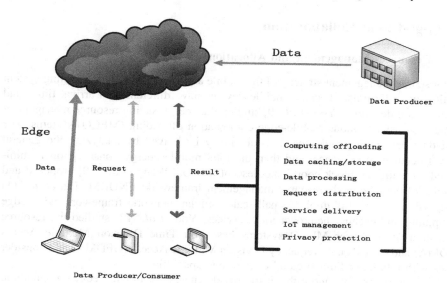

Fig. 3. Edge calculation model

2.3 Programming Model

In cloud computing, users can write and compile code on the target platform and then run it in the cloud server, so users don't need to know the infrastructure. The edge computing model is different from cloud computing. The tasks in edge computing can be divided into several subtasks, the task functions can be migrated to different edge devices for execution, and the execution of the task needs to meet the mobility, which means that the task migration is a necessary condition for data processing on the edge device. Data Distribution: It is both a requirement for the edge computing model to process data sets and a feature of edge computing.

In order to the limited resources of edge devices that can handle more tasks in edge computing scenarios on the object device, Li *et al.* [7] designed a lightweight programming language, EveryLite. The experiment result show that compared to Jerry-Script and Lua respectively, the execution time of EveryLite is lower 77% and 74%, and the memory footprint is 18.9% and 1.4%. Therefore, the programming model under the edge computing scene has a lot of research space, and the demand is urgent. Zhang *et al.* [8] proposed a firework model (Firework) that is a programming model based on edge calculation, which mainly includes Firework manager and Firework node. In the era of Internet of Everything, data production and consumption are migrated to edge devices, which adding large data distributed sharing and processing, besides, private data can be processed on data stakeholder devices that are different fireworks model nodes.

3 Edge-Cloud Collaboration

3.1 Resources Management and Allocation

The resource management strategy of the mobile asynchronous edge computing system is difficult to formulate because mobile devices have different data arrival times and computation deadlines. You *et al.* [9] studied the energy-saving resource management strategy of asynchronous mobile-edge computation offloading (MECO) systems. The best data partitioning and time division policy is derived by analyzing the general arrival detail date sequence, and then the total mobile energy consumption is minimized by using the block coordinate descent method. Wang *et al.* [10] proposed and developed the edge node resource management framework: ENORM. Tan *et al.* [11] designed a virtual full-duplex small-scale cellular network framework with edge computing and caching heterogeneous services. You *et al.* [12] studied the resource allocation of multiuser MECO systems based on Time Division Multiple Access (TDMA) and Orthogonal Frequency Division Multiple Access (OFDMA) and consider cases with infinite or limited cloud computing capabilities.

It is very expensive and difficult to provide energy for moving edge computation. Although there are many advantages for the offsite renewable energy is used to power the mobile edge calculation, the intermittent and unpredictable nature of renewable energy poses a huge challenge for high quality unloading services. In order to solve this problem, Yu *et al.* [13] describe the problem as a Markov decision process and proposed an efficient online resource-based reinforcement resource management algorithm which can reduce system service latency and operating costs by real-time learning of the best strategies for dynamic job offloading and edge server provisioning. Unlike traditional reinforcement learning algorithms, this online learning algorithm achieves high learning rate and runtime performance through decomposition value iteration and reinforcement learning.

3.2 Task Partitioning

Which part of the task is offloaded to the edge, which part is offloaded to the cloud, and which part is left to be executed locally. It is a good way to optimize the application using the compute partition. Much of the work focused on partitioning applications from the perspective of mobile users currently which often optimize individual mobile users to minimize the cost of execution of time or energy consumption on the device.

Qiu *et al.* [14] proposed an optimization algorithm to reduce the energy consumption of the data center by reasonably scheduling virtual machines. Wang *et al.* [15] proposed a computation offloading scheme, they calculated the optimal program partition for a set of training execution options, and then determines which partition to be used at runtime, for the case where the optimal program partition varies with different execution options, and also implements the computation shunt scheme in GCC. Yang *et al.* [16] proposed and developed the Joint Computing Partitioning and Resource Allocation Problem (JCPRP) for delay-sensitive applications in the field of mobile edge clouds for the first time, and designed an efficient heuristic method - multidimensional search and adjustment (MDSA) to solve this problem. Niu *et al.* [17]

proposed a bandwidth-based partitioning scheme to improve static partitioning and avoid the high cost of dynamic partitioning.

4 Decision Making of Computation Offloading

4.1 What to Offload

The Internet of Things will connect a large number of heterogeneous devices with powerful computing power, but for many of these devices, local computing resources are not enough to run complex applications. A possible strategy for resolving these problems is to enable resource-constrained mobile devices to offload their energy-intensive tasks to other servers with more resourceful. Regarding what to offload, we have summarized the work of others.

Yuan et al. [18] used a representative ecommerce benchmark and studied many partitioning strategies extensively and find that offloading and caching on edge proxy servers can achieve significant advantages without migrating the database to the vicinity of the client, a 2–3x delay reduction can be achieved in the typical user boring mode and network conditions. To alleviate the pressure of rapid growth in demand for caching and computing services, Zhou et al. [19] proposed a new information-centric heterogeneous network framework for content caching and computing. Lin et al. [20] pointed out that edge computing has become an important technology for delivering Web content to growing users via the Internet. Kumar et al. [21] proposed the problem of offloading computation to save energy and the difference between cloud computing and existing models is the adoption of virtualization technology which allows service providers to run any application from a different client on a virtual machine without managing the programs running on the server.

4.2 When to Offload

With the popularity of smart mobile devices, users have higher requirements for the computing power of mobile devices, while the research existing on mobile computing offloading defaults to smart computing devices that use fixed computing speeds, which are not optimal for mobile devices. To solve this problem, Wang et al. [22] explored dynamic voltage-frequency adjustment (DVFS). They introduce dynamic voltage-frequency adjustment technology into the computation offloading problem of smart mobile devices, which enable smart mobile devices to adjust computational speeds based on computation demands dynamically to reduce energy consumption and computation time. Ko et al. [23] proposed a real-time data prefetching architecture for mobile computing offloading based on task level computing prefetching and cloud computing simultaneously, which control the size of the corresponding prefetching data to minimize the energy consumption by dynamically selecting the prefetching task, and this real time prefetching technique avoids excessive data offloading but retains the advantage of reducing program execution time and power consumption through prediction.

4.3   Where to Offload

A good offloading strategy requires both high service performance and minimum power consumption. The choice of the destination of the offloading is based on the following aspects. One is based on the type of computation offloading tasks, the second is according to the system status.

Effective offloading decisions can infer when and where offloading will improve performance. In order to make efficient offloading decisions, many researchers have proposed a variety of solutions to determine when and where to perform computational offloading. The problem is that making such an unloading decision relies on monitoring several metric parameters periodically, but these operations usually are computation intensive tasks that can cause additional overhead when running on a mobile device. In this regard, Rego et al. [24] proposed a new method for defining an offloading strategy using a decision tree to examine the offloading decision based on the decision tree, but all computation intensive operations related to the offloading decision creation are transferred to the remote server for execution, while the mobile device only needs to parse the constructed decision tree previously. Meurisch et al. [25] proposed a new method of making offloading decisions. First, detect unknown available offloading systems, such as nearby edge nodes, cloudlets, or remote clouds, in an energy efficient manner at runtime to make better offloading decisions. The experimental results show that the Meurisch's solution can predict the performance of the unknown offloading system after running a micro-task that takes two milliseconds successfully, with an accuracy of 85.5%. In virtualized systems, different hypervisor has different energy efficiency even when the same applications are executed and provisioned on top of it [26]. Therefore, energy efficiency of targeted platform must also be considered when deciding where to offloading.

4.4   Tradeoff Between Computation and Communication

Saving energy and enhancing processing power are the benefits of computing offloading to mobile devices, but communication between mobile devices and edge nodes and cloud servers can cause certain execution delays, which can affect program performance. Therefore, the balance between computing and communication is critical to the development of computing offloading. Jiang et al. [27] optimized inter-VM I/O communication with shared memory. Wang et al. [28] developed a joint optimization problem that uses offloading to reduce the energy consumption of mobile devices while minimizing application execution latency. They described the problem as MinED and modeled it as a 0–1 integer linear programming (ILP) problem and give the optimal solution for the polynomial time based on weighted double matching for special cases where there is sufficient residual energy on the mobile device and each application requires the same amount of resources.

5 Examples of Computation Offloading Approaches

5.1 Gaming and Cooperation Based Offloading Between Edge and the Cloud

In the application of the in-vehicle system, the service can be improved by computation offloading, however, in the case of traffic intensive, the MEC server may become a bottleneck affecting the quality of the offloading service due to computation limitations. To solve this problem, Zhang *et al.* [29] proposed a layered cloud-based VEC offloading framework that compensates for the shortcomings of the MEC server's computation resources by sharing backup servers nearby.

Some literature focuses on offloading computations to local edge servers, but there is a potential for local edge servers to be unwilling to participate in computation offloading, which requires better incentives to stimulate cloud service operators and edge server owners to participate in computation offloading. Liu *et al.* [30] regarded the economic interaction between cloud service operators and edge server owners as a Stackelberg game, which enable cloud service operators to allocate computation based on the valuation of edge servers to maximize the benefit of cloud service operators and edge servers. Regarding offloading of competing users on shared channels, Meskar *et al.* [31] studied a group of mobile users using cloud computing offloading who offload computing tasks to the cloud server through shared transport channels to reduce energy consumption on the shared channel. Chen *et al.* [32] used game theory to solve such problems, they propose that game theory is a useful framework for designing decentralized mechanisms first which enables mobile device users in the system to self-organize into satisfactory computational offload decisions, and the self-organizing function can add maintainability to the mobile cloud computing system automatic alleviate the heavy burden of complex centralized management of the cloud. Chen *et al.* [33] study the multi-user computing offloading problem of mobile edge cloud computing in multi-channel wireless interference environment, proposes a game theory method for computing unloading decision problems among multiple mobile device users for mobile edge cloud computing, and design a distributed computing offloading algorithm.

5.2 Heuristics Based Offloading

The development of an online offloading strategy is a difficult problem. Jia *et al.* [34] introduced an online task offload algorithm in order to minimize the execution time of applications on mobile devices. The starting point of the algorithm is that if a task is unloaded, the tasks adjacent to it may also be unloaded. In addition, you can reduce the execution time of your tasks by offloading tasks into the cloud, maximizing parallelism between clouds and mobile devices. They found that sequential tasks can be offloaded to the cloud as best tasks. For parallel tasks, load balancing heuristics can be used to offload tasks into the cloud to maximize parallelism between mobile and cloud.

5.3   Optimization Based Offloading

In addition to the classical computation offloading methods mentioned above, researchers also proposed a variety of computation offloading schemes for different application scenarios and research directions. When designing the computation offloading methods in mobile cloud computing scenario, Deng *et al.* [35] designs a new offloading strategy by using the optimization method of genetic algorithm, and solves the above three problems by adding dependencies between components, designing the moving model and introducing fault tolerance mechanism. For smartphone usage scenarios, Lin *et al.* [36] developed an offloading framework called Triple Decision Makers (TDM) to reduce energy consumption and response time. Compared with the existing offloading decision method, the proposed method can save up to 75% execution time and 56% power consumption. Zhou *et al.* [37] studied the impact of mobile device context on offloading decisions and proposed a context-aware offloading framework called mCloud. Similar to the work of Wang *et al.* [15], Bowen Zhou didn't consider the communication problems between different cloud resources when designing mCloud.

For the computation offloading scenarios of multiple mobile users, Sardellitti *et al.* [38] studied MIMO multi-cell systems and proposed an iterative algorithm based on convex optimization to calculate the local optimal solution. Kuang *et al.* [39] proposed an agent-based offloading framework for mobile cloud computing, aiming at shortening the request delay of mobile users, alleviating the overhead of network communication and reducing the excess energy consumption caused by invalid transmission requests. Kao *et al.* [40] proposed Hermes, a full polynomial time approximation scheme, to trade off delays and resources within acceptable performance constraints. Terefe *et al.* [41] proposed a multi-site offloading strategy for mobile devices. By analyzing the data-intensive and computation-intensive modules of the application, the author uses a mathematical model to simulate the execution energy consumption of the multi-site application. Mao *et al.* [42] use the cost of execution delay and task failure as a performance metric to evaluate the offloading strategy, and propose a dynamic computation offloading algorithm based on Lyapunov optimization. For data center operation, computation offloading decision making must also consider the data center wide resources utilization for better QoS guarantee especially for co-located data centers with online services and batch jobs [43].

6   Conclusions and Future Work

This paper is a survey of edge computing, the emergence of edge computing enhances the response ability of services, protects privacy data, improves data security and alleviates the pressure of network bandwidth and data center greatly. Computation offloading is the core technology of edge computing that can divide tasks according to the computing capacity of current devices dynamically to reduce network data transmission and improve system performance. The core problems of computation offloading are as follows. Which to offload? When to offload? Where to offload? What to offload? How to offload? In a word, a good offloading strategy requires a balance between energy consumption and system performance. Finally, we summarize, classify and compare the existing computation offloading strategies and hope to propose our own computation offloading strategies for edge computing.

Acknowledgments. This work is supported by Natural Science Foundation of China (61472109, 61572163, 61672200, 61602137, and 61802093), Key Research and Development Program of Zhejiang Province (No. 2018C01098, 2019C01059, 2019C03134, 2019C03135) and the Natural Science Foundation of Zhejiang Province (NO. LY18F020014).

References

1. Varghese, B., Buyya, R.: Next generation cloud computing: new trends and research directions. Future Gener. Comput. Syst. **79**, 849–861 (2018)
2. Ramırez, W., et al.: Evaluating the benefits of combined and continuous fog-to-cloud architectures. Comput. Commun. **113**, 43–52 (2017)
3. Masip-Bruin, X., Marin-Tordera, E., Jukan, A., Ren, G.J.: Managing resources continuity from the edge to the cloud: architecture and performance. Future Gener. Comput. Syst. **79**, 777–785 (2018)
4. Shi, W., Cao, J., Zhang, Q., Li, Y., Xu, L.: Edge computing: vision and challenges. IEEE Internet Things J. **3**(5), 637–646 (2016)
5. Liu, L., Chang, Z., Guo, X., Mao, S., Ristaniemi, T.: Multi-objective optimization for computation offloading in fog computing. IEEE Internet Things J. **5**(1), 283–294 (2018)
6. Shi, W.S., Liu, F., Sun, H.: Edge Computing, 1st edn. Science Press, Beijing (2018)
7. Li, Z., Peng, X., Chao, L., Xu, Z.: Everylite: a lightweight scripting language for micro tasks in IoT systems. In: 2018 IEEE/ACM Symposium on Edge Computing (SEC), pp. 381–386. IEEE (2018)
8. Zhang, Q., Zhang, X., Zhang, Q., Shi, W., Zhong, H.: Firework: big data sharing and processing in collaborative edge environment. In: 2016 Fourth IEEE Workshop on Hot Topics in Web Systems and Technologies (HotWeb), pp. 20–25. IEEE (2016)
9. You, C., Zeng, Y., Zhang, R., Huang, K.: Asynchronous mobile-edge computation offloading: energy-efficient resource management. IEEE Trans. Wireless Commun. **17**(11), 7590–7605 (2018)
10. Wang, N., Varghese, B., Matthaiou, M., Nikolopoulos, D.S.: Enorm: a framework for edge node resource management. IEEE Trans. Serv. Comput. (2017)
11. Tan, Z., Yu, F.R., Li, X., Ji, H., Leung, V.C.: Virtual resource allocation for heterogeneous services in full duplex-enabled SCNs with mobile edge computing and caching. IEEE Trans. Veh. Technol. **67**(2), 1794–1808 (2018)
12. You, C., Huang, K., Chae, H., Kim, B.H.: Energy-efficient resource allocation for mobile-edge computation offloading. IEEE Trans. Wireless Commun. **16**(3), 1397–1411 (2017)
13. Xu, J., Ren, S.: Online learning for offloading and autoscaling in renewable-powered mobile edge computing. In: 2016 IEEE Global Communications Conference (GLOBECOM), pp. 1–6. IEEE (2016)
14. Qiu, Y., Jiang, C., Wang, Y., Ou, D., Li, Y., Wan, J.: Energy aware virtual machine scheduling in data centers. Energies **12**(4), 646 (2019)
15. Wang, C., Li, Z.: A computation offloading scheme on handheld devices. J. Parallel Distrib. Comput. **64**(6), 740–746 (2004)

16. Yang, L., Liu, B., Cao, J., Sahni, Y., Wang, Z.: Joint computation partitioning and resource allocation for latency sensitive applications in mobile edge clouds. IEEE Trans. Serv. Comput. (2019)
17. Niu, J., Song, W., Atiquzzaman, M.: Bandwidth-adaptive partitioning for distributed execution optimization of mobile applications. J. Network Comput. Appl. **37**, 334–347 (2014)
18. Yuan, C., Chen, Y., Zhang, Z.: Evaluation of edge caching/off loading for dynamic content delivery. IEEE Trans. Knowl. Data Eng. **16**(11), 1411–1423 (2004)
19. Zhou, Y., Yu, F.R., Chen, J., Kuo, Y.: Resource allocation for information-centric virtualized heterogeneous networks with in-network caching and mobile edge computing. IEEE Trans. Veh. Technol. **66**(12), 11339–11351 (2017)
20. Lin, Y., Kemme, B., Patino-Martinez, M., Jimenez-Peris, R.: Enhancing edge computing with database replication. In: 2007 26th IEEE International Symposium on Reliable Distributed Systems (SRDS 2007), pp. 45–54. IEEE (2007)
21. Kumar, K., Lu, Y.H.: Cloud computing for mobile users: can offloading computation save energy? Computer **4**, 51–56 (2010)
22. Wang, Y., Sheng, M., Wang, X., Wang, L., Li, J.: Mobile-edge computing: Partial computation offloading using dynamic voltage scaling. IEEE Trans. Commun. **64**(10), 4268–4282 (2016)
23. Ko, S.W., Huang, K., Kim, S.L., Chae, H.: Live prefetching for mobile computation offloading. IEEE Trans. Wireless Commun. **16**(5), 3057–3071 (2017)
24. Rego, P.A., Cheong, E., Coutinho, E.F., Trinta, F.A., Hasan, M.Z., de Souza, J.N.: Decision tree-based approaches for handling offloading decisions and performing adaptive monitoring in MCC systems. In: 2017 5th IEEE International Conference on Mobile Cloud Computing, Services, and Engineering (Mobile Cloud), pp. 74–81. IEEE (2017)
25. Meurisch, C., Gedeon, J., Nguyen, T.A.B., Kaup, F., Muhlhauser, M.: Decision support for computational offloading by probing unknown services. In: 2017 26th International Conference on Computer Communication and Networks (ICCCN), pp. 1–9. IEEE (2017)
26. Jiang, C., et al.: Energy efficiency comparison of hypervisors. Sustain. Comput. Inf. Syst. (2019)
27. Jiang, C., et al.: Interdomain I/O optimization in virtualized sensor networks. Sensors **18**(12), 4395 (2018)
28. Wang, X., Wang, J., Wang, X., Chen, X.: Energy and delay tradeoff for application offloading in mobile cloud computing. IEEE Syst. J. **11**(2), 858–867 (2017)
29. Zhang, K., Mao, Y., Leng, S., Maharjan, S., Zhang, Y.: Optimal delay constrained offloading for vehicular edge computing networks. In: 2017 IEEE International Conference on Communications (ICC), pp. 1–6. IEEE (2017)
30. Liu, Y., Xu, C., Zhan, Y., Liu, Z., Guan, J., Zhang, H.: Incentive mechanism for computation offloading using edge computing: a stackelberg game approach. Comput. Netw. **129**, 399–409 (2017)
31. Meskar, E., Todd, T.D., Zhao, D., Karakostas, G.: Energy aware offloading for competing users on a shared communication channel. IEEE Trans. Mob. Comput. **16**(1), 87–96 (2017)
32. Chen, X.: Decentralized computation offloading game for mobile cloud computing. IEEE Trans. Parallel Distrib. Syst. **26**(4), 974–983 (2015)
33. Chen, X., Jiao, L., Li, W., Fu, X.: Efficient multi-user computation offloading for mobile-edge cloud computing. IEEE/ACM Trans. Networking **24**(5), 2795–2808 (2016)
34. Jia, M., Cao, J., Yang, L.: Heuristic offloading of concurrent tasks for computation intensive applications in mobile cloud computing. In: 2014 IEEE Conference on Computer Communications Workshops (INFOCOM WKSHPS), pp. 352–357. IEEE (2014)

35. Deng, S., Huang, L., Taheri, J., Zomaya, A.Y.: Computation offloading for service workflow in mobile cloud computing. IEEE Trans. Parallel Distrib. Syst. **26**(12), 3317–3329 (2015)
36. Lin, Y.D., Chu, E.T.H., Lai, Y.C., Huang, T.J.: Time-and-energy-aware computation offloading in handheld devices to coprocessors and clouds. IEEE Syst. J. **9**(2), 393–405 (2015)
37. Zhou, B., Dastjerdi, A.V., Calheiros, R.N., Srirama, S.N., Buyya, R.: mCloud: a context-aware offloading framework for heterogeneous mobile cloud. IEEE Trans. Serv. Comput. **10**(5), 797–810 (2017)
38. Sardellitti, S., Scutari, G., Barbarossa, S.: Joint optimization of radio and computational resources for multicell mobile-edge computing. IEEE Trans. Sig. Inf. Process. Over Netw. **1**(2), 89–103 (2015)
39. Kuang, Z., Guo, S., Liu, J., Yang, Y.: A quick-response framework for multi-user computation offloading in mobile cloud computing. Future Gener. Comput. Syst. **81**, 166–176 (2018)
40. Kao, Y.H., Krishnamachari, B., Ra, M.R., Bai, F.: Hermes: latency optimal task assignment for resource-constrained mobile computing. IEEE Trans. Mob. Comput. **16**(11), 3056–3069 (2017)
41. Terefe, M.B., Lee, H., Heo, N., Fox, G.C., Oh, S.: Energy-efficient multisite offloading policy using markov decision process for mobile cloud computing. Pervasive Mob. Comput. **27**, 75–89 (2016)
42. Mao, Y., Zhang, J., Letaief, K.B.: Dynamic computation offloading for mobile edge computing with energy harvesting devices. IEEE J. Sel. Areas Commun. **34**(12), 35903605 (2016)
43. Jiang, C., Han, G., Lin, J., Jia, G., Shi, W., Wan, J.: Characteristics of co-allocated online services and batch jobs in internet data centers: a case study from Alibaba cloud. IEEE Access **7**, 22495–22508 (2019)

An Edge Computing Platform for Intelligent Internet Data Center Operational Monitoring

Yeliang Qiu[1,2], Congfeng Jiang[1,2(✉)], Tiantian Fan[1,2], and Jian Wan[3]

[1] Key Laboratory of Complex Systems Modeling and Simulation,
Hangzhou Dianzi University, Hangzhou 310018, China
cjiang@hdu.edu.cn
[2] School of Computer Science and Technology, Hangzhou Dianzi University,
Hangzhou 310018, China
[3] School of Information and Electronic Engineering, Zhejiang University
of Science and Technology, Hangzhou 310023, China

Abstract. The explosive growth in cloud-based services, big data analytics, and artificial intelligence related services provisioning leads to the rapid growth of construction of large scale Internet data centers (IDCs). Modern IDCs are equipped with various sensors to monitor its healthy operation and maintenance states, such as temperature, thermal distribution, air flow, etc. However, fine-grained, single-node level and even mainboard level monitoring including server resource consumption and power consumption is still needed for more progressive resource multiplexing and job scheduling in IDCs. In this paper, we propose an edge computing platform for intelligent Internet data center operational monitoring, which integrates wireless sensors and on-board built-in sensors to sense and collect the data of data center operation and maintenance. The edge computing based solution reduces the latency for data transportation to central clouds and reduces the amount of data and enhances the real time resource capping decisions in data centers.

Keywords: Edge computing · Data center · Monitoring · Intelligent operation and maintenance · Energy efficiency

1 Introduction

The ever-increasing demand of cloud services, big data analytics, e-commerce, artificial intelligence and other industries and technologies lead to continuous construction of large-scale Internet data centers (IDCs). Global data center IP traffic is expected to triple from 2014 to 2019, with a compound annual growth rate (CAGR) of 25% [1]. Meanwhile, according to the report from Laurentian Berkeley National Laboratory (LNBL), energy consumption in IDCs will increase to 73 billion KWH by 2020 [2]. The data center's electricity bill is $13 billion and emits nearly 100 m tons of carbon pollution a year [3]. One of the major sources of energy consumption in the data center (about 37% [4]) is the cooling energy. Energy consumption often leads to thermal management issues, cost issues, and system reliability issues. And many existing approaches are based on an approximated system model that often incorporates

© Springer Nature Singapore Pte Ltd. 2019
C. Hu et al. (Eds.): HPCMS 2018/HiDEC 2018, CCIS 913, pp. 16–28, 2019.
https://doi.org/10.1007/978-981-32-9987-0_2

first-order effects of thermal, electrical, and mechanical principles [5–9]. However, large-scale data center server hardware devices are often highly heterogeneous posing challenges to data management. Efficient operation and maintenance data centers have various requirements, such as environmental monitoring of the data center, resource monitoring of the server, and reasonable task scheduling based on the application layer and server operation information. Therefore, with the rapid increase in the complexity of data center management and operation and maintenance, how to effectively monitor and manage the data center has become an urgent problem in the industry. In [10–12], the authors use machine learning algorithm to predict the service quality and throughput of the data center, and effectively package the workload into available resources to improve the service quality of the data center. As cloud service quality and operational costs increase, administrators want to be able to perform joint constrained operations on the data center. Joint constraints include cluster power, cluster performance, cluster environment, and quality of service. In order to run the data center under these constraints, administrators need to monitor all clusters, IDC environments, and other related real-time operational status. In addition, they need to mine the characteristics of the server and understand the power ratio and load behavior of the server to schedule tasks reasonably and effectively and reduce the power consumption of IDC. Existing monitoring methods for data centers are often single items, such as IDC environment (temperature, humidity, smoke), or monitoring only the server resources (CPU, Mem, I/O, and Network). Therefore, there is a lack of integrated monitoring system for data center, which can monitor all relevant information in the IDC, such as single-point server power consumption, server cabinet energy consumption, data center environment, and server system resources.

This paper proposes an intelligent IDC management platform based on the edge computing framework, which can integrate various types of monitoring data, process the data acquired by the sensor in real time, store the data permanently, and the data is presented graphically to the user for review and analysis. Users can also use machine learning, artificial intelligence and other algorithms to predict the operating characteristics of the data center, including hardware health status trends, load operation quality, load forecasting and other information. This platform can provide decision-making for intelligent operation and maintenance.

The reminder of this paper is organized as follows. In Sect. 2, we introduce the background techniques and related work for data center monitoring. Then we introduce the architecture design of our intelligent data center monitoring system in Sect. 3, and we evaluate explain the prototypical implementation in Sect. 4. Finally, we summarize our work in Sect. 5.

2 Background and Related Work

Existing cluster resource monitoring systems [13–18] aim to detect and monitor thousands of nodes, such as Ganglia [17], an open source cluster monitoring project initiated by UC Berkeley. The server of Ganglia can collect data of all clients on the same network segment through a client. The design of this architecture shows that, through different layers, a server can manage tens of thousands of servers. As one of other different types of monitoring systems, Cacti is a set of network traffic monitoring graphic analysis tools based on PHP, MySQL, SNMP, and RRDTool. It acquires data by SNMPget and draws graphics by RRDtool. With the combination with LDAP, it can verify users and add templets by itself. When the users call for the data, the RRDtool produces icons and presents them to the users. Compared to the Ganglia, it's more difficult for Cacti to extend. However, with a built-in information sending system, Cacti can inform the operation and maintenance staff immediately in case of emergency. Above monitoring only take system resource into consideration, which might cause the incomprehensive information, so it is impossible to meet the joint constraints required by the service provider.

With the expansion of the scale of data centers, the scale of data generated by IDC and the demand of data processing is increasing constantly. Understand resource and task information in the datacenter can help better workload placement and energy savings for hybrid resource scheduling in data centers [19]. Many work [20–23] to perform task scheduling by analyzing the server resource and characteristics of the application. Jiang et al. [24] improve data center service quality by optimizing virtual machine communication mechanisms. As an emerging platform, edge computing has gained widespread attention in recent years. Data is increasingly being generated at the edges of networks; As a result, processing data at the edge of the network is also more efficient. Previous work, such as clone cloud [25], cloudlet [26] and fog computing [27, 28], has been introduced into the community. Shi et al. [29] define edge computing as the enabling technologies allowing computation to be performed at the edge of the network, on downstream data on behalf of cloud services and upstream data on behalf of IoT services. Yi et al. built a proof-of-concept platform in [30] to run a face recognition application, reducing the response time from 900 ms to 169 ms by moving computing from the cloud to the edge. In virtualized systems, different hypervisor has different energy efficiency even when the same applications are executed and provisioned on top of it [31]. Therefore, good knowledge of server's runtime energy efficiency can help make better energy aware workload placement. This also urges the intelligent data center wide operational monitoring.

The aim of edge computing is to unify the scattered resources that close to each other in spatial or network distance to provide applications with the services of computing, storage and network. When it comes to the monitoring of IDC, we made the whole monitoring platform easier to extend by introducing edge computing. By processing all kinds of information on edge nodes, the real-time performance of the platform is enhanced. At the same time, the operation and maintenance personnel can immediately observe the information and make the task scheduling decision intelligently through analysis.

3 Architecture Design

We proposed a smart operation and maintenance monitoring framework based on an edge computing platform, which is used to collect information about the IDC and make intelligent operation and maintenance decisions based on related information.

The framework consists of the following parts:

Data Collection: Data collection consists of three parts of information

(1) Collection of data center environmental information, including data center temperature, humidity, smoke, intrusion detection, etc.
(2) Collection of data center cluster system resources, including CPU utilization, memory utilization, disk information, and I/O information, etc.
(3) Data center server hardware information collection, including cabinet energy consumption, server power consumption, CPU power consumption, RAM power consumption, server-related hardware information, etc.

This platform can access all kinds of monitoring data by opening interfaces, such as CPU data analysis in Intel RAPL, which can achieve millisecond-level monitoring.

Streaming Engine: A stream processing engine that processes monitored data in real-time. The engine can use algorithms such as machine learning and artificial intelligence to predict data center operations in the future based on real-time data and historical data characteristics. Through the data center temperature, humidity, server energy consumption and other related information, we can predict the data center hardware status trends. By collecting the resource information of the server cluster system, it is possible to predict the future workload quality, mission failure probability, and load situations. Through the stream processing engine, the data in the IDC can also be modeled to provide data security for intelligent operation and maintenance, help the operation and maintenance personnel to understand the situation of the data center in advance, and make timely decisions.

Edge Server: Due to the large number of data center servers, we can divide the data center into multiple grids according to the logical function or geographical location, and each grid is responsible for collecting and preprocessing the monitoring data of this grid. As shown in Fig. 2, because the edge server is close to the data source, it can process the data in real time and present it to the user. Finally, the edge server will send the processed data to the data aggregation server.

Data Aggregation Server: The data aggregation server collects data from the edge server and forms a hierarchy with the edge server. The server stores the detected IDC information persistently and uses the chart drawing technology such as Echarts and Jfreechart on the server to display the data in a line chart, bar chart, and other legends to facilitate the management. Because the Data aggregation server has a global view, it can make more global scheduling, such as analyzing the operation of the entire data center and scheduling tasks according to the performance of each grid.

Task Schedule There are many ways to schedule tasks. Here we propose a method to optimize the energy efficiency of data centers. Through the historical information of various servers in the data center, we can analyze the energy efficiency chart of various servers, as shown in Fig. 1. The red line in the figure is the ideal proportion curve of the server, and blue is the true server energy equality curve. It can be seen that this server has a better workload range. Between 60% and 90%, putting the server in this load situation will be the best case for energy efficiency. If we can put each type of server in the entire data center into the appropriate working range, it will greatly help reduce the overall energy consumption of the data center. Simulation experiments show that when the total power of the data center is certain, the server that is turned on is running at the peak energy efficiency utilization point, which can not only increase the number of servers to be turned on, but also increase the total throughput of the data center, that is, the number of tasks completed in a unit of time. For example, running the server at the peak energy efficiency point can achieve an average of 47.3% more nodes than running the server at the 100% utilization point, and the total number of tasks in the entire data center increases by 3.69%. Of course, the task scheduling should also make decisions based on a variety of related resources, such as CPU resources, memory resources, hard disk resources, network delays, etc., and the resources collected in the edge server can help task Schedule to make a more reasonable decision-making.

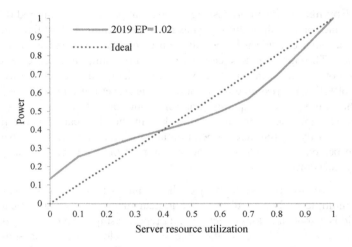

Fig. 1. The energy efficiency curve (Color figure online)

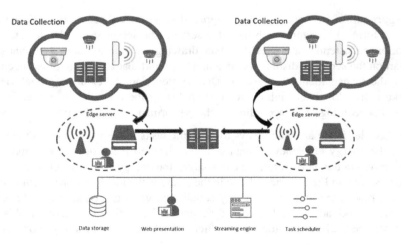

Fig. 2. Data center intelligent operation and maintenance platform

The monitoring network in the monitoring framework is isolated from the network in the IDC and is not coupled with the existing network in the IDC, so as not to increase the complexity of the existing network, making the monitoring network easy to expand and improve the reliability of monitoring. Even the network in IDC is abnormal, the monitoring network can also work normally. As shown in Fig. 2, in the server environment, we can arrange various sensors in the room and use WSN (Wireless Sensor Network) to connect them. We set up an intelligent AP and edge server for environmental data collection and processing. Due to the large scale of the IDC, different clusters may have different service functions. We can divide the clusters into different grids according to their logical functions. This grid can be expanded or changed on its own according to the service needs. In order to ensure real-time monitoring and mapping of data, we can set up an edge server under each grid. Its functions are as follows:

(1) Collect IDC information of the grid and show to the user. Because it is close to the data source, it has better real-time performance.
(2) The sensor data can be pre-processed, processed into intermediate results, and reduced in data volume. For example, the monitoring data in a period of time can be averaged and then transmitted to the edge for storage.
(3) It can be used as a distributed dispatch agent to make local decisions and perform reasonable task scheduling according to the task type of owning grid. Since the edge server has a global view and has all the data of each grid, it can analyze and process information of the entire data center through the streaming engine and can use machine learning and artificial intelligence algorithms to count or predict the future load situation of the entire data center. The network, power usage, task completion status, task failure status, etc.

The framework also provides the following data and strategy support for smart operation and maintenance:

(1) With these global data, such as the temperature and humidity of the entire engine room for years, it is possible to predict the hardware lifetime and then predict the server's damage rate in the future based on the server's own information.
(2) According to the temperature sensor and air flow sensor in each cabinet, the air flow path can be optimized to reduce the intelligent cost of the data center.
(3) According to each grid's response time and task completion situation can further optimize the data center task division, because each grid configuration and performance will be different, so we can put those tasks that need priority services assigned to high-performance grid to implement.
(4) With global data, we can also calculate the energy efficiency comparison block diagram for each type of server. IDC administrators can use this data to maintain the entire center in an energy-efficient state and can also perform data based on these data. The equipment selects the server, eliminates those servers with low energy efficiency and efficiency in a timely manner, and optimizes the energy efficiency structure of the data center server, thereby saving data center energy consumption.

The monitoring system framework has the characteristics of high scalability, high reliability. The edge server in the framework can rely on its advantage of being close to the data source, processing and analyzing the data of the grid near the data source and reducing the data volume by central processing the data. The edge server can perform data analysis and prediction or perform distributed task scheduling by using machine learning or artificial intelligence algorithms based on the monitored cluster information.

4   Prototypical Implementation

In this section, we implement a prototype monitoring system for a small-size data center according to the above proposed framework.

4.1   Data Center Environment Information Collection

To effectively monitor the environmental conditions of data center zone such as temperature, humidity, smoke, light, intrusion detection and so on, we adopted wireless sensor network (WSN). WSN defined as a multi-hop, self-organizing network system formed by wireless communication between a large number of low-cost spatially dispersed micro sensors. WSN aimed to cooperatively sense, collect and process the information of the perceived objects in the network coverage area and then send them to the observers.

The wireless sensor network-based environmental monitoring system has the following advantages:

(1) With a high autonomy, normal operation of the entire network will not be affected by the joining and leaving of the nodes.
(2) The wireless sensor network monitoring system is a non-intrusive monitoring system, so it is free of deploying more complex network equipment in an already complex data center network.
(3) Because of the significant benefit of low-energy-consumption features, sensor nodes can run by the heat generated by the servers of data center.

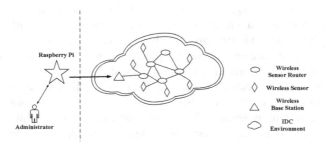

Fig. 3. Wireless sensor network architecture

Figure 3 illustrates the high-level overview of the wireless sensor network architecture. In such an architecture following a certain requirement, the micro nodes will be deployed to form a network in a self-organizing way. These nodes integrated with sensors, data processing units and communication modules. With the aid of the sensors embedded in it, the nodes can measure the ambient environmental data directly. To bring the communication modules into operation, wired, wireless, and Bluetooth are available. However, short distance wireless low-power-consumption technology is generally used as the medium in the industry. As shown in Fig. 3, by utilizing ZigBee, the data collected from the sensor nodes can be send to the other routing nodes in the network, and finally to the base station node of the connection management platform. The base station node stores the data into the database and updates it to the monitor interface of the administrator with Web Server (Fig. 4).

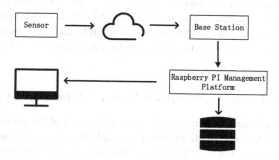

Fig. 4. Monitoring system monitoring information channel

We adopt Arduino as sensor nodes collection platform, ZigBee as wireless data transmission protocol and Raspberry Pi as edge server. By building web server and database server in Raspberry Pi, visualization monitoring service is provided for user. In the term of hardware configuration, DHT-11 temperature and humidity sensor, MQ2 smoke sensor, infrared detector and light-sensitive resistors are used to collect temperature, humidity, delay, intrusion and brightness data respectively. The MCU uses Mega 8 chip Arduino Platform of Atmel, while the network module uses XBee module of the wireless sensor network of Digi company.

In order to guarantee the scalability of the node, a tree topology supported by the ZigBee protocol is introduced in the network topology. As shown in Fig. 5, the coordinator establishes an initial network, whose branch nodes are composed of routers that equipment connected to. In this topology, the terminal device does not participate in message forwarding. The routing nodes can establish a subnet independently of the coordinator and forward the message. In this design, in order to ensure the scalability of the nodes, a tree topology is adopted, the coordinator is used as a base station node, and the remaining nodes are topologically networked in a tree topology manner.

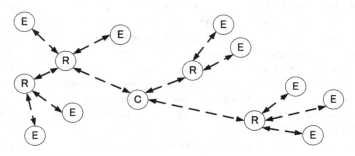

Fig. 5. Tree topology

The environmental detection module ensures the whole monitoring in the computer room global, autonomous and non-invasive. The utilization of Raspberry Pi, Arduino module and necessary sensors can process the data and then send them to edge server, which has realized the basic functional requirements of the IDC environment monitoring system.

4.2   Data Center Hardware and System Resource Information Collection

In this section we implemented server hardware monitoring of the prototype system. As shown in Fig. 6, we use the IPMI protocol to implement accurate and real-time collection of power consumption data for servers and provide more convenient monitoring tools for the server operation and maintenance managers. IPMI is called the intelligent platform management interface, which is an industrial standard for hardware devices. With IPMI, users can obtain physical status such as voltage, power and temperature of servers.

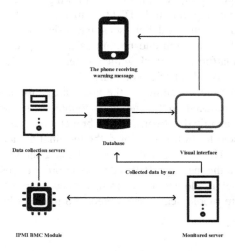

Fig. 6. Monitoring system function structure

The edge server polls the host to be monitored according to the configuration at intervals (2 s–3 s), obtains parameters such as CPU operating temperature and power supply, and then writes them to the database. The monitoring host also uses the sar command to obtain information such as the CPU and memory usage and disk conditions of the target monitoring host, and then write it to the database. The obtained information can also be displayed in the form of a line chart in real time. The system also allows the user to set the listening parameter threshold in advance. The client monitors the parameter. In case the parameter is abnormal for a period of time, an alarm is issued and then sent as a short message.

4.3 Server Cabinet Energy Consumption Information Collection

The object collected by the prototype system is the Sugon cabinet, which provides the query of baud rate, input maximum current, and version number. In the display data information mode, you can view the input and output data information of PDM, including the voltage of three-phase L1, L2 and L3, total current, active power, apparent power and the branch current corresponding to the three-phase output. The collection process consists of two parts: he extraction and analysis of power information from the cabinet PDM and display the information on the Web page for visual display. The functions of the two modules are as follows:

(1) The information extraction module includes two functional modules, which are the extraction and analysis of electrical information. The data is read by the edge server through the RS485 interface of the PDM. The process is mainly to open the serial port, after proper configuration, the serial data can be read in a complete and effective way. Then the serial port data is analyzed and written to the database through the Java program installed in the edge server.

(2) This module realizes information visualization on Web pages, in which charts can be displayed by using Echart.

It provides data support for data center management and task scheduling by collecting circuit information of cabinets in data center.

4.4 Real-Time Information Display

Relative to a large number of raw data, user is more willing to see data in the form of images or diagrams, which will show them the server information in a more intuitive and more visual way. In order to enable data to be displayed in real time and ensure interactivity between system and users, we use Websocket technology, which is one of the new features of HTML5. Compared with traditional polling, Websocket is more prevalent because of its better performance. We use Node.js-engine-driven Javascript to build Websocket server. The visualization process is as follows: Firstly, background open Websocket service and wait for access from browsers. Once the browser's connection event is monitored, the database begins to be polled at a certain time interval. Once the data collected from the data acquisition module is updated, the new updated data is sent to the front desk through the Websocket interface. At the same time, because the front-end uses echarts.js, the front-end pushes received data into the original array, and realizes the dynamic update of the broken line graph.

Whenever the front-end receives the data from the Websocket, it is necessary to match the preset threshold. Once the threshold is exceeded or below the threshold, the value is continuously monitored. If the time exceed a certain length, the abnormal situation is reported to the background through the Websocket, and the SMS interface is called by the background to send short message to the administrator's cell phone. If the normal situation is not achieved for a period of time, it will continue to send short messages until the abnormal situation is resolved.

5   Conclusion

This paper proposes a framework of monitoring platform based on edge of computing. The platform uses sensor networks, IPMI, and other tools to collect data center environment information, system resource information, and power consumption information. By dividing the logic of the data center cluster into grids and placing edge servers in each grid, we can perform data processing, data analysis, task prediction, and task scheduling in the vicinity of the data source, improving the real-time performance of the system and reducing data transmission and data volume. In the aggregation server, we have global information about the data center. Based on this information, we can use algorithms such as deep learning and artificial intelligence to analyze the new energy efficiency situation, mission failure, and energy consumption of the IDC. According to the specific energy efficiency of each grid, the energy efficiency of the data center is optimized to keep it in a state of high energy efficiency and reduce data center energy consumption and overhead. We implemented a prototype system to demonstrate the feasibility of this monitoring system.

In the future work, we will implement a stream processor that can schedule tasks in this grid, improve service quality and reduce resource overhead. We will conduct experiments under real scenarios in large data centers to verify the effectiveness of this platform.

Acknowledgments. This work is supported by Natural Science Foundation of China (61472109, 61572163, 61672200, 61602137, and 61802093), Key Research and Development Program of Zhejiang Province (No. 2018C01098, 2019C01059, 2019C03134, 2019C03135) and the Natural Science Foundation of Zhejiang Province (No. LY18F020014).

References

1. Cisco Global Cloud Index: Forecast and Methodology. http://www.cisco.com/c/en/us/solutions/collateral/service-provider/global-cloud-index-gci/CloudIndexWhitePaper.html. Accessed 7 Apr 2019
2. United States data center energy usage report. https://eta.lbl.gov/sites/all/files/publications/lbnl-1005775_v2.pdf. Accessed 7 Apr 2019
3. America's data centers consuming and wasting growing amounts of energy. http://www.nrdc.org/energy/data-center-efficiency-assessment. Accessed 7 Apr 2019

4. Data Centre Energy Efficiency Benchmarking - E2 Singapore. http://www.e2singapore.gov.sg/DATA/0/docs/Resources/NEADCEnergyBenchmarkingSummary-FinalReport.pdf. Accessed 7 Apr 2019
5. Farrell, A., Hoffmann, H.: {MEANTIME}: achieving both minimal energy and timeliness with approximate computing. In: 2016 USENIX Annual Technical Conference (ACT), vol. 16, pp. 421–435. USENIX (2016)
6. Hoffmann, H.: Jouleguard: energy guarantees for approximate applications. In: Proceedings of the 25th Symposium on Operating Systems Principles, pp. 198–214. ACM (2015)
7. Imes, C., Kim, D.H., Maggio, M., Hoffmann, H.: Poet: a portable approach to minimizing energy under soft real-time constraints. In: 21st IEEE Real-Time and Embedded Technology and Applications Symposium, pp. 75–86. IEEE (2015)
8. Mishra, N., Zhang, H., Lafferty, J.D., Hoffmann, H.: A probabilistic graphical model-based approach for minimizing energy under performance constraints. In: ACM SIGPLAN Notices, vol. 50, pp. 267–281. ACM (2015)
9. Wu, Q., et al.: Dynamo: facebook's data center-wide power management system. In: 2016 ACM/IEEE 43rd Annual International Symposium on Computer Architecture (ISCA), pp. 469–480. IEEE (2016)
10. Barroso, L.A., Hölzle, U.: The datacenter as a computer: an introduction to the design of warehouse-scale machines. Synth. Lect. Comput. Architect. 4(1), 1–108 (2009)
11. Crankshaw, D., Wang, X., Zhou, G., Franklin, M.J., Gonzalez, J.E., Stoica, I.: Clipper: a low-latency online prediction serving system. In: 14th USENIX Symposium on Networked Systems Design and Implementation (NSDI 17), pp. 613–627 (2017)
12. Delimitrou, C., Kozyrakis, C.: Quasar: resource-efficient and QoS-aware cluster management. In: ACM SIGARCH Computer Architecture News, vol. 42, pp. 127–144. ACM (2014)
13. Wang, T., et al.: Towards bandwidth guaranteed energy efficient data center networking. J. Cloud Comput. 4(1), 9 (2015)
14. Wang, X., Wang, X., Xing, G., Chen, J., Lin, C.X., Chen, Y.: Towards optimal sensor placement for hot server detection in data centers. In: 2011 31st International Conference on Distributed Computing Systems. pp. 899–908. IEEE (2011)
15. Chan, H., et al.: A robot as mobile sensor and agent in data center energy management. In: Proceedings of the 8th ACM International Conference on Autonomic Computing, pp. 165–166. Citeseer (2011)
16. Katsaros, G., Subirats, J., Fito, J.O., Guitart, J., Gilet, P., Espling, D.: A service framework for energy-aware monitoring and VM management in clouds. Future Gener. Comput. Syst. 29(8), 2077–2091 (2013)
17. Massie, M., et al.: Monitoring with Ganglia: tracking dynamic host and application metrics at scale. O'Reilly Media Inc., Massachusetts (2012)
18. Bose, R., Sahana, S., Sarddar, D.: An adaptive cloud service observation using billboard manager cloud monitoring tool. Int. J. Softw. Eng. Appl. 9(7), 159–170 (2015)
19. Jiang, C., Han, G., Lin, J., Jia, G., Shi, W., Wan, J.: Characteristics of co-allocated online services and batch jobs in internet data centers: a case study from Alibaba cloud. IEEE Access 7, 22495–22508 (2019)
20. Kalyani, N.: An energy efficient dynamic schedule-based server load balancing approach for cloud data center. Int. J. Future Gener. Commun. Netw. 8(3), 123–136 (2015)
21. Qiu, Y., Jiang, C., Wang, Y., Ou, D., Li, Y., Wan, J.: Energy aware virtual machine scheduling in data centers. Energies 12(4), 646 (2019)
22. Qu, J., Li, L., Liu, L., Tian, Y., Chen, J.: Smart temperature monitoring for data center energy efficiency. In: Proceedings of 2013 IEEE International Conference on Service Operations and Logistics, and Informatics, pp. 360–365. IEEE (2013)

23. Cuervo, E., et al.: Maui: making smartphones last longer with code offload. In: Proceedings of the 8th International Conference on Mobile Systems, Applications, and Services, pp. 49–62. ACM (2010)
24. Jiang, C., et al.: Interdomain I/O optimization in virtualized sensor networks. Sensors **18**(12), 4395 (2018)
25. Chun, B.G., Ihm, S., Maniatis, P., Naik, M., Patti, A.: Clonecloud: elastic execution between mobile device and cloud. In: Proceedings of the Sixth Conference on Computer Systems, pp. 301–314. ACM (2011)
26. Satyanarayanan, M., Bahl, P., Caceres, R., Davies, N.: The case for VM-based cloudlets in mobile computing. IEEE Pervasive Comput. **4**, 14–23 (2009)
27. Bonomi, F., Milito, R., Zhu, J., Addepalli, S.: Fog computing and its role in the internet of things. In: Proceedings of the First Edition of the MCC Workshop on Mobile Cloud Computing, pp. 13–16. ACM (2012)
28. Dastjerdi, A.V., Buyya, R.: Fog computing: helping the internet of things realize its potential. Computer **49**(8), 112–116 (2016)
29. Shi, W., Cao, J., Zhang, Q., Li, Y., Xu, L.: Edge computing: vision and challenges. IEEE Internet Things J. **3**(5), 637–646 (2016)
30. Yi, S., Hao, Z., Qin, Z., Li, Q.: Fog computing: platform and applications. In: 2015 Third IEEE Workshop on Hot Topics in Web Systems and Technologies (HotWeb), pp. 73–78. IEEE (2015)
31. Jiang, C., et al.: Energy efficiency comparison of hypervisors. Sustainable Computing: Informatics and Systems (2019)

Big Data Analytics for Water Resources Sustainability Evaluation

Yinghui Zhao[1,2] and Ru An[1(✉)]

[1] School of Earth Science and Engineering,
Hohai University, Nanjing 210098, Jiangsu, China
anrunj@163.com
[2] Department of Water Resources, Zhejiang Tongji Vocational College
of Science and Technology, Hangzhou 311231, Zhejiang, China

Abstract. With the advances in remote sensing and computing technology, water resource sustainability evaluation is ingested with high volume data acquired from heterogeneous sources. However, traditional theories and methods for comprehensive water resources sustainability evaluation are challenged by the large quantity, high velocity, and high diversity of those data sets. In this paper, we propose a framework for big data analytics based water resource sustainability evaluation. We build a prototype for regional water resource sustainability evaluation based on big data of regional economic and social development. We build the relationship between economic development and water demand is modeled through regression analysis on water vertical industrial usage distribution, population, and water supply capacity. In our prototype, users can model and predict regional water resource demand and sustainability under constraints of population and industrial development. Results show that the proposed prototype can be used to evaluate regional water resource sustainability and environmental performance in practice and provide scientific basis and guidance to formulate water supply policies.

Keywords: Big data · Sustainability · Water resources · Cloud computing · Remote sensing

1 Introduction

Big data generally refer to massive volumes of data that are too large or complex to be readily deal with by the usual data processing tools and application software. Environmental and hydrological sciences are witnessing a rapid increase in the amount of relevant monitoring data. For example, a large share of these data is the result of environmental monitoring, either in situ or via remote sensing that is being made available by government institutions [1]. With the advances in communications and sensor technology, wireless sensors are deployed in smart cities, smart homes, autonomous vehicles, and industrial environments [2, 3]. All these sensors and devices help build a smart world with Internet of Things (IoT) and Edge computing, as well as generate huge volume of data in almost all kind of scenarios. In order to leverage the data generated, Big Data analytics is becoming the basic decision making technique in

© Springer Nature Singapore Pte Ltd. 2019
C. Hu et al. (Eds.): HPCMS 2018/HiDEC 2018, CCIS 913, pp. 29–38, 2019.
https://doi.org/10.1007/978-981-32-9987-0_3

both academia and industry [4]. Data driven analysis framework can ingest large scale data and leverage latest algorithms in machine learning and artificial intelligence to infer and derive statistical and predicative results. The advent of Big Data related algorithms and processing techniques deliver the cost-effective prospect to improve decision-making in almost all areas such as health care, economic productivity, and security [5–7]. Developments in sensing technology, data processing and visualization, and wireless communication technologies, are creating a wide range of new opportunities for water resources big data analytics. For example, advanced technology for hydrological data collection, such as robust, cheap, and low-maintenance wireless sensor equipment provide unprecedented opportunities for data collection in all contexts [8–10]. By using various big data toolkits, scientific researchers and government administrators can speed up the data collection and knowledge generation for water resources research and management.

With the tremendous progress in our abilities to store, retrieve, and process large quantities of data, big data analytics in water resources can help create new hydrological knowledge, especially in relation to the characterization of water cycle and energy consumption in different regions and under different human activities [11–13]. Currently, the water resource management is under huge pressure to integrate big data analysis capabilities for sustainable practices and management. There are some case studies on big data and cloud computing based water resource analysis framework [14, 15]. However, traditional theories and methods for comprehensive water resources sustainability evaluation are challenged by the large quantity, high velocity, and high diversity of those data sets. With the emergency of cloud computing and big data, more and more data analytics are conducted in cloud platforms in data center and thus in the last decade, electricity use by data centers increased, due largely to explosive growth in both the number and density of data centers. It is estimated that United States data centers consumed about 70 billion kilowatt hours of kilowatt hours of electricity in 2014, representing 2% of the United States total energy consumption [16].

In this paper, we first present the theories and technologies regarding big data analysis and the opportunities and applications for water resources sustainability evaluation. Then we propose to leverage big data analytics for water resource sustainability evaluation, including its framework, pipeline for data processing, and a case study. We build a prototype, namely, *WaterRE*, for regional water resource sustainability evaluation based on big data of regional economic and social development. With *WaterRE*, users can manage the massive water resources data efficiently, including data collection and ingestion, ETL (extraction, transformation, and loading), and data analysis. *WaterRE* also provides advanced analysis method such as predictive analysis, data mining, statistical analysis, and data visualization. In *WaterRE*, the relationship between economic development and water demand is modeled through various machine learning algorithms on water vertical industrial usage distribution, population, and water supply capacity.

The rest of the paper is organized as follows. In Sect. 2, we describe the framework of *WaterRE*, including its methodology, architecture, and components for water resources sustainability evaluation. We provide experiment results for regional water resources sustainability evaluation in Zhoushan City as a case study in Sect. 3.

In Sect. 4 we review some related work on big data analytics in water resources and identify our unique approach. We conclude the paper with some future research directions in Sect. 5.

2 The WaterRE Platform

2.1 Architecture and System Design

Although there are many different types of sensors, lots of them share similar goal of data sensing and transmission. For intelligent water resources management, we argue that it should contain three capabilities:

(1) Sustainable big data management system including data collection, storage, and transmission. Firstly, all sensors send downstream data of various water resources related usage, performance, and device healthy data to clients, which is similar to traditional SCADA (Supervisory control and data acquisition) systems. Ultimately, all data will be converged to build a Big Data management system.

(2) Machine learning algorithms enabled big data analytics. The big data management system shall support all kind of analysis based on different machine learning algorithms and parameters configuration. Newly invented algorithms can easily plug into the system and ready for use.

(3) Artificial intelligence enabled analytics. The analytics platform shall read data automatically from different sources including the Internet to learn and identify new analysis opportunities. For example, in case of emergency in water resources (such as earthquakes, floods, etc.), the system can provide real time analysis and provide estimation of water resource sustainability under current conditions.

Once we configure the water demand, and water supply, we can calculate the water shortage under different conditions compared to the baseline condition. We can compare the performance and accuracy of a set of possible predicting algorithms by changing parameters of demand or supply and re-execute the water resource sustainability analysis. Reversely, we can also model the water resource sustainability analysis by setting a fixed number of each parameter in the target time period and calculate the water shortage under that final condition.

Take the water consumption of the agriculture category of Zhoushan City as an example. In WaterRE, the correlation data between the per capita GDP of Zhoushan (gpdpc) and the Water consumption per 10000 GDP (RMB) of agriculture output value (water10 k) is used. The regression analysis shows that there is a negative correlation between gpdpc and water10 k. That is, with the growth of per capita GDP, the water consumption per unit value of agricultural decreases gradually. When regional economy grown in the earlier state, the water consumption of per 10,000 yuan of agriculture output value decreased rapidly with the increase of per capita GDP, i.e., gpdpc grows faster. Then when the per capita GDP reaches a certain value after long term development, the downward trend is gradually slow. Therefore, with the improvement of the social and economic development level, the water consumption per unit value of agricultural should be stabilized within a basic constant range, that is, no great change will occur. This boundary is the bound limit of agricultural water savings. The system implementation consists of four layers as described as follows:

(1) Hardware layer, which is responsible for hardware interconnection, data generation and data aggregation,
(2) Communication layer, which is responsible for all types of inter-device communication between, for instance, sensors, relays, base stations, and the Internet,
(3) Middleware layer, which is responsible for data management and processing using various big data analysis support
(4) Application layer, which is responsible for application and usage of the data analysis services and the results generated and visualization.

To speed up the big data analysis, we first separate the data sets into different chunks, which can be processed on a Hadoop cluster based on MapReduce. At each computing node, computation can be conducted on local data chunk and data block using different statistical and machine learning algorithms.

The architecture of WaterRE is listed in Fig. 1.

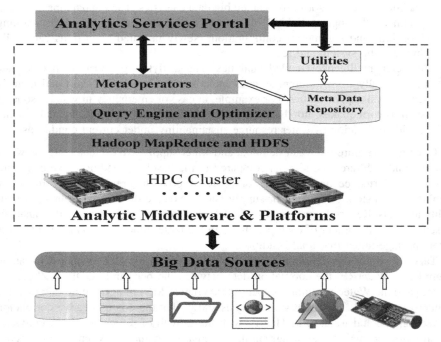

Fig. 1. WaterRE architecture.

In order to conduct parallel analysis on large data sets, we first decompose the analysis task into sub-parallel tasks and then execute the subtasks on multiple machines. The decomposition flow is listed in Fig. 2.

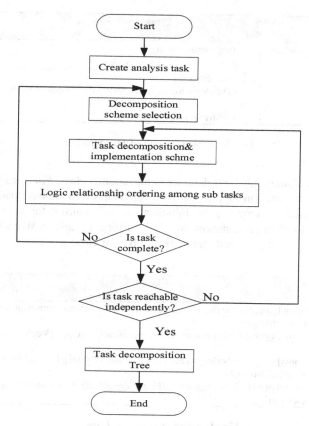

Fig. 2. Parallel analytics task decomposition

2.2 Data Structure and Classes Design

To facilitate the big data based modeling and analysis, we build four subcomponents for data processing, namely, economy, society, population, and water resources. The economy subsystem includes agricultural submodule, industrial submodule and services industry submodule and it includes added values of agriculture, and services industry respectively. The society subsystem consists of the regional development patterns and future planning. The population distribution subsystem includes the number of urban population, rural population, and the remote regions. And the water resources subsystem includes water supply sub module (local water resources, water diversion, and sewage reuse) and water demand module.

In order to process pure text data and row-column data efficiently, we define a data class, namely, **DataStruct**, for easier data storage and operation. **DataStruct** has 2 member variables, one is **dataName**, and another is **data**. The member **data** has a type of *Vector* <*Vector*<*String*≫, which stores the actual data. Its class structure is listed in Fig. 3.

Class DataStruct	
Member variables	dataName: String data: Vector<Vector<String>>
Methods	+DataStruct() +DataStruct(dataName:String,data:Vector<Vector<String>>) +toString():String

Fig. 3. Class structure of DataStruct

For easier manipulation of text data, we define another class, ***Form***, to process table data. Its structure is listed in Fig. 4. All the methods in Form are overloaded. The first method is designed for empty table initialization and waiting for user's input, the remaining 3 are for data presentation. In a typical form created in ***WaterRE***, user can edit it and the data will be saved automatically before close it.

Class Form	
Methods	+<u>showForm</u>(title:String,owner:JFrame,rowCount:int,columnCount:int):Vector<Vector<String>> +<u>showForm</u>(title:String,owner:JFrame,datas:Object[][]):Vector<Vector<String>> +<u>showForm</u>(title:String,owner:JFrame,datas:Object[][],isEnabled:Boolean):Vector<Vector<String>> +<u>showForm</u>(title:String,owner:JFrame,<u>datas</u>:Vector<Vector<String>>):Vector<Vector<String>>

Fig. 4. Class structure of ***Form***

WaterRE provides comprehensive visualization functions for water resources sustainability evaluation based on JFreeChart. Figures, including line graphs or histograms, can be generated according to settings of the data. Moreover, it supports multiple data source such as texts and Microsoft Excel tables. Attributes of the corresponding graph can be edited dynamically, such as the title, the coordinate axis information, etc. The generated graphs can also be saved in JPG, PNG, or TIFF form in hard disk.

We define a class, namely, ***GraphTemplate***, for figures generation and editing. Its class structure is listed in Fig. 5.

Most of the members in the ***GraphTemplate*** class are used to set the properties of the graph and chart. In ***GraphTemplate***, we reuse the most of the members of class Template in JFreeChart. In order to reference its instance in controls like *JComboBox*, we rewrite its *toString()* method. Moreover, we rewrite the *clone()* method to create a graph template quickly and copy all members into the newly created graph instance.

Class GraphTemplate	
Member variables	+templateName: String
	+templateType: ChartType
	+chartName: String
	+xName: String
	+xUnitName: String
	+yName: String
	+yUnitName: String
	+showNode: boolean
	+showNodeValue: boolean
	+saveAuto: boolean
	+showInNewWindow: boolean
	+height: int
	+width: int
	+imageSavePath: String
	+colors: Color[]
	+bgColor: Color
	+titleFont: Font
	+axesFont: Font
Methods	+toString():String
	+clone():GraphTemplate

Fig. 5. Class structure of *DataStruct*

3 Case Study

We choose Zhoushan City as a case study because such coastal island cities are typical regions that suffer from water shortages because there are no long ground run-offs. Moreover, continued regional population growth and climate change may bring even greater adaptation challenges for water resource sustainability, such as reduced water supplies and increased water demands. Zhoushan city area is 1140 square kilometers. In Zhoushan, the main freshwater resources are river run offs and a small amount of shallow groundwater. And the total water resource volume is 8.11 million cubic meters. On the basis of historical data, the simulation results of model simulation analysis and data simulation analysis are calculated respectively, and the simulation analysis results of industrial, agricultural, the services industry and domestic water usage are calculated. The results of the water demand forecast for Zhoushan city are shown in Table 1.

Table 1. Water resources demand forecast for Zhoushan City (unit: 100 million m^3)

Year	Industry	Agriculture	Services	Inhabitants	Environment	Total
2020	0.621	0.223	0.251	0.402	0.070	1.567
2023	0.693	0.201	0.276	0.412	0.080	1.662
2025	0.776	0.181	0.302	0.422	0.080	1.761
2028	1.085	0.127	0.381	0.450	0.090	2.133
2030	1.343	0.098	0.436	0.468	0.100	2.445

4   Related Work

IoT is providing a growing number of inputs from various sensors. And IoT is driving a revolution of sensing technologies and communication platforms, spurring the development of advanced sensors that will provide access to new data streams for the waste industry. Therefore, parallel processing of big data is essential for large data sets based decision making. Moreover, characteristics of hardware platforms and the software stack also have a significant impact on big data analytics [17]. Ahmed et al. [18] survey the recent advances in big data analytics for IoT systems as well as the key requirements for managing big data and for enabling analytics in an IoT environment. Badiezadeh et al. [19] propose a big data approach for performance evaluation of sustainable supply chain management. They propose an NDEA model for calculating optimistic and pessimistic efficiency, which can incorporate undesirable outputs and rank supply chains in terms of efficiency scores.

Song et al. [20, 21] review the theories and technologies regarding big data and the opportunities and applications for environmental performance evaluation. Fu et al. [22] use big data analysis from social micro-blog platform to form the public's acceptance level of recycled water.

Cloud computing based services are becoming the main platforms for water resources big data analytics [23]. Researchers identify the unique characteristics of water resource big data [19] and the feasibility of cloud computing based water resource analytics [12, 14], such as the data management framework for water resources, data situational analysis model, data monitoring and warning based on the cloud computing platform [15]. Chalh et al. [24] propose a big data open platform for water resources management based on J2EE. The platform can simulate and compare the effects of different current and future management scenarios and make choice to preserve the environment and natural resources.

In Big data based resource analysis, Li et al. [25] utilized the big data theory to analyze the relevant data of China's forestry resources including economic, social and ecological factors for resource assessment.

5   Conclusions

Due to the wide development of water quality sensors, there is more data than ever for operators, engineers, plant managers and other stakeholders to analyze these data. However, since these data is often stored in various platforms including relational database, Excel spreadsheets, text documents, these data are under-utilized. With the advancements in big data analytics tools and platform, harnessing the power of historical and real-time data to compliment traditional operational decision support systems is actively needed in order to transform these data into informative insights and decision support. Shortening analysis time allows operators to identify problems earlier, allowing them to be proactive rather than reactive in their response. Big data driven decision support tools can also be used to provide real-time treatment process optimization resulting in increased energy efficiency and reduced waste. Big data analytics plays a significant role in improving the quality of current water resources sustainability evaluation. Our experiences show that Big Data analytics for water resource sustainability evaluation outperforms the traditional generalized analysis techniques. The case study presented in this paper reflects the opportunities in the integration of big data analytics in water resources sustainability evaluation and water resources management. Sustainability analysis combined with industrial development can identify water usage characteristics in target regions. It can also help evaluate the effectiveness of improvements in water usage efficiency in regional sustainable development focuses on finding effective ways to achieve sustainable development.

Acknowledgments. This research was funded by the Science and Technology Planning Program of Department of Water Resources of Zhejiang Province (Grant No. RC1843).

References

1. Vitolo, C., Elkhatib, Y., Reusser, D., Macleod, C., Buytaert, W.: Web technologies for environmental Big Data. Environ. Model Softw. **63**, 185–198 (2015)
2. Li, R., Li, H., Mak, C., Tang, T.: Sustainable smart home and home automation: big data analytics approach. Int. J. Smart Home **10**(8), 177–187 (2016)
3. Jiang, C., et al.: Interdomain I/O optimization in virtualized sensor networks. Sensors **18**, 4395 (2018)
4. Kambatla, K., Kollias, G., Kumar, V., Grama, A.: Trends in big data analytics. J. Parallel Distrib. Comput. **74**(7), 2561–2573 (2014)
5. Hilbert, M.: Big data for development: a review of promises and challenges. Dev. Policy Rev. **34**(1), 135–174 (2016)
6. Sun, Z., Du, K., Zheng, F., Yin, S.: Perspectives of research and application of big data on smart agriculture. J. Agric. Sci. Technol. **15**(6), 63–71 (2013)
7. Rathore, M., Ahmad, A., Paul, A., Rho, S.: Urban planning and building smart cities based on the Internet of Things using Big Data analytics. Comput. Netw. **101**, 63–80 (2016)
8. Koo, D., Piratla, K., Matthews, C.: Towards sustainable water supply: schematic development of Big Data collection using Internet of Things (IoT). Procedia Engineering **118**, 489–497 (2015)
9. Han, G., Liu, L., Zhang, W., Chan, S.: A hierarchical jammed-area mapping service for ubiquitous communication in smart communities. IEEE Commun. Mag. **56**(1), 92–98 (2018)
10. Jiang, C., et al.: Energy efficiency comparison of hypervisors. Sustainable Computing: Informatics and Systems (2017)
11. Chen, Y., Han, D.: Big data and hydroinformatics. J. Hydroinformatics **18**(4), 599–614 (2016)
12. Kim, Y., Kang, N., Jung, J., Kim, H.: A review on the management of water resources information based on big data and cloud computing. J. Wetlands Res. **18**(1), 100–112 (2016)
13. Uddameri, V.: Big data, computing, and water resources hazards. J. Am. Water Resour. Assoc. **54**(4), 765–766 (2018)
14. Suciu, G., Suciu, V., Dobre, C., Chilipirea, C.: Tele-monitoring system for water and underwater environments using cloud and big data systems. In: Proceedings of 20th International Conference on Control Systems and Computer Science, pp. 809–813 (2015)
15. Ai, P., Yue, Z., Yuan, D., Liao, H., Xiong, C.: A scene analysis model for water resources big data. In: Proceedings of 2015 14th International Symposium on Distributed Computing and Applications for Business Engineering and Science, pp. 280–283(2015)

16. Qiu, Y., Jiang, C., Wang, Y., Ou, D., Li, Y., Wan, J.: Energy aware virtual machine scheduling in data centers. Energies **12**, 646 (2019)
17. Jiang, C., Han, G., Lin, J., Jia, G., Shi, W., Wan, J.: Characteristics of co-allocated online services and batch jobs in internet data centers: a case study from Alibaba cloud. IEEE Access **7**, 22495–22508 (2019)
18. Ahmed, E., Yaqoob, I., Hashem, I., Khan, I., et al.: The role of big data analytics in Internet of Things. Comput. Netw. **129**, 459–471 (2017)
19. Badiezadeh, T., Saen, R., Samavati, T.: Assessing sustainability of supply chains by double frontier network DEA: a big data approach. Comput. Oper. Res. **98**, 284–290 (2018)
20. Song, M., Fisher, R., Wang, J., Cui, L.: Environmental performance evaluation with big data: theories and methods. Ann. Oper. Res. **270**(1–2), 459–472 (2018)
21. Song, M., et al.: How would big data support societal development and environmental sustainability? Insights and practices. J. Clean. Prod. **142**(2), 489–500 (2017)
22. Fu, H., Li, Z., Liu, Z., Wang, Z.: Research on Big Data digging of hot topics about recycled water use on micro-blog based on particle swarm optimization. Sustainability **10**, 2488 (2018)
23. Romero, J., Hallett, S., Jude, S.: Leveraging Big Data tools and technologies: addressing the challenges of the water quality sector. Sustainability **9**, 2160 (2017)
24. Chalh, R., Bakkoury, Z., Ouazar, D., Hasnaoui, M.: Big data open platform for water resources management. In: Proceedings of 2015 International Conference on Cloud Technologies and Applications, pp. 1–8 (2015)
25. Li, L., Hao, T., Chi, T.: Evaluation on China's forestry resources efficiency based on big data. J. Clean. Prod. **142**(2), 513–523 (2017)

Exploring Water Resource Changes of Artificial Reservoir Using Time-Series Remote Sensing Images from Landsat Sensors and in Situ Data

Yifan Chang[1,2], Hailei Wang[1(✉)], Wenbo Li[1], Xuelian Wu[1], and Bingyu Sun[3]

[1] Institute of Technology Innovation, Hefei Institute of Physical Science, Chinese Academy of Sciences, Hefei 230088, China
{cyflz,hailei}@mail.ustc.edu.cn, wbli@iim.ac.cn, xlwu@rntek.cas.cn
[2] The Department of Automation, University of Science and Technology of China, Hefei 230026, China
[3] Institute of Intelligent Machines, Chinese Academy of Sciences, Hefei 230031, China
bysun@iim.ac.cn

Abstract. Periodic and accurate assessments of the water resources changes of artificial reservoirs are important for water resource management. Danjiangkou Reservoir (DJKR) is the largest artificial freshwater lake in Asia and is the freshwater source for Middle Route of South-to-North Water Diversion Project (MRSNWDP) in China. Remote sensing images of long time-series Landsat sensors and in situ observed storage data from 1993 to 2014 were used to monitor water resource variations of the DJKR. The results show significant monthly surface water area changes of the DJKR. Precipitation variations in the upper Hanjiang River Basin and reservoir operation missions are primarily responsible for these changes. In addition, the relationship between surface water area and reservoir storage of the DJKR can be described as a cubic polynomial model.

Keywords: Landsat sensor · Water resources · Surface water area · Reservoir storage · Change monitoring

1 Introduction

Lakes and rivers are the most accessible freshwater resources for ecosystems and human consumption [1]. Artificial reservoirs make freshwater resources available to industrial, irrigation, hydropower, and environmental water use sectors [2]. Periodic and accurate assessments of the water resources changes of artificial reservoirs are important for water resource management [3]. The relationship between water storage and surface water area of a given reservoir can be estimated [1]. Once this relationship is established, changes in freshwater storage can be estimated using only remote sensing images without field survey data.

The objective of this study is to comprehensively characterize the changes in the surface water area and the relationship between the surface water area and storage of the DJKR using remote sensing images and *in situ* data from 1993 to 2014.

2   Study Area and Materials

2.1   Study Area

The DJKR lies in the upstream region of the Hanjiang River [4]. The outline of the DJKR forms a "V" shape. The section that contains the Hanjiang River is long and narrow, while the section that contains the Danjiang River is wide [5]. Shuttle Radar Topography Mission (SRTM) Digital Elevation Model (DEM) data show that the elevations of the upstream Hanjiang River Basin range from 73 m to 3533 m above sea level (Fig. 1).

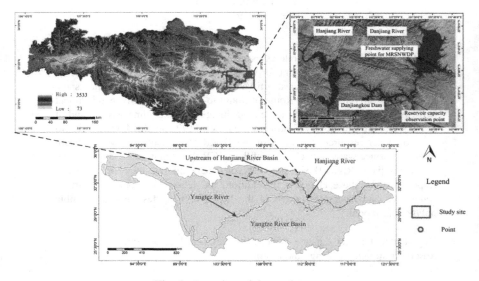

Fig. 1. Location of the study area.

2.2   Materials

Landsat series multispectral images from the sensors of TM (Thematic Mapper) [6], ETM+ (Enhanced Thematic Mapper Plus) [7, 8], and OLI (Operational Land Imager) [9–11], which have a high spatial resolution of 30 m, were selected as primary data sources. To process these remote sensing images, users can rent online cloud services from cloud computing providers to setup remote sensing big data analysis platform, rather than build their own but not powerful computing clusters [12, 13, 14].

Further information regarding the specifications of the selected Landsat time-series sensors are provided in Table 1.

Seventy-eight (path/row 125/37) of the TM, ETM+ , and OLI data covering the study area were selected in this study. The selected Landsat series multispectral data include thirty-nine TM data, twenty-eight ETM+ data, and eleven OLI data. The selected seventy-eight data all archived on the United States Geological Survey (USGS) server and Daily observed in situ DJKR storage data archived on the Hydrology and Water Resources Survey Bureau of China (HWRSB) server were used for this study.

Table 1. Specifications of the TM, ETM+ , and OLI sensors used in this study.

Sensor	Band	Wavelength/μm	Sensor	Band	Wavelength/μm
TM	B1 (Blue)	0.45–0.52	ETM+	B1(Blue)	0.450–0.515
TM	B2 (Green)	0.52–0.60	ETM+	B2 (Green)	0.525–0.605
TM	B3 (Red)	0.63–0.69	ETM+	B3 (Red)	0.63–0.69
TM	B4 (NIR)	0.76–0.90	ETM+	B4 (NIR)	0.75–0.90
TM	B5 (SWIR)	1.55–1.75	ETM+	B5 (SWIR)	1.55–1.75
TM	B7 (SWIR)	2.08–2.35	ETM+	B7 (SWIR)	2.09–2.35
OLI	B1a (Coastal)	0.43–0.45	OLI	B1b (Blue)	0.45–0.51
OLI	B2 (Green)	0.53–0.59	OLI	B3 (Red)	0.64–0.67
OLI	B4 (NIR)	0.85–0.88	OLI	B5 (SWIR1)	1.57–1.65
OLI	B7 (SWIR2)	2.11–2.29			

3   Methodology

3.1   Extraction of Surface Water Area

We selected the modified NDWI (MNDWI) [15], which is a classical water area extraction method, as a primary tool for extracting surface water areas of the DJKR from long time-series Landsat remotely sensed images in this study.

3.1.1   Surface Water Area Extraction Model

Water bodies have low reflectance from the visible to infrared range. Thus, MNDWI is defined as:

$$MNDWI = \frac{\rho_{Green} - \rho_{SWIR}}{\rho_{Green} + \rho_{SWIR}} \tag{1}$$

where ρ_{Green} and ρ_{SWIR} are the reflectances of the green and SWIR bands, respectively. Band 2 (0.52–0.60 μm) and Band 5 (1.55–1.75 μm) of TM, Band 2 (0.525–0.605 μm) and Band 5 (1.55–1.75 μm) of ETM+ and Band 2 (0.53–0.59 μm) and Band 5 (1.57–1.65 μm) of OLI, were chosen for green channel and the SWIR channel respectively.

3.1.2   Pre-Processing of Landsat Data

The TOA reflectance of TM and ETM+ data is given by the following equation:

$$\rho_\lambda = \frac{\pi \cdot L_\lambda \cdot d^2}{ESUN_\lambda. \cos \theta_s} \qquad (2)$$

where ρ_λ is the TM or ETM+ TOA reflectance of wavelength λ [unitless], d is the earth-sun distance [astronomical units], $ESUN_\lambda$ is the mean exo-atmospheric solar irradiance [W/(m^2 μm)], θ_λ is the solar zenith angle [degrees], and L_λ is the spectral radiance at wavelength λ at the sensor's aperture [W/(m^2 sr μm)]. L_λ can be obtained from the ND value, which is given by the following equation:

$$L_\lambda = (\frac{LMAX_\lambda - LMIN_\lambda}{Q_{cal\ max} - Q_{cal\ min}})(Q_{cal} - Q_{cal\ min}) + LMIN_\lambda \qquad (3)$$

where $LMAX_\lambda$ is the spectral at-sensor radiance that is scaled to $Q_{cal\ max}$ [W/(m^2 sr μm)], $LMIN_\lambda$ is the spectral at-sensor radiance that is scaled to $Q_{cal\ min}$ [W/(m^2 sr μm)], $Q_{cal\ max}$ is the maximum DN value, $Q_{cal\ min}$ is the minimum DN value, and Q_{cal} is the DN value.

The USGS standard Landsat-8 level 1 OLI products can be rescaled to the TOA reflectance using the following equation:

$$\rho_\lambda = \frac{\rho_{\lambda'}}{\cos(\theta_{SZ})} = \frac{\rho_{\lambda'}}{\sin(\theta_{SE})} \qquad (4)$$

where ρ_λ is the OLI TOA reflectance of wavelength λ [unitless], $\rho_{\lambda'}$ is the planetary TOA reflectance of wavelength λ, θ_{SE} is the local sun elevation angle, θ_{SE} is the local solar zenith angle, and $\theta_{SE} = 90° - \theta_{SE}$.

The parameter $\rho_{\lambda'}$ can be obtained from the DN value (Q_{cal}), as follows:

$$\rho_{\lambda'} = M_\rho \cdot Q_{cal} + A_\rho \qquad (5)$$

where M_ρ is the band-specific multiplicative rescaling factor and A_ρ is the band-specific additive rescaling factor.

3.1.3   Image Threshold Segmentation

The Otsu method [16] was employed to determine different thresholds to divide the MNDWI image into two classes, a non-water class and a water class. The optimal threshold t^* for the segmentation of the MNDWI images can be determined from the between-class variance of the non-water class and the water class by using the following equation:

$$t* = Arg \underset{a \leq t \leq b}{Max} \left\{ \sigma^2 = P_w \cdot (M_w - M)^2 + P_{nw} \cdot (M_{nw} - M)^2 \right\} \qquad (6)$$

where σ is the between-class variance of the non-water and water for MNDWI images, $-1 \leq t^* \leq 1$, P_w is the water class probability, M_w is the water class mean value, M is

MNDWI image mean value, P_{nw} is the non-water class probability, and M_{nw} is the non-water class mean value.

The parameters in the Eq. (6) can be obtained from statistical analysis of the MNDWI images, and have the following relationships:

$$\begin{cases} M = P_{nw} \cdot M_{nw} + P_w \cdot M_w \\ P_{nw} + P_w = 1 \end{cases} \tag{7}$$

3.2   Reservoir Surface Water Area-Storage Curve Fitting

In this study, polynomial functions were used. Two statistical indexes, the root mean square error (RMSE) and coefficient of determination (R-squared: R^2), were used to validate the fits of the curves to the data. The RMSE is expressed as follows:

$$RMSE = \sqrt{\frac{1}{n} \sum_{i=1}^{n} (y_i - \hat{y}_i)^2} \tag{8}$$

where y_i is the daily in situ observed DJKR storage data, corresponding to the Landsat images derived from the HWRSB server, $\hat{y}_i$ is the corresponding value that is estimated in this study, i is the index of the variables, and n is the number of samples. R^2 is expressed as follows:

$$R^2 = \frac{\sum_{i=1}^{n} (\hat{y}_i - \bar{y}_i)^2}{\sum_{i=1}^{n} (y_i - \bar{y}_i)^2} = 1 - \frac{\sum_{i=1}^{n} (y_i - \hat{y}_i)^2}{\sum_{1=i}^{n} (y_i - \bar{y}_i)^2} \tag{9}$$

where $\bar{y}_i$ is the mean value of y_i.

4   Results

We first monitored changes in the surface water area of the DJKR from 1993 to 2014. Next, we analyzed these changes. Finally, we estimated the relationship between the surface water area and reservoir storage of the DJKR.

4.1   Changes in the Surface Water Area of the DJKR from 1993 to 2014

Table 2 shows the surface water areas of the DJKR from 1993 to 2014.

Figure 2 shows the changes in the surface water area of the DJKR during the wet and dry seasons from 1993 to 2014.

Figure 3 shows Changes in the average monthly surface water area of the Danjiangkou Reservoir and the average monthly precipitation in the upper Hanjiang River Basin.

Table 2. Surface water areas of the Danjiangkou Reservoir derived from TM, ETM+ , and OLI multispectral data from 1993 to 2014. (Surface Water Area: SWA)

Time	SWA (km²)	Time	SWA (km²)	Time	SWA (km²)
24.Sep.1993	442.31	17.Nov.2001	367.34	2.Apr.2005	394.83
17.Nov.1995	416.98	27.Dec.2001	333.02	11.Oct.2005	506.64
1.Jan.1996	381.93	4.Jan.2002	325.31	4.Mar.2006	423.25
5.Feb.1996	362.58	12.Jan.2002	323.37	23.May.2006	389.66
25.Apr.1996	329.59	28.Jan.2002	325.56	24.Jun.2006	370.66
27.May.1996	342.31	21.Feb.2002	299.65	10.Jul.2006	361.51
31.Aug.1996	417.77	9.Mar.2002	306.60	12.Sep.2006	335.24
18.Oct.1996	468.31	2.Apr.2002	305.25	14.Oct.2006	363.13
1.Sep.1999	313.79	18.Apr.2002	306.87	11.Jun.2007	328.39
22.Dec.1999	292.34	7.Jul.2002	407.84	14.Aug.2007	437.66
19.Mar.2000	297.38	24.Aug.2002	374.81	15.Sep.2007	440.68
27.Mar.2000	305.69	1.Sep.2002	360.46	18.Jul.2009	416.16
4.Apr.2000	298.12	25.Sep.2002	350.45	23.Nov.2009	430.75
12.Apr.2000	296.68	27.Oct.2002	338.05	2.May.2010	380.34
28.Apr.2000	294.37	4.Nov.2002	326.80	9.Aug.2011	442.07
15.Jun.2000	309.88	28.Nov.2002	303.03	25.Aug.2011	464.99
17.Jul.2000	450.59	30.Dec.2002	304.97	11.Jun.2013	357.01
10.Aug.2000	440.88	7.Jan.2003	314.92	14.Aug.2013	415.23
24.Dec.2000	481.62	20.Mar.2003	314.07	15.Sep.2013	387.63
18.Feb.2001	438.17	5.Apr.2003	314.55	18.Nov.2013	375.28
1.May.2001	376.43	7.May.2003	333.27	4.Dec.2013	362.23
18.Jun.2001	349.40	16.Jun.2003	347.23	21.Jan.2014	343.87
4.Jul.2001	362.20	14.Mar.2004	414.45	10.Mar.2014	329.42
5.Aug.2001	380.60	17.May.2004	347.82	26.Mar.2014	313.25
21.Aug.2001	374.69	4.Jul.2004	336.26	27.Apr.2014	336.85
9.Nov.2001	380.64	8.Oct.2004	456.15	1.Aug.2014	366.98

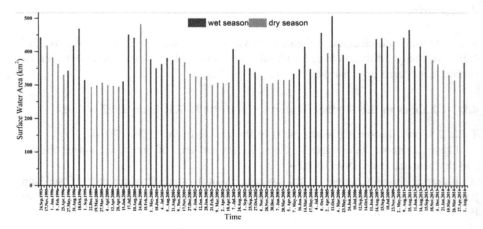

Fig. 2. Changes in the surface water area of the Danjiangkou Reservoir during the wet season and dry season from 1993 to 2014.

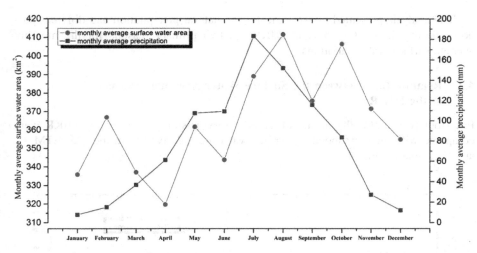

Fig. 3. Changes in the average monthly surface water area of the Danjiangkou Reservoir and the average monthly precipitation in the upper Hanjiang River Basin.

From Fig. 3, precipitation gradually increased from January to April while the monthly average surface water area fluctuated. The phenomenon resulted from two factors. First, the precipitation during the dry season is less. Second, the main tasks for the DJKR in March and April are hydroelectric power, agricultural irrigation, and flood preparedness for the wet season. When come to the wet months, the average monthly surface water area in May is greater than April because May has more precipitation and the main task is flood preparedness. The monthly surface water area in May is greater than that in June because the DJKR is mainly used for flood control. Maximum precipitation occurs in July and the average monthly surface water area is greater than in June because the inflow from the upper Hanjiang River is greater than the outflow and the DJKR can rely on the reservoir flood regulation capacity to store freshwater. The maximum average monthly surface water area is in August because DJKR can use the reservoir flood regulation capacity to store more freshwater. In September, the average monthly surface water area is lower than that in July and August because the precipitation is less and the Danjiangkou Hydropower plant can use more freshwater stored from July and August to generate electricity. The average monthly surface water area is greater in September than May and June because September has greater precipitation. However, less precipitation occurs in October than September. Nevertheless, the average monthly surface water area is greater in October than September. The largest surface water area occurred during October (11 Oct. 2005) because heavy autumn rain of West China occurred. In November, the monthly average surface water area was greater than that in May and June because May and June are the wet season months and the primary task is flood preparedness and control as well as freshwater storage and hydroelectric power. In December, the monthly average surface water area is less than that in November, primarily because less precipitation in December than November.

The analysis presented above indicates the natural precipitation and different purposes during different months in DJKR are two primary reasons for the monthly average surface water variations.

4.2   Relationships Between the Surface Water Area and Storage of the DJKR

Fifty-four records for the in situ observed reservoir storage data of the DJKR were compared with the corresponding surface water areas derived from the TM, ETM + , and OLI images (Fig. 4).

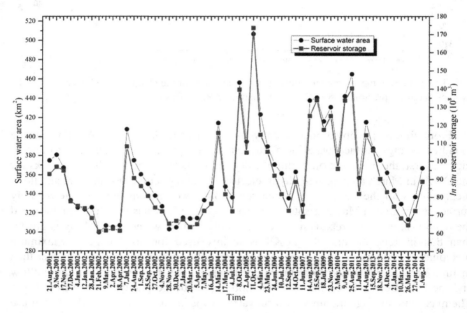

Fig. 4. Changes in the surface water area and in situ reservoir storage in the Danjiangkou Reservoir.

We calculated eight polynomial fitting curves and used the RMSE and R2 to quantitatively analyze the performance of the different fitting functions. Table 3 shows the polynomial functions and the corresponding results of the quantitative assessment.

The function with smaller RMSE values and larger R-squared values has better fitting performance. Based on comprehensive considerations of the RMSE, R-squared, and complexity, we recommend a cubic polynomial function as the better choice for representing the relationship between the surface water area and storage in the DJKR.

Table 3. Polynomial functions and the corresponding quantitative assessment results

Order	Function	RMSE $(10^8 m^3)$	R^2
1	$V = 4.99 \times 10^{-1}S - 92.03$	3.536	0.975
2	$V = 9.1 \times 10^{-4}S^2 - 0.179S + 32.29$	3.070	0.982
3	$V = -1.359 \times 10^{-5}S^3 + 1.63 \times 10^{-2}S^2 - 5.891S + 734.5$	2.878	0.985
4	$V = -5.87 \times 10^{-8}S^4 + 7.55 \times 10^{-5}S^3 - 3.4 \times 10^{-2}S^2 + 7.67S - 431.3$	2.905	0.985
5	$V = 4.53 \times 10^{-10}S^5 - 9.2 \times 10^{-7}S^4 + 7.3 \times 10^{-4}S^3 - 0.28S^2 + 52.5S - 3840$	2.942	0.985
6	$V = -7.6 \times 10^{-11}S^6 + 1.74 \times 10^{-7}S^5 - 1.7 \times 10^{-7}S^4 + 8.3 \times 10^{-2}S^3 - 23.52S^2 + 3526S - 2.19 \times 10^5$	2.943	0.985
7	$V = -4.14 \times 10^{-12}S^7 + 1.09 \times 10^{-8}S^6 - 1.22 \times 10^{-5}S^5 + 7.6 \times 10^{-3}S^3 - 2.81S^3 - 625.6S^2 + 7.68 \times 10^4 S + 4.02 \times 10^6$	2.839	0.986
8	$V = -4.11 \times 10^{-16}S^8 - 2.91 \times 10^{-12}S^7 + 9.27 \times 10^{-9}S^6 - 1.1 \times 10^{-5}S^5 + 7.0 \times 10^{-3}S^4 - 2.65S^3 + 594.2S^2 - 7.35 \times 10^4 S + 3.87 \times 10^6$	2.880	0.986

5 Conclusions

Time-series Landsat remote sensing images (TM/Landsat-5, ETM +/Landsat-7, and OLI/Landsat-8) were used to monitor changes in the surface water area of the DJKR from 1993 to 2014. The results show that the variations of precipitation and reservoir operation missions primarily caused the changes and a cubic polynomial function can fit the relationship between the surface water area and reservoir storage of the DJKR.

6 Discussions

Extraction of the surface water area is a main cause of uncertainty. The first factor is the selection of the MNDWI image segmentation threshold. The Otsu method was used, but the Otsu method alone is not always precise enough to determine the optimal threshold for segmenting different MNDWI images. The second factor is the spatial resolution of Landsat remote sensing imagery. The pixels located at the water-land boundaries are often mixed pixels. The third factor is the accurate assessment of the surface water area extraction results.

Additional uncertainty results from the in situ observation reservoir storage data. The first factor is the data synchronization issue. The first factor is the data synchronization issue. In this study, in situ observation reservoir storage data measured at 8:00 a.m. are used, and the passing time of the Landsat satellites is approximately 10:30 a.m. In addition, the sample number issue is considered. only fifty-four records of in situ observation reservoir storage and Landsat images were selected for the limited temporal resolution of the Landsat series satellites and the influences of clouds.

Acknowledgments. This paper is financially supported by the National Key Research and Development Program of China (No. 2016YFB0502600), the National Natural Science Foundation of China (No. 41701594, No.41871302). We are indebted to the U.S. Geological Survey server for preprocessing data and providing the TM/Landsat-5, ETM +/Landsat-7, OLI/Landsat-8, and DEM data used in this manuscript. In addition, we are indebted to the Hydrology and Water Resources Survey Bureau of China for offering reservoir storage data.

References

1. Zhu, W., Jia, S., Lv, A.: Monitoring the fluctuation of lake Qinghai using multi-source remote sensing data. Remote Sens. **6**(11), 10457–10482 (2014)
2. Duan, Z., Bastiaanssen, W.G.M.: Estimating water volume variations in lakes and reservoirs from four operational satellite altimetry databases and satellite imagery data. Remote Sens. Environ. **134**, 403–416 (2013)
3. Dubey, A.K., Gupta, P., Dutta, S., Kumar, B.: Evaluation of satellite-altimetry-derived river stage variation for the braided Brahmaputra river. Int. J. Remote Sens. **35**(23), 7815–7827 (2014)
4. Li, W., Qin, Y., et al.: Estimating the relationship between dam water level and surface water area for the Danjiangkou Reservoir using Landsat remote sensing images. Remote Sens. Lett. **7**(2), 121–130 (2016)
5. Yin, D., Zheng, L., Song, L.: Spatio-temporal distribution of phytoplankton in the Danjiangkou Reservoir, a water source area for the South-to-North Water Diversion Project (Middle Route) China. J. Oceanol. Limnol. **29**(3), 531–540 (2011)
6. Campos, J.C., Sillero, N., Brito, J.C.: Normalized difference water indexes have dissimilar performances in detecting seasonal and permanent water in the Sahara-Sahel transition zone. J. Hydrol. **464–465**, 438–446 (2012)
7. Li, W., Du, Z., Ling, F., et al.: A comparison of land surface water mapping using the normalized difference water index from TM, ETM + and ALI. Remote Sens. **5**(11), 5530–5549 (2013)
8. Margono, B.A., Bwangoy, J.R.B., Potapov, P.V., et al.: Mapping wetlands in Indonesia using Landsat and PALSAR data-sets and derived topographical indices. Geo-Spatial Inf. Sci. **17**(1), 60–71 (2014)
9. Du, Z., Li, W., Zhou, D., et al.: Analysis of Landsat-8 OLI imagery for land surface water mapping. Remote Sens. Lett. **5**(7), 672–681 (2014)
10. Rokni, K., Ahmad, A., Selamat, A., Hazini, S.: Water feature extraction and change detection using multitemporal Landsat imagery. Remote Sens. **6**(5), 4173–4189 (2014)
11. Zhai, K., Wu, X., Qin, Y., et al.: Comparison of surface water extraction performances of different classic water indices using OLI and TM imageries in different situations. Geo-Spatial Inf. Sci. **18**(1), 32–42 (2015)
12. Jiang, C., Han, G., Lin, J., Jia, G., Shi, W., Wan, J.: Characteristics of co-allocated online services and batch jobs in internet data centers: a case study from Alibaba cloud. IEEE Access **7**, 22495–22508 (2009). https://doi.org/10.1109/access.2019.2897898
13. Qiu, Y., Jiang, C., Wang, Y., Ou, D., Li, Y., Wan, J.: Energy aware virtual machine scheduling in data centers. Energies **12**, 646 (2019)

14. Jiang, C., Fan, T., Qiu, Y., Wu, H., Zhang, J., Xiong, N., Wan, J.: Interdomain I/O optimization in virtualized sensor networks. Sensors **18**, 4395 (2018)

15. Xu, H.: Modification of normalised difference water index (NDWI) to enhance open water features in remotely sensed imagery. Int. J. Remote Sens. **27**(14), 3025–3033 (2006)

16. Otsu, N.: A threshold selection method from gray-level histograms. IEEE Trans. Syst., Man, and Cybern. **9**(1), 62–69 (1979)

A Deep Learning Based Objection Detection Method for High Resolution Remote Sensing Image

Hailei Wang[1,2,5], Sumin Li[3], Bingyu Sun[1], Ronghua Du[3], Ling Zhao[4], Wenbo Li[5(✉)], and Yifan Chang[2,5]

[1] Institute of Intelligent Machines, Chinese Academy of Sciences, Hefei 230031, China
hailei@mail.ustc.edu.cn, bysun@iim.ac.cn

[2] The Department of Automation, University of Science and Technology of China, Hefei 230026, China
{hailei,cyflz}@mail.ustc.edu.cn

[3] School of Architecture, Changsha University of Science and Technology, Changsha 410076, China
lisumin57@gmail.com, csdrh@163.com

[4] School of Geosciences and Info-Physics, Central South University, Changsha 410083, China
17693608@qq.com

[5] Institute of Technology Innovation, Hefei Institute of Physical Science, Chinese Academy of Sciences, Hefei 230088, China
wbli@iim.ac.cn

Abstract. Automatic building detection from remote sensing images plays an important role in a wide range of applications. In this paper, we apply improved U-NET and HF-FCN as main models to detect small building which is more difficult than big building. MUL-Pan Sharpen and PAN data used as the training data. Improved U-NET and HF-FCN were selected as main models. In order to detect small building, we oversample small building areas and under sample large building areas. We adapt morphological methods to dilate and erode output of the mod-el. With the optimization of model's outputs, we can fill in the disconnected area, but also eliminates part of the false detection noise.

Keywords: Deep learning · Building extraction · Remote sensing · U-NET · HF-FCN

1 Overview

Buildings are the most artificial prominent features in the earth's surface. Building information has significance for urban planning, cartographic mapping, emergency responses, and so on. On the other hand, different features detection is one of the most important techniques for remote sensing applications. High resolution remote sensing data have been proved to be a useful tool and resource for detection buildings features [1]. With the increasing availability of high resolution remote sensing images, it is

© Springer Nature Singapore Pte Ltd. 2019
C. Hu et al. (Eds.): HPCMS 2018/HiDEC 2018, CCIS 913, pp. 50–56, 2019.
https://doi.org/10.1007/978-981-32-9987-0_5

possible to identify detailed building changes occurring at the level of ground structures. However, the development of high resolution remote sensing techniques poses challenges to the traditional change detection methods [2]. High resolution remote sensing data are absolutely required for tackling the specific problem, while any spectral information more than the standard RGB enhance significantly the discrimination capabilities between the different man-made objects [3]. Recently, Convolution Neural Networks have been employed in object detection from high resolution remote sensing data and machine learning applications [3]. Deep-learning algorithms have been introduced into the remote sensing big data analysis community such as features information detection [4]. Under different background conditions, different objects may have similar spectral signatures and objects of the same type may appear with different spectral signatures, so building detection from high resolution remote sensing images is still a challenge [1].

Modeling population dynamics is of great importance for disaster response and recovery, and detection of buildings and urban areas are key to achieve so. We would like to pose the challenge of automatically detecting buildings from satellite images. This problem is formulated as a binary segmentation problem to localize all building polygons in each area. The evaluation will be based on the overlap of detected polygons with the ground truth. The task of this study is to automatically detect building from high resolution remote sensing images, which can be viewed as a standard semantic segmentation task. We compute the area of overlap between the predicted bounding box (polygons) and the ground-truth bounding box.

In this study, U-Net model [5], a semantically segmented deep neural network is widely used in recent years. Meanwhile, we notice that the requirement for the outline of building was relatively high. The network of Holistically-Nested Edge Detection (HED) [6] achieved a good effect on the extraction of the outline. We selected HF-FCN [7], a mature HED network, to extract building profiles as accurately as possible.

In general, our solution mainly includes the following points:

1. Selecting U-Net and HF-FCN as the models;
2. Selecting the MUL-Pan Sharpen and PAN data as training data of 9 bands;
3. Over-sample small building areas and under-sample large building areas;
4. Using multi-scaled patch and sliding window generate training data, and at edges the windows are overlapped to cover the entire image;
5. Building a calibration model;
6. Selecting morphological processing on the final predictions to close the building area and remove non-building discrete noise.

First we get our training data of nine channel. Then we get our ensemble model trained. Final, with some after-treatments, we get our final result. The overall idea is shown in Fig. 1.

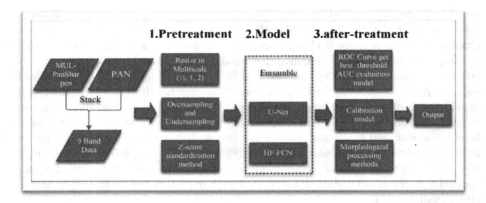

Fig. 1. Overall idea.

2 Data Preprocessing

The data used in this study came from the challenge which is governed by DeepGlobe Rules. The data for the Deep Globe Building Extraction Challenge is hosted on the SpaceNet Repository on AWS [8].

The competition offers four data types: MUL, MUL-PanSharpen, PAN, RGB-PanSharpen [8]. MUL-PanSharpen contains 8 bands. After detailed analysis of each data type, we choose MUL-Pan Sharpen and PAN as our training data. In order to understand the characteristics of remote sensing images, we visualize the data distribution of the eight bands of MUL-Pan Sharpen. We find that the distribution of the data is inconsistent. We perform zero center and normalizing for each band of each original image, making the distribution of each bands in MUL-Pan Sharpen as consistent as possible. It is conducive to model training.

The most important feature of buildings are its color, shape, texture, etc [9, 10]. With some pre-processing methods, we expect the building features will become more prominent and facilitate model learning. Nowadays, mainstream cloud services vendors provide online services including storage and parallel processing of remote sensing images [11, 12, 13].The cloud services can significantly speed up the feature extraction process by using deep learning approaches.

Training set of images and corresponding labels are shown in Fig. 2. The left picture shows the RGB-PanSharpen image, and the right picture shows the mask converted from the corresponding geographic coordinate file. We can know from the pictures that the area needed to be detected is mainly urban areas. Vegetation shelters, lighting effects, road vehicle influences increase difficulties for building detection.

It should be noted that this normalization method loses certain information which influence the mean of data. It is not conducive to the generalization of the model. We enhance the data by randomly changing the mean variance to ensure the generalization of the model.

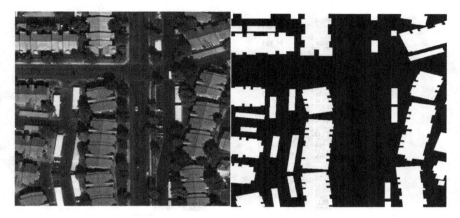

Fig. 2. Training data and label.

We notice that when the slider is sampled on the original image, it will divide the entire building into parts, which is not conducive to detect building as a whole. In order to reduce this edge effect, we use a multi-scale plus sampling window to cover the cropped edge in a small-step-sliding manner.

For some small buildings, we have over-sampled to reduce the probability of missed detection of small building, and at the same time under-sampled those building that are regularly shaped and common. Making the proportion of various types of building more reasonable.

3 Detection Method

3.1 Selection of Models

In combination with the building identification tasks, we try different depths of U-Net networks, we use cross-validation methods and AUC to evaluate the model's classification capabilities. Finally we chose 4 groups of 2*conv+maxpool structures. In order to make the distribution of parameters in each layer more reasonable, we add a BN layer to each set of convolutions. The adding of BN layer also solve the disappear of gradient. To suppress over fitting, a dropout layer was add to the upsampling process. The specific network structure is shown as Fig. 3.

Meanwhile, we notice that the HF-FCN network has a significant effect in segmenting building boundaries. It is proven that HF-FCN set to achieve good score in the competition data. We also use 4 groups of 2*conv+maxpool structures.

In order to make full use of the respective features of U-Net and HF-FCN, we use ensemble learning method for training. The score of model integration is better than a single model.

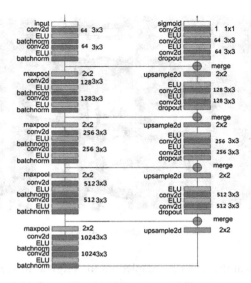

Fig. 3. U-Net structure.

3.2 Model Training Details

We stack 8-band MUL-Pan Sharpen and 1-band PAN data as training data.

Using random changes in mean, variance, and contrast to enhance the data and improve the model's generalization ability.

Building three scales of 325*325, 650*650, 1300*1300, and use a 160*160 window to sample in 80 steps.

We combine the cross entropy with iou as the loss function, defined as:

$$iou\_loss = bce - \log(iou) \tag{1}$$

$$bce = -\sum (y_t) \log y_p + (1 - y_t) \log (1 - y_p) \tag{2}$$

$$iou = \sum_{i=1}^{N} \frac{\sum (y_t \times y_p)}{\sum y_t + \sum y_p - \sum (y_t \times y_p)} / N \tag{3}$$

We choose the higher point of val_iou as the convergence point.

Determining the threshold by the ROC curve.

At prediction phase, we use the overlap slider prediction method to average the overlapping regions.

3.3 Optimization of Model's Output

In order to enhance the reliability of the final recognition, we integrate the prediction results of the integrated model with the RGB-PanSharpen data to build a new training data. We use the fine-tune method to train a shallow U-Net as a calibration model based on this dataset. The calibration rules are filtered according to the coincidence between the old output and the new output, as shown in Fig. 4.

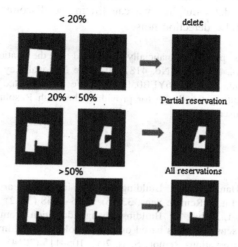

Fig. 4. Calibration rules.

The visualization of some prediction results reveals a phenomenon that the building prediction area is disconnected. Morphological preprocessing is added after the prediction, which not only fills in the disconnected area, but also eliminates part of the false detection noise. We set the size of the closed operation to 10*10 and the size of the open operation to 8*8. The effect of Morphological dilate and erode shown in Fig. 5.

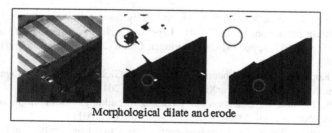

Fig. 5. Morphological methods

4 Conclusion

In order to make full use of the data, we combine the MUL-Pan Sharpen and PAN data as the training data. We apply improved U-NET and HF-FCN as main models. We want the models pay more attention to the small building which is more difficult to detect, so, we oversample small building areas and under sample large building areas.

We adapt multi-scaled patch and sliding window to promote the generalization of the models. We have a calibration model to make our result more reliability. On the other hand, we adapt morphological methods to dilate and erode output of the model. With the optimization of model's outputs, we can fill in the disconnected area, but also eliminates part of the false detection noise.

Acknowledgments. This paper is financially supported by the National Natural Science Foundation of China (No. 41701594, No. 41871302), the National Key Research and Development Program of China (No. 2016YFB0502600). We are indebted to DeepGlobe 2018 Satellite Image Understanding Challenge for providing the High Resolution Remote Sensing Images used in this manuscript.

References

1. Chen, L., Zhao, S., Han, W., et al.: Building detection in an urban area using lidar data and QuickBird imagery. Int. J. Remote Sens. **33**(16), 5135–5148 (2012)
2. Huang, X., Zhang, L., Zhu, T.: Building change detection from multitemporal high-resolution remotely sensed images based on a morphological building index. IEEE J. Sel. Top. Appl. Earth Observations Remote Sens. **7**(1), 105–115 (2014)
3. Vakalopoulou, M., Karantzalos, K., Komodakis, N., et al.: Building detection in very high resolution multispectral data with deep learning features. In: 2015 IEEE International Geoscience and Remote Sensing Symposium (IGARSS), pp. 1873–1876, IEEE (2015)
4. Zhang, L., Zhang, L., Du, B.: Deep learning for remote sensing data: A technical tutorial on the state of the art. IEEE Geosci. Remote Sens. Mag. **4**(2), 22–40 (2016)
5. Ronneberger, O., Fischer, P., Brox, T.: U-Net: convolutional networks for biomedical image segmentation. In: Navab, N., Hornegger, J., Wells, W.M., Frangi, A.F. (eds.) MICCAI 2015. LNCS, vol. 9351, pp. 234–241. Springer, Cham (2015). https://doi.org/10.1007/978-3-319-24574-4_28
6. Xie, S., Tu, Z.: Holistically-nested edge detection. Int. J. Comput. Vis. **125**(1–3), 3–18 (2017)
7. Zuo, T., Feng, J., Chen, X.: HF-FCN: hierarchically fused fully convolutional network for robust building extraction. In: Lai, S.-H., Lepetit, V., Nishino, K., Sato, Y. (eds.) ACCV 2016. LNCS, vol. 10111, pp. 291–302. Springer, Cham (2017). https://doi.org/10.1007/978-3-319-54181-5_19
8. Demir, I., Koperski, K., Lindenbaum, D., et al.: DeepGlobe 2018: A Challenge to Parse the Earth through Satellite Images. arXiv preprint arXiv, 2018, 1805.06561
9. Noronha, S., Nevatia, R.: Detection and modeling of buildings from multiple aerial images. IEEE Trans. Pattern Anal. Mach. Intell. **23**(5), 501–518 (2001)
10. Li, E., Femiani, J., Xu, S., et al.: Robust rooftop extraction from visible band images using higher order CRF. IEEE Trans. Geosci. Remote Sens. **53**(8), 4483–4495 (2015)
11. Jiang, C., Han, G., Lin, J., Jia, G., Shi, W., Wan, J.: Characteristics of co-allocated online services and batch jobs in internet data centers: a case study from Alibaba cloud. IEEE Access **7**, 22495–22508 (2019). https://doi.org/10.1109/access.2019.2897898
12. Qiu, Y., Jiang, C., Wang, Y., Ou, D., Li, Y., Wan, J.: Energy aware virtual machine scheduling in data centers. Energies **12**, 646 (2019)
13. Jiang, C., Fan, T., Qiu, Y., Wu, H., Zhang, J., Xiong, N., Wan, J.: Interdomain I/O optimization in virtualized sensor networks. Sensors **18**, 4395 (2018)

A Case Study for User Rating Prediction on Automobile Recommendation System Using MapReduce

Zikai Nie[1], Jiao Sun[2(✉)], and Zhehua He[3]

[1] National University of Defense Technology, Changsha, China
zikai93@163.com
[2] Tsinghua University, Beijing, China
j-sun16@mails.tsinghua.edu.cn
[3] Jilin University, Changchun, China

Abstract. Recommender systems have been widely used in contemporary industry and plenty of work has been done in this field to help users to identify items of interest. Collaborative Filtering (CF, for short) algorithm is an important technology in recommender systems. However, less work has been done in automobile recommendation system with the sharp increase of the amount of automobiles. Whats more, the computational speed is a major weakness for collaborative filtering technology. Therefore, using MapReduce framework to optimize the CF algorithm is a vital solution to this performance problem. In this paper, we present a recommendation of the users comment on industrial automobiles with various properties based on real world industrial datasets of user-automobile comment data collection, and provide recommendation for automobile providers and help them predict users comment on automobiles with new-coming property. Firstly, we solve the sparseness of matrix using previous construction of score matrix. Secondly, we solve the data normalization problem by removing dimensional effects from the raw data of automobiles, where different dimensions of automobile properties bring great error to the calculation of CF. Finally, we use the MapReduce framework to optimize the CF algorithm, and the computational speed has been improved times. UV decomposition used in this paper is an often used matrix factorization technology in CF algorithm, without calculating the interpolation weight of neighbors, which will be more convenient in industry.

Keywords: Automobile recommendation · Data normalization · Collaborative filtering · MapReduce

1 Introduction

Recommender systems analyze patterns of user interest in items or products to provide personalized recommendations of items that will suit a users taste [1, 2], recommendation aim at predicting a few items (movies, books and etc.) of interest to a particular user [17]. Few systems make recommendation for automobile customers, and this brings a huge loss to the automobile electrical commerce. Meanwhile, for the recommendation

© Springer Nature Singapore Pte Ltd. 2019
C. Hu et al. (Eds.): HPCMS 2018/HiDEC 2018, CCIS 913, pp. 57–68, 2019.
https://doi.org/10.1007/978-981-32-9987-0_6

system of vehicles, users direct taste upon a kind of vehicle is hard to measure, but users demand for properties of vehicles is clear. Then we may use users demand to exclude users comments upon this kind of vehicle according to past records, then make the recommendation.

Therefore, after having users comments upon various vehicles, we should make recommendation for them to satisfy their taste, while maximizing users utilities are also very important, in this work, we use users experience to value their utilities, and what we focus on is to maximize their experience in different dimensions.

Generally speaking, recommender systems use two strategies, the content based approach and collaborative filtering. And the development of collaborative filtering mainly follows several independent directions. The first direction, which accounts for the majority of works in CF, is the development of algorithms, such as memory-based techniques, matrix factorization algorithms, probabilistic models and ensemble methods [13, 15, 20]. In contrast to other CF technologies, such as K-nearest neighborhood (KNN, for short) method, matrix factorization algorithms don't require for calculating the weight interpolation of similar users or items and the correlation between two of them. Similarity calculation techniques would be suitable for cross-ontology terms across different ontologies [19], but it might not be feasible for industrial automobile recommendation, due to fact that the differences between some properties of automobile are hard to distinguish, such as the model of cars, open-topped car or SUV. And the specific CF technology used in this paper is the matrix factorization algorithm.

As for the recommendation part, we have the predicted users comment upon this property of vehicle, then we should choose the best vehicle for user to satisfy his demand and optimize his experience to improve click rate of website or increase the probability of consuming. In this project, there're many consumers want to buy cars, and various cars with different properties, we may wonder if it can be modeled as a stable matching problem, and the answer is no for the amount of resources in stable matching problem is limited, while in this case the amount of cars is unlimited on the website, or though the amount of cars in reality is limited, after being recommended for different users, maybe none of them accept the recommendation and buy the car. Therefore, we shouldn't regard it as a stable matching problem, while many requirements in the vehicle case can be modeled as constraints satisfaction problems. The category of constraint satisfaction problems is too wide to specify this case.

In many cases, constraints are classified into hard constraints and soft constraints, meaning the former must be satisfied, and the latter may remain violated if its difficult to satisfy them. In the framework of weighted constraint satisfaction problem, both hard constraint problem and soft constraint problem can be processed on the same mathematical basis by adjusting the weight of penalty function, in this case, we consider it as a weighted constraint satisfaction problem.

The main components of matrix factorization algorithms are the input matrix construction, data normalization. And the computational speed of matrix factorization is a vital index to evaluate the algorithm. Accordingly, we revisit these three items and suggest novel methods to significantly improve the accuracy of matrix factorization approach on the automobile score dataset and significantly improve the computational speed of matrix factorization. Our three main contributions are:

- The previous construction of the matrix in matrix factorization algorithm is to have the rows representing users, and the columns representing items, then the values of the matrix presenting the score given by the certain user. However, it might not be feasible for the automobile score dataset, because most of users only bought two automobiles at most in the dataset, which causes the score matrix extremely sparse and leads to the great inaccuracy of calculating result. We present a new method of constructing the matrix and efficiently solve the sparseness problem that can be used to nearly all the automobile datasets.
- The dimensional and order of magnitude between different property of automobile are of great difference. For instance, the model of automobile may consist of SUV, open-topped car, van, etc. while the engine of the car is usually about 100 to 300 in horsepower. Therefore, we come up with a method to normalize the raw data, which can be applied to nearly all the automobile score datasets.
- The computational speed of the matrix factorization algorithm is a very important component to evaluate the efficiency of the algorithm. Instead of optimizing the algorithm itself. We concentrate on the speed up of the algorithm in running time. And we optimize the algorithm by using MapReduce framework, and the running time of the algorithm has been reduced times.

The paper is organized as follows. In Sect. 2, we introduce the background task of this paper, including some introduction to the principle of MapReduce Framework and the collection of datasets we used in this paper. In Sect. 3, we introduce our improved CF algorithm and optimize it in running time by using MapReduce framework. In Sect. 4, we show the experiments of automobile recommendation system using MapReduce in Hadoop. Then we draw a conclusion and make a discussion about the future work.

2   Background Task and Dataset

MapReduce is a programming model for processing and generating large datasets [5]. The framework provides an abstraction consists of mapper and reducer functions, and their function of processing data is shown in Fig. 1. We use Hadoop streaming for python to realize the MapReduce process. Accordingly, the input data is split by the mapper, and output key-value pairs based on the program implementation, which is provided by the mapper function automatically. Then the map result was shuffled and sorted, values with same key are grouped together, becoming the input to the reducer program using Hadoop streaming, then user can complete their implementation in the reducer program using the grouped values, such as matrix factorization. Finally, the output of reducer program makes up the final result of MapReduce program.

In the past few years, the amount of automobiles all over the world has been increased sharply, the changes in Automobile sales volume in China in the past ten years is shown in Fig. 2.

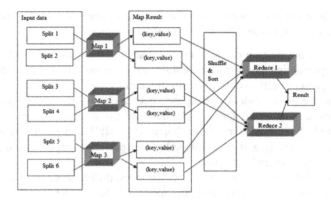

Fig. 1. The procedure of data processing using MapReduce Frame.

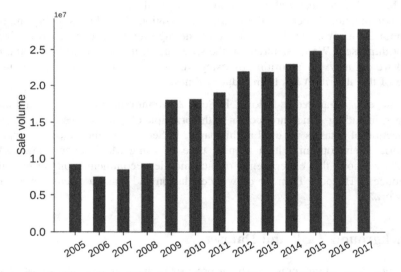

Fig. 2. Illustration of the changes in automobile sales volume in China.

And several websites begin to sell the automobiles specifically and collect users comments on cars they have bought, in the same way like e-commerce leader Amazon.com collects users volume in China comments on items. We have crawled users comments upon automobiles theyve bought from Autohome website, which is the largest automobile interaction platform in China, the number of registered users in Autohome has increased a lot, as is shown in Fig. 3. Whats more, it covers 87.46% of automobile series in sale, 68.85% of automobile brand and 73.34% of automobiles in sale. In addition, it collects 4,91,464 users comments of automobiles. Therefore, we think the data collected from Autohome is comprehensive and convincing. Accordingly, we have also crawled the basic properties of automobiles user has commented, including motor, horsepower, automobile model, average oil cost of automobile owners and price, 5 dimensions in total. And the dataset we collected contains 27,895 records. Whats more, the users comments on certain automobiles also consist of 8 dimensions, including decoration inside the automobile, the power, the comfort, the appearance, the space, the oil cost, the cost performance, and the manipulability. All the comment scores range from 1 to 5, higher score it gets, more satisfied the customer is. And we only collect the property of automobiles that user has commented on, instead of collecting all automobiles properties in the website by using DFS search in website crawler.

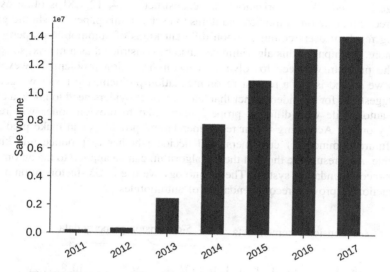

Fig. 3. Illustration of the changes in registered users of Autohome.

In a word, the dataset we used is a real-world industrial automobile dataset, including 5-dimension property data and 8-dimension comment data.

3   Automobile Recommendation System with CF Using MapReduce Framework

The algorithm used in this paper is to build an automobile recommendation system to recognize the users taste upon automobiles with certain kind of properties, so the sellers can make recommendation.

According to the result of prediction. For real-world automobile datasets, we shall take the matrix construction, data normalization and computational speed into consideration to improve the accuracy and efficiency of the CF algorithm. In this section, firstly, we will introduce the CF algorithm we used and some related work including the matrix construction and data normalization which can be applied to nearly all automobile datasets. Then we will introduce how to optimize the CF algorithm using

MapReduce framework. Subsequently, we will introduce the improved tabu search method for WCSP taking users preference into consideration and avoid confining the search into a restricted region that satisfy the constraints with large weights while the user may dont care too much about.

3.1 The Automobile Recommender System with CF

Collaborative Filtering techniques are often used in recommendation systems with extremely sparse inputs [6, 8]. One of their most publicized use was the Netflix Challenge [3], and UV- factorization and reconstruction [4, 12, 18] is often used to provide recommendation of movies and items to users. In this paper, we should get the predicting result of users comment upon different kinds of automobile property data. Whats more, the input of this algorithm can also be constructed as a matrix, so we can regard the problem we need to solve as a recommendation problem. However, the problem we solved is not a regular recommendation problem, the result we get is to make suggestions for providers rather than customers. Providers need to know a certain kind of automobile with different property compared to previous ones will receive popularity or not. According to our recommendation, providers can make predictions on the future comment of customers, and decide whether to produce this kind of automobile. As a result, we thought the CF algorithm can be applied to the automobile-provider recommendation system. The technology we use is UV-factorization and PQ reconstruction to provide recommendation of automobiles.

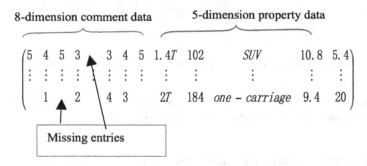

Fig. 4. The automobile-score matrix.

(1) **Matrix Construction.** In previous construction of score matrix, the row of matrix represents user, and the columns of matrix represents various items, thus the items of the matrix represent the users comment or score upon certain item. However, it might not feasible for automobile dataset, because a user in our dataset only bought two automobiles at most. Therefore, the comment a user has make is also up to two, and if we construct the matrix as pervious work, the resulting matrix will be extremely sparse. And the extreme sparseness will bring great inaccuracy to the calculation of UV factorization. To solve this problem, we reconstruct a matrix with the specific series of automobile as rows, such as Boxster2.7L in

2006, Audi A1 1.4TFSIEgo in 2012, BMW 2012 series 116I manual block 1, etc. and 5-dimension property data and 8-dimension comment data, as is described in Sect. 2. In doing so, the matrix were constructed is hardly sparse with some missing entries we should estimate, as shown in Fig. 4.

(2) **Data Normalization.** Data Normalization is an essential part of data mining, and especially important for automobile datasets due to the huge difference between dimensions of automobile property data. For instance, the range of motor is around 1T- 20T, the horsepower is from 100 to 300, even higher, the model of automobile consists of SUV, one-carriage car, two-carriage car and so on, while the price of various automobiles is of great difference. As a result, we have to normalize the property data of automobile.

First of all, we remove the unit from each property data, such as T and million. Secondly, we make a list of each model of automobile by using the enumeration of normalization, and rank the one-carriage car 1, two-carriage car 2, three-carriage car 3, SUV 4, open-topped car 5 and so on. And all the property data is numerical and easy to analyze. Thirdly, we have to normalize each dimensional property data.

The Z-score normalization is a familiar statistical method in both neuro-imaging [11] and psychological studies [10], [7] among others. And we can also apply it to the each column of property data by using Z-score normalization shown in Eq. 1, where μ and σ is the mean and variance of property data in each column.

$$x^* = (x - \mu)/\sigma. \tag{1}$$

Then, all property data in each column is map to [0, 1] and Obey standard normal distribution. In order to shorten the difference between comment data and property data, we also map the property data in each column into [1, 5] using standard partition table shown in Fig. 5.

α / β_i	3	4	5	6	7	8	9	10
β_1	-0.43	-0.67	-0.84	-0.97	-1.07	-1.15	-1.22	-1.28
β_2	0.43	0	-0.25	-0.43	-0.57	-0.67	-0.76	-0.84
β_3		0.67	0.25	0	-0.18	-0.32	-0.43	-0.52
β_4			0.84	0.43	0.18	0	-0.14	-0.25
β_5				0.97	0.57	0.32	0.14	0
β_6					1.07	0.3-67	0.43	0.25
β_7						1.15	0.76	0.52
β_8							1.22	0.84
β_9								1.28

Fig. 5. Illustration of standard partition table.

(3) **UV Factorization and PQ Reconstruction.** The input of UV factorization in this case is the reconstructed matrix mentioned above. If we let R be the input matrix containing all the score and normalized property data that various kinds of automobiles have got. Assuming the number of missing entries is K, then our task is to find two metrics $P(a|U| \times K)$ matrix). and Q (a $K \times |V|$ matrix) to estimate the missing entry of $R\left(R \approx P \times Q^T = \widehat{R}\right)$. Whats more, the result of UV factorization is approximate rather than accurate, so the efficiency of UV factorization is higher than SVD, which is also often used in industry. Then we use PQ-reconstruction with Stochastic Gradient Descent (SGD), a simple latent-factor model to reconstruct the missing entries. Firstly, the output of UV factorization provides an initial reconstruction of A. Subsequently, SGD iterates over all elements of reconstructed matrix of R until convergence. For each element r_{ui}:

$$e_{ij}^2 = \left(r_{ij} - \widehat{r}_{ij}\right)^2 = \left(r_{ij} - \sum_{k=1}^{K} p_{ik}q_{ki}\right)^2. \tag{2}$$

$$p'_{ik} = p_{ik} + 2\alpha e_{ij}q_{kj}. \tag{3}$$

$$q'_{ik} = q_{ik} + 2\alpha e_{ij}p_{kj}. \tag{4}$$

SGD iterates over all elements until e_{ij} becomes marginal or the iteration times reach the maximum which is settled by the program. Generally speaking, the loss of property data in relatively rare compared to the comment data. And we can estimate the new coming certain series of automobile according to its property data. Starting with the prediction of users score, sellers can make recommendation according to it accurately.

3.2   Optimize the CF Algorithm Using MapReduce Framework

It is well known that dense matrix factorization can be implemented efficiently on distributed memory parallel computers [8, 9, 14, 16]. And we use the MapReduce framework to parallelize the CF algorithm in distributed environment. As is described in Sect. 2, we should focus on the implementation of mapper and reducer program, and the function of data processing can be illustrated as follows:

$$Map: data \rightarrow (key, value)pairs$$

$$Reduce: List(key) \rightarrow List'(key),$$

$$Generally, Length(List) > Length(List')$$

And we should focus on the chosen of key and value of the reconstructed matrix in Sect. 3.1. In order to divide the matrix into small matrices easy to calculate, we chose the property data with 5 phases as the key of map program, and comment data with 8 phases as the value of map program. Then the raw data was mapped into a list where the records was sorted and grouped by the property data. After the execution of mapper program, the reducer program do the UV factorization and PQ reconstruction for each value list with same property of automobile, which can be described as follows:

$$Map : \ data \rightarrow (property, comment)pairs$$

$$Reduce : \ List(property) \rightarrow CF(List(property))$$

The CF mentioned in this formula is the CF algorithm, including UV factorization and PQ reconstruction as modeled in Sect. 3.1. Accordingly, the input of CF algorithm in the reduce program is the list of comment data of automobile with the same property, so that the original matrix can be divided into several matrics to make up the input of CF algorithm separately, as a result, the running time of algorithm has been reduced sharply. The data transmission is the key of MapReduce, and Fig. 6 shows the MapReduce based algorithm. The map function emits the key of MapReduce is the comment data of automobile. The reduce function distinguish different property data using the output of the map function. All the function is completed by Hadoop streaming using python code.

```
Mapper procedure;
    start
        for all line in dataset do
            (key,value) = (property,comment)
    end

Reducer procedure:
    start
    last_key = None,count = 0
    for all line from mapper's output do:
        if key = last_key or last_key = None:
            count + 1
            add this to this key's input matrix of CF
        else:
            if key != last_key:
            if the length of last_key's matrix > 1:
                CF(last_key's matrix)
                add the result of CF to result matrix
            else
                add this line to result matrix
    end
```

Fig. 6. Pseudocode of the CF algorithm using the MapReduce algorithm.

4 Experimenta and Analysis

We used a cluster of 4 nodes, all machines involved in the experiments has 4 Intel(R) Core(TM) i5-3230 m 2.60 GHz processors and 8 GB of memory and were running CentOS 6.7 (64 bit) Linux operating system on VMware Workstation 12 Pro. Hadoop version 2.5.2 and java 1.7.0 60 were used for the benchmarks and Eclipse 4.4.1 was used for the java code, while python version is 2.7 and PyCharm 4.5.3 is used for the python code.

The dataset we used has been described in Sect. 2, the automobile dataset crawled from Autohome, containing 27,895 records in total. The algorithms were run on a sample of 10,000 and it was sampled sequentially. The sample sizes are 20, 200, 853, 2000, 10000 which are selected randomly among the remaining dataset after the pre-processing of data mentioned in Sect. 3.1.

There are three experiments based on automobile recommendation system and presented here. The first one is collaborative filtering using brute force, without using MapReduce. The second is collaborative filtering under Hadoop stand-alone operation. And the third one is implemented in parallel for Hadoop in the cluster of 4 nodes, which is a real distributed environment.

In order to test the accuracy of CF algorithm, we use 80% of every sample dataset as training set and the remaining 20% of every sample as testing set to test the accuracy of CF algorithm used in this paper. Whats more, we also count the consumption of running time upon every property of machine, including brute force, stand-alone and real distributed environment of MapReduce. Then we add the interpolation weight to every error between the result of predicting data and realistic data, and the interpolation weight is the number of missing values.

Table 1. Change in accuracy of predicting result

Sample size	20	200	853	2000	10000
Broute force	67.06%	72.20%	81.73%	88.54%	89.43%
Hadoop	66.60%	71.12%	80.05%	87.20%	88.65%

Then we use the ε to divide the dimension of comment data which need to predict, and derive the accuracy percent of predict. According to different property of machine, we derive different accuracy of predicting using different sample dataset, which is shown in Table 1. We can know that after using the MapReduce frame, we can see the loss of accuracy is extremely tiny which is up to 2% and can be nearly ignored compared to the improvement of running time. Besides, we can also see the CF algorithm used in this paper is efficient and accurate, and the rate of accuracy is over 80% with the increase of sample sizes. Meanwhile, the increase of accuracy for predicting result using MapReduce framework is as obvious as brute force method, thus we needn't to worry about the decrease of accuracy using MapReduce framework with the increase of sample sizes.

Figure 7 shows the change in time consumption over samples size of automobiles were selected for test mentioned above, after the overwriting of the normal UV factorization, we see the shorten of running time consumption is extremely obvious at the beginning, whereas with the increase of automobiles samples, the optimization of running time is not as obvious as previous. The change in time consumption over samples size of automobile in the real distributed environment for Hadoop, and we can discover the great optimization of running time consumption. The MapReduce program divide the matrix after preprocessing of CF into several parts, where each part has its own property data, and the CF algorithm can be applied for parallel running, so that the running consumption can be reduced a lot. We can see the time consumption of 2,000 automobiles recommendation is about 8 min, which is definitely feasible for the industry.

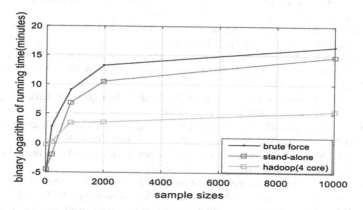

Fig. 7. Pseudocode of the CF algorithm using the MapReduce algorithm.

5 Conclusion and Future Work

The specialty of automobile dataset makes it difficult to estimate the users taste upon certain kind of automobile, and the computational cost of UV factorization is pretty high. In this paper, we come up with a CF algorithm to make recommendation of automobiles by using MapReduce framework, and the dataset we used for experiment is the property data and comment data of kinds of automobiles in Autohome, which is convincing and comprehensive. Then after the experiment, we get pretty good result, and the CF algorithm in this paper is pretty efficient and feasible for industrial use.

In addition, we also come up with the method of data pre- processing of automobile dataset, which can be used for most of datasets in industry, and the accuracy of recommendation algorithm can be improved screamingly.

However, the algorithm used in this paper is often-used collaborative filtering technology in recommendation system and we hardly optimize the algorithm itself. Whats more, the algorithm using for MapReduce is not self-adapting, we may do some work about making it self-adapting to get the globally optimal solution of the whole matrix in reducer program rather than the globally optimal solution of each divided matrix.

References

1. Adomavicius, G., Tuzhilin, A.: Toward the next generation of recommender systems: a survey of the state-of-the-art and possible extensions. IEEE Trans. Knowl. Data Eng. **17**(6), 734–749 (2005)
2. Bell, R.M., Koren, Y.: Scalable collaborative filtering with jointly derived neighborhood interpolation weights. In: The Seventh IEEE International Conference on Data Mining (ICDM), vol. 7, pp. 43–52. IEEE (2007)
3. Bell, R.M., Koren, Y., Volinsky, C.: The bellkor 2008 solution to the netflix prize. Statistics Research Department at AT&T Research, 1 (2008)
4. Bottou, L.: Large-scale machine learning with stochastic gradient descent. In: Lechevallier, Y., Saporta, G. (eds.) Proceedings of COMPSTAT 2010, pp. 177–186. Springer, Heidelberg (2010). https://doi.org/10.1007/978-3-7908-2604-3_16
5. Chen, L.C., Kuo, P.J., Liao, I.E.: Ontology-based library recommender system using MapReduce. Cluster Comput. **18**(1), 113–121 (2015)
6. Delimitrou, C., Kozyrakis, C.: Quasar: resource-efficient and QoS-aware cluster management. ACM SIGPLAN Not. **49**(4), 127–144 (2014)
7. Fruchter, B., Fruchter, D.A.: Factor content of the wais with separate digits-forward and digits-backward scores for a borderline and mentally retarded sample. Monogr. Am. Assoc. Ment. Defic. (1), 67 (1973)
8. Gallivan, K.A., Plemmons, R.J., Sameh, A.H.: Parallel algorithms for dense linear algebra computations. SIAM Rev. **32**(1), 54–135 (1990)
9. Geist, G.A., Romine, C.H.: Lu factorization algorithms on distributed-memory multiprocessor architectures. SIAM J. Sci. Stat. Comput. **9**(4), 639–649 (1988)
10. Guilford, J.P.: Structure-of-intellect abilities in preliterate children and the mentally retarded. Monogr. Am. Assoc. Ment. Defic. **1**, 46–58 (1973)
11. Ishii, K., et al.: A diagnostic method for suspected alzheimer's disease using h 2 15 O positron emission tomography perfusion Z score. Neuroradiology **42**(11), 787–794 (2000)
12. Kiwiel, K.C.: Convergence and efficiency of subgradient methods for quasiconvex minimization. Math. Program. **90**(1), 1–25 (2001)
13. Koren, Y., Bell, R., Volinsky, C.: Matrix factorization techniques for recommender systems. Computer **42**(8), 30–37 (2009)
14. Kumar, V., Grama, A., Anshul, G., Karypis, G.: Introduction to parallel computing: design and analysis of algorithms. Benjamin/Cummings Publishing Company **18**, 82–109 (1994)
15. Marlin, B.: Collaborative filtering: a machine learning perspective. University of Toronto (2004)
16. O'Leary, D.P., Stewart, G.W.: Assignment and scheduling in parallel matrix factorization. Linear Algebra Appl. **77**, 275–299 (1986)
17. Pradel B., et al.: A case study in a recommender system based on purchase data. In: Proceedings of the 17th ACM SIGKDD International Conference on Knowledge Discovery and Data Mining, pp. 377–385. ACM (2011)
18. Rajaraman, A., Ullman, J.: Textbook on mining of massive datasets (2011)
19. Rodriguez, M.A., Egenhofer, M.J.: Determining semantic similarity among entity classes from different ontologies. IEEE Trans. Knowl. Data Eng. **15**(2), 442–456 (2003)
20. Su, X., Taghi, M.K.: A survey of collaborative filtering techniques. Adv. Artif. Intell. **2009**, 4 (2009)

Diverse Demands Estimation and Ranking Based on User Behaviors

Liandong Chen[1], Shigang Li[3], Chunbao Zhou[2], Fang Liu[2(✉)], Rui Xu[1], Shuo Li[2,4], Jue Wang[2], and Boyao Zhang[2,4]

[1] State Grid Hebei Electric Power Supply Co., Ltd., Shijiazhuang, China
`{ldchen, rxu}@sgcc.com.cn`
[2] Computer Network Information Center, Chinese Academy of Science, Beijing, China
`{zhoucb, liufang, lis, wangjue, zhangby}@sccas.cn`
[3] Institute of Computing Technology, Chinese Academy of Sciences, Beijing, China
`lixg@ict.ac.cn`
[4] University of Chinese Academy of Sciences, Beijing, China

Abstract. In the big data era, users can get massive information from the Internet, but the value density is very low. In order to help users find the information they need more quickly, this paper presents the mechanism of diverse demands estimation and ranking based on user behaviors. Firstly, a definition of classification system for users query intent is proposed. Secondly, in order to mine the documents on the websites of specific classification, LDA model is used to cluster and annotate the websites. To speed up the inference process of LDA, we take advantage of MPI and OpenMP hybrid parallelism techniques to reduce both internode and intra-node communication cost. Lastly, according to the historical behaviors of users and the search engine return results, we rank the classifications on Map-Reduce platform and present the top-ranking ones to users

Keywords: Big data · LDA · MPI · OpenMP · Clustering · Ranking

1 Introduction

LDA can be considered as an unsupervised machine learning technology. It is a clustering tool that has attracted many people's attention. It can identify potential topic information in a large-scale set of documents, and it can also predict and infer which topics a new document is related. LDA uses the bag of words method. Each document is regarded as a vector of word frequency. If two different words often appear together in the same document, then the LDA training algorithm tends to classify these two words to one category (with the same topic).

LDA is a generative model. The LDA first assumes a process of generating documents, and then it leans the chararteritis of the generating process according to a large set of real documents. LDA assumes that there are K topics for each document, and each topic can be considered of as a distribution of words). To generate a document, we

C. Hu et al. (Eds.): HPCMS 2018/HiDEC 2018, CCIS 913, pp. 69–78, 2019.
https://doi.org/10.1007/978-981-32-9987-0_7

first generate a topic distribution for the document, and then we generate a collection of words. To generate a word, we randomly select a topic according to the topic distribution of the document, and then we randomly generate a word based on the distribution of words in that topic.

In general, the implementation of LDA includes two parts: the training algorithm and the prediction algorithm. The training algorithm refers to learning the LDA model based on the existing set of documents, which has a great influence on the effects and the convergence of the LDA model. The number of iterations can usually reach hundreds or thousands. The prediction algorithm refers to using the learned LDA model to infer the topic distribution of a new document.

The process of LDA training includes a large number of iterations. In each iteration, all the words in all the training documents need to be searched, and the document - theme matrix (matrix size is $D * K$, where D is the document number, K number, theme) together with the theme - word matrix (the size of $K * V$, where V is the number of) should be updated in each iteration. The whole process is very time-consuming, so the demand for a new parallel training algorithm is urgent.

2   Related Works

Blei et al. [2] first proposed Latent Dirichlet Allocation (LDA) to model documents, of which computational complexity is dominated by the number of topics multiplied by the vocabulary size in the document collection.

Some works resort to the techniques of parallel computing to speed up the inference for LDA model. Newman et al. [12] proposed two distributed inference schemes approximate distributed inference for LDA, AD-LDA and HD-LDA. AD-LDA achieves speedup easily, but without convergence guarantees. HD-LDA has a theoretical convergence guarantee but with high computational cost. Wang et al. [18] implemented parallel LDA (PLDA) on both MPI and MapReduce, and showed that MPI-PLDA got better performance than MapReduce-PLDA but still with high message passing communication cost. Liu et al. [11] presented PLDA+, which uses a series of optimizations to reduce inter-node communication cost of PLDA. Asuncion et al. [1] presented asynchronous distributed inference for LDA (Async-LDA), which eliminates the global synchronization in AD-LDA. Tora et al. [14] implemented AD-LDA in hybrid MPI and OpenMP programming to reduce intra-node communication cost, which is the most recent work for parallel LDA. The LDA model used in this paper is based on the hybrid MPI/OpenMP implementation [14] and future optimized by preprocessing and selecting the best combination of threads and processes.

The inference process of LDA can be accelerated using MPI [5] and OpenMP [4] hybrid parallelism techniques. The Message Passing Interface (MPI) [5] is a message-passing library interface specification, which is always used for communication in parallel applications [8–10]. The MPI is widely used in HPC (High Performance Computing) area [16, 17, 20]. Most of the cloud computing services providers now offer online parallel and distributed machine learning and artificial intelligence platform and support latest machine learning framework [21–23]. OpenMP [4] is an application programming interface (API) for parallel programming on multiprocessors [15] which is a framework dedicated to systems with shard memory. OpenMP offers a powerful new way to achieve scalability in parallel program [3].

Hybrid MPI and OpenMPI is also an alternative way to speed up the progress [13, 19]. In this paper, we make an implementation of this kind of hybrid computing model for PLDA.

3 Clustering the Websites by LDA Model

3.1 LDA Model

LDA is an unsupervised machine learning techniques, which is able to identify the potential topics from large-scale documents information and predict the inference. Generally LDA includes training part and prediction part. In the training part, the LDA model is learned from an existing set of documents. In the prediction part, the LDA model learned in the training phase is used to infer the topic distribution of a new document. Assume that there are total D documents, K latent topics and W words. LDA models each document as a mixture of K latent topics and each topic is a multinomial distribution over W words.

Figure 1 illustrates the LDA model, in which α and β denote hyperparameters of the Dirichlet priors, and Nj denotes the number of words in document j. For document j, the multinomial parameters $\theta_{k|j}$ are drawn from Dirichlet prior distribution $Dir(\alpha)$. For topic k, the multinomial parameters $\phi_{w|k}$ are drawn from Dirichlet prior distribution $Dir(\beta)$.

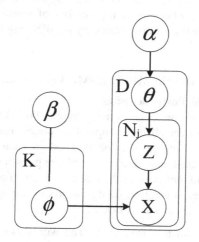

Fig. 1. LDA model

For the i-th word w in document j:

(1) Topic zij is drawn from multinomial distribution $Mult(\theta_j)$.
(2) Word w is drawn from multinomial distribution $Mult(\phi_{z_{ij}})$.

The posterior distributions can be estimated by collapsed Gibbs sampling [7], in which the probability of zij can be Given the current state of all but one variable zij, the conditional probability of zij is:

$$p(z_{i,j} = k|z^{-ij}, x, \alpha, \beta) \propto (\alpha + n_{k|j}^{-ij}) \frac{\beta + n_{x_{ij}|k}^{-ij}}{W\beta + n_k^{-ij}}$$

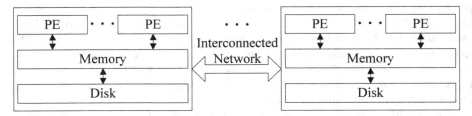

Fig. 2. Multi-core cluster architecture

LDA requires a lot of training iterations. Each iteration needs to traverse all the words of the training documents, constantly update the document-topic matrix (size D × K, where D is the number of documents, K is the number of topics) and the topic-word matrix (size K × W, where W is the number of words), which is very time-consuming. Thus, to reduce the training period by parallelizing the algorithm is in great demand.

3.2   Speed Up LDA by Hybrid MPI/OpenMP Parallelism

3.2.1   Preprocessing and Postprocessing

We speed up LDA on multi-core clusters using hybrid MPI/OpenMP parallelism. The documents are distributed over all the computation nodes. Each node has a copy of topic-word matrix, and the matrix will be updated in each iteration. The size of document-topic matrix on each node decreases with the growth of the number of nodes, while the size of topic-word matrix on each node is constant. To reduce the storage load of the related data structures, several pre- and post-processing operations are carried out for the input and output files, as stated below:

(1) Remove the words with low frequency. The words that seldom appear are not concerned. For example, the words that appear less than 10 times are removed from the documents set.
(2) Add a unique number (ID) for each word in the input file. Each word is represented by a tripe <word (string), the word ID (integer), the frequency of the word

appears in the documents (integer)>. During processing, the word ID is used instead of the word string to reduce the memory cost.

(3) During the postprocessing phase, the word IDs are mapped back to the actual word strings.

3.2.2 Parallel Inference for LDA

We parallelize the LDA algorithm on multi-core clusters by hybrid MPI/OpenMP programming. Multi-core clusters consist of shared memory within a node and distributed memory between nodes, as shown in Fig. 2.

Figure 3 illustrates the LDA execution model on multi-core clusters, where the solid line represents the MPI processes and OpenMP threads and the dashed line represents the loop iteration.

In the parallel LDA algorithm, the D training documents are distributed to P MPI processes, and each MPI process launches T OpenMP threads. For load balancing, each process is assigned to D/P documents. All the T threads within a process share the D/P documents and each thread processes D/P/T documents. The t-th thread in the p-th process the documents set W(p, t), and the topics set (corresponding to the words in the documents set) is Z(p, t), where $p \in [1, P]$ and $t \in [1, T]$. The documents set processed by p is $W_p = \{W(p, t)\}_{t=1}^{T}$ and the corresponding topics set is $Z_p = \{Z(p, t)\}_{t=1}^{T}$.

During each iteration of Gibbs sampling, thread t assigns value to z(p, t, i, j) by the posterior distribution, as noted below:

$$P(z_{(p,t,i,j)} = k | Z_{-(p,t,i,j)}, W_{-(p,t,i,j)}, W_{(p,t,i,j)} = v)$$
$$\propto (C^{doc}_{(p,t,i,k)-(p,t,i,j)} + \alpha) \times (C^{mod}_{(v,k)-(p,t,i,j)} + \beta)/(C^{mod}_{(k)-(p,t,i,j)}$$
$$+ V \times \beta)$$

Where k is one of the K topics and $k \in [1, K]$; v is one of the V words and $v \in [1, V]$; $w_{(p,t,i,j)}$ is the j-th word in the i-th document processed by the t-th thread of the p-th process; z(p, t, i, j) is the corresponding topic of $w_{(p,t,i,j)}$; $C^{doc}_{(p,t,i,k)-(p,t,i,j)}$ is the number of times that topic k appears in the i-th document processed by the t-th thread of the p-th process (except w(p, t, i, j) and z(p, t, i, j)); $C^{mod}_{(v,k)-(p,t,i,j)}$ is the number of times that the topic of word is assigned to the k (except w(p, t, i, j) and z(p, t, i, j)); $C^{mod}_{(k)-(p,t,i,j)} = \sum_{v=1}^{V} C^{mod}_{(v,k)-(p,t,i,j)}$.

The process of the parallel algorithm is illustrated as follows:

(1) Launch P processes and read the input file. Assign the value to z(p, t) by sampling;

(2) Each process initiates the document related data structures (including the documents-topics matrix S doc, etc.) and the model related data structures (including the topics-words matrix S_p^{mod}, etc.);

(3) Each process accumulates the partial results of S_p^{mod} by MPI_Allreduce;

(4) Launch T threads for each process;

(5) The time-step iteration:

(5.1) Each thread processes D/P/T documents. For each word in the document d:

    (5.1.1) Lock;

    (5.1.2) Update $z(p, t, i, j)$ by sampling collection through $C^{mod}_{(v,k)-(p,t,i,j)}$, $C^{mod}_{(k)-(p,t,i,j)}$ and $C^{doc}_{(p,t,i,k)-(p,t,i,j)}$;

    (5.1.3) Recalculate $C^{mod}_{(v,k)-(p,t,i,j)}$ and $C^{mod}_{(k)-(p,t,i,j)}$;

    (5.1.4) Unlock;

    (5.1.5) Recalculate $C^{doc}_{(p,t,i,k)-(p,t,i,j)}$;

(5.2) Thread synchronization;

(5.3) The main thread of each process to obtain the local topics-words matrix S^{mod}_p;

(5.4) Each process accumulates the partial results of S^{mod}_p by MPI_Allreduce;

(5.5) thread synchronization.

Note that: (1)–(4) correspond to the step0 in Fig. 3; (5.1) corresponds to the step1 in Fig. 3; (5.2) corresponds to the step2 in Fig. 3; (5.3) and (5.4) correspond to the step3 in Fig. 3; (5.5) corresponds to the step4 in Fig. 3.

4 Classification Ranking

4.1 Quality Evaluation

Most websites offer data through XML file with predetermined format. XML is stored by category, which includes several the center words and the data related to each word. In this section, we use XML data as an example to illustrate the evaluation of the results quality.

The quality of XML data is judged online considering the query results of common websites. The low-quality results will decrease its ranking position in the searching results based on a threshold value, or be filtered directly. We use VSM (Vector Space Model) to train the data offline and judge the quality online.

(1) Data training offline.

Prepare the corpus:

Pick up words randomly from the user log and capture the titles and abstracts of the Top10 searching results. These selected data are used as the corpus under the actual query distribution, which is denoted as SetA;

Capture the titles and abstracts of Top10 results searching by the center word of XML, which are used as a specific classification of corpus and denoted as SetB;

For SetA, remove the unused words and select the Top20000 terms in terms of frequency. Use the selected terms to generate the feature vectors and the set of the terms is denoted as VectorKey.

Calculating eigenvectors of the classifications:

Calculate the tf-idf of each term in the VectorKey, which is used as the feature vectors of a specific classification and denoted as VectorClass. In practice, there is eigenvector for each XML classification.

(2) Quality judging online.

When a user initiates a query, use the Top10 webpage results instead of SetB to calculate the tf-idf of the VectorKey, which is used as the feature vector of the current query and denoted as VectorQuery. The quality f a specific classification is judged by computing the cosine distance of VectorClass and VectorQuery.

4.2 Parallelize the Ranking Algorithm Under Map-Reduce Framework

The ranking algorithms involve features with thousands of dimensions. The extraction and preprocessing of these features are usually time-consuming. The massive scale of Internet data and real-time demands of the users require that the data should be processed quickly. We resort to the distributed computing based Map-Reduce framework to speed up the features calculation.

In the Map-Reduce programming model, all data are represented based on the key-value pairs. The output of Map stage is the input of Reduce stage. The output of Reduce stage is the final result. In the Map stage, all the key-value pairs that need processed are specified. In the Reduce stage, all the values with the same key are processed on the same Reduce node.

During the ranking based on the user behaviors, the feature calculation is very time-consuming. In the searching logs, only Top10 results are considered, and each session can be expressed as <query,url1,click1,url2,click2, ... , url10,click10>.

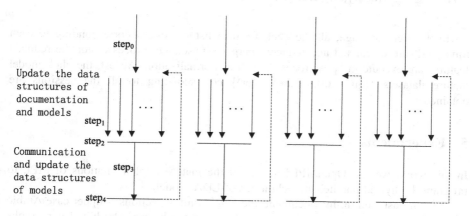

Fig. 3. Multi-core cluster architecture

Mapper algorithm:

```
1:     Class Mapper
2:     Method Map(session)
3:     query<-session.query,
4:        for i =1,2,…,10 do
5:           url<-session.urli, feature<-extract_click_features(i,clicki)
6:           EMIT((query,url),feature)
```

In the Map stage, (query,url) is extracted from each session as the click feature, which is used as the input of the Reduce stage. The method "extract_click_features" is the specific feature extraction module, which can be defined as extracting the information of the last click, first click, single click, click position and so on. "feature" is the numeric array or string corresponding to those click features.

Reducer algorithm:

```
1:     Class reducer
2:     Method Reduce((query,url),list<feature>)
3:     newVector<-new feature space for merging features
4:     For each feature in list<feature> do
5:           newVector[i]=newVector[i]+feature[i], for i=0,1,…feature.length-1
6:     featureVector<-postprocess(newVector)
7:     EMIT((query,url), featureVector)
```

In the Reduce stage, all the click features list <features> corresponding to each (query,url) are calculated and reduced merger. Subsequent processes for the reduced features are execute in "postprocess", such as normalization. At last, the click model feature datasets {(query,url,featureVector)} corresponding to all the sessions are obtained.

5   Experiments

In this work, we use OpenMPI [6], one of the mature implementations of MPI, to program the hybrid parallelism techniques of LDA model.

As demonstrated in this document, the numbering of sections is upper case Arabic numerals, then upper case Arabic numerals, separated by periods. Initial paragraphs after the section title are not indented. Only the initial, introductory paragraph has a drop cap (Table 1).

Table 1. Input test data

Iterations	Topics	Documents	No.	α	β
1200	300	150 Million	1892263	0.1	0.01

The test results on a batch of 256 cores experimental data is shown in the following Table 2, where 1p * 8t means one process with 8 threads per process are launched on each node, 2p * 4t means 2 processes with 4 threads per process, and 4p * 2t means 4 processes with 2 threads per process. Weekly we update the documents, and the model will be retrained accordingly.

Table 2. Experiment result

	1p * 8t	2p * 4t	4p * 2t
Operating Time	31 h	25 h and 6 min	27 h and 5 min
Speedup	96	120	110

6 Conclusions

This paper presents the mechanism of diverse demands estimation and ranking based on user behaviors by proposing a definition of classification system for the query intent of the users. Then the mining of the documents on the websites of specific classifications are accomplished using the LDA model. The inference process of the LDA model are accelerated using MPI and OpenMP hybrid parallelism techniques, which yields a speedup of around a hundred of times on a typical set of test data.

Acknowledgements. This work is jointly supported by Grant 2017YFB0203504 in the National Major Research High Performance Computing Program of China, and the State Key Program of National Natural Science Foundation of China (No. 91530324).

References

1. Asuncion, A.U., Smyth, P., Welling, M.: Asynchronous distributed learning of topic models. In: Proceedings of International Conference on Neural Information Processing Systems, Vancouver, British Columbia, Canada, December, pp. 81–88. DBLP (2008)
2. Blei, D.M., Ng, A.Y., Jordan, M.I.: Latent Dirichlet allocation. J. Mach. Learn. Res. **3**, 993–1022 (2003)
3. Chandra, R., Dagum, L., Kohr, D., Maydan, D., Mcdonald, J.: Parallel Programming in OpenMP. Morgan Kaufmann Publishers, Burlington (2001)
4. Dagum, L., Enon, R.: OpenMP: an industry-standard API for shared-memory programming. IEEE Comput. Sci. Eng. **5**, 46–55 (1998)
5. Forum, M.P.: MPI: A Message-passing interface standard. University of Tennessee (1994)

6. Gabriel, E., Fagg, G.E., Bosilca, G., et al.: Open MPI: goals, concept, and design of a next generation MPI implementation. In: Proceedings of Recent Advances in Parallel Virtual Machine and Message Passing Interface, European Pvm/mpi Users' Group Meeting, Budapest, Hungary, 19–22 September 2004, Proceedings, pp. 97–104. DBLP (2004)

7. Griffiths, T.L., Steyvers, M.: Finding scientific topics. Proc. Natl. Acad. Sci. U.S.A **101** (Suppl. 1), 5228–5235 (2004)

8. Gropp, W., Lusk, E., Skjellum, A.: Using MPI: Portable Parallel Programming with the Message-Passing Interface. MIT Press, Cambridge (1994)

9. Li, S., Zhang, Y., Hoefler, T.: Cache-oblivious MPI all-to-all communications based on Morton order. IEEE Trans. Parallel Distrib. Syst. **PP**(99), 1 (2018)

10. Li, S., Zhang, Y., Hoefler, T.: Cache-oblivious MPI all-to-all communications on many-core architectures. ACM SIGPLAN Not. **52**(8), 445–446 (2017)

11. Liu, Z., Zhang, Y., Chang, E.Y.: Sun, M: PLDA+: parallel latent dirichlet allocation with data placement and pipeline processing. ACM Trans. Intell. Syst. Technol. (TIST) **2**(3), 26 (2011)

12. Newman, D., Asuncion, A.U., Smyth, P., Welling, M.: Distributed inference for Latent Dirichlet allocation. In: Proceedings of International Conference on Neural Information Processing Systems, Vancouver, British Columbia, Canada, pp. 1–6. DBLP, December 2007

13. Rabenseifner, R., Hager, G., Jost, G.: Hybrid MPI/OpenMP parallel programming on clusters of multi-core SMP nodes. In: Proceedings of Euromicro International Conference on Parallel, Distributed and Network-Based Processing, pp. 427–436. IEEE (2009)

14. Tora, S., Eguchi, K.: MPI/OpenMP hybrid parallel inference for Latent Dirichlet allocation. In: Proceedings of The Workshop on Large Scale Data Mining: Theory and Applications, p. 5. ACM (2011)

15. Vrenios, A.: Parallel programming in C with MPI and OpenMP [book review]. IEEE Distrib. Syst. Online **5**(1), 7.1–7.3 (2004)

16. Wang, J., Liu, C., Huang, Y.: Auto tuning for new energy dispatch problem: a case study. Futur. Gener. Comput. Syst. **54**(C), 501–506 (2016)

17. Wang, J., Gao, F., Vazquez-Poletti, J.L., Li, J.: Preface of high performance computing or advanced modeling and simulation of materials. Comput. Phys. Commun. **211**, 1 (2017)

18. Wang, Yi, Bai, Hongjie, Stanton, Matt, Chen, Wen-Yen, Chang, Edward Y.: PLDA: parallel Latent Dirichlet allocation for large-scale applications. In: Goldberg, Andrew V., Zhou, Yunhong (eds.) AAIM 2009. LNCS, vol. 5564, pp. 301–314. Springer, Heidelberg (2009). https://doi.org/10.1007/978-3-642-02158-9_26

19. Wu, B., Li, S., Zhang, Y., et al.: A hybrid optimization strategy for the communication of large-scale Kinetic Monte Carlo simulation. Comput. Phys. Commun. (2016)

20. Zhang, Y., Li, S., Yan, S., et al.: A cross-platform SpMV framework on many-core architectures. ACM Trans. Arch. Code Optim. **13**(4), 33 (2016)

21. Jiang, C., Han, G., Lin, J., Jia, G., Shi, W., Wan, J.: Characteristics of co-allocated online services and batch jobs in Internet data centers: a case study from Alibaba cloud. IEEE Access **7**, 22495–22508. https://doi.org/10.1109/access.2019.2897898

22. Qiu, Y., Jiang, C., Wang, Y., Ou, D., Li, Y., Wan, J.: Energy aware virtual machine scheduling in data centers. Energies **12**, 646 (2019)

23. Jiang, C., et al.: Interdomain I/O optimization in virtualized sensor networks. Sensors **18**, 4395 (2018)

Energy Aware Edge Computing: A Survey

Tiantian Fan[1,2], Yeliang Qiu[1,2], Congfeng Jiang[1,2(✉)], and Jian Wan[3]

[1] Key Laboratory of Complex Systems Modeling and Simulation,
Hangzhou Dianzi University, Hangzhou 310018, China
cjiang@hdu.edu.cn
[2] School of Computer Science and Technology, Hangzhou Dianzi University,
Hangzhou 310018, China
[3] School of Information and Electronic Engineering,
Zhejiang University of Science and Technology, Hangzhou 310023, China

Abstract. Edge computing is an emerging paradigm to meet the ever-increasing computation demands from pervasive devices such as sensors, actuators, and smart things. Though the edge devices can execute complex applications, it is necessary for some applications to migrate to centralized servers. By offloading the computation from the edge nodes to the edge servers or cloud servers, the quality of computation experience could be greatly improved. However, it may cause delay and increase network overheads, and energy consumption eventually. Therefore, an optimal offloading strategy should take into account what task should be offloaded, when to offload and where to offload to avoid the overheads. Thus, it is important to tradeoff between energy consumption, computation delay and throughput when the system makes the computation offloading to achieve high energy efficiency. In this paper, we conduct a survey of energy aware edge computing, including the existing work on computation offloading frameworks and strategies in edge computing. Specifically, we describe the strategies from the perspective of energy aware offloading, energy optimization offloading and offloading algorithms.

Keywords: Edge computing · Energy efficiency · Computation offloading · Energy aware computing · Task partitioning

1 Introduction

With the advances in computing, sensors, and wireless communications, mobile devices and smart things are widely deployed in industrial, individual, and ambient places. These things are ubiquitous in terms of functionality, mobility, connectivity, and sustainability. For example, in a smart home, security systems, home appliances, ambient and entertainment equipment, PCs and smart phones, can be connected to collaborate in personal daily life and provide safer, easier, and healthier quality living. With more powerful computing, storage, and communication capabilities, these things are no longer constrained to provide one single function, such as sensing, data storage,

© Springer Nature Singapore Pte Ltd. 2019
C. Hu et al. (Eds.): HPCMS 2018/HiDEC 2018, CCIS 913, pp. 79–91, 2019.
https://doi.org/10.1007/978-981-32-9987-0_8

or data transmission. Instead, these things are capable of providing complex services for diverse requirements [1]. Edge computing is an emerging paradigm that can take full advantage of the computing capability of mobile devices. Edge computing refers to the enabling technologies that allow computation to be performed at the network edge so that computing can be occurred near data sources. Besides, putting the data to be processed at the edge could gain efficient processing, shorter response times, and put less pressure on the network bandwidth. Therefore, it can improve the user experience for time-sensitive application significantly. Edge computing has attracted wide attention in the community since it was firstly proposed [2, 3].

However, since the edge devices are resource constrained and have limited computation ability and power supply, they may not have the ability to solve the applications which require high power supply and a large amount of processing services, the constraint yields a significant barrier to the full enjoyment for users to leverage edge devices to process the highly demanding applications [4]. To tackle these problems, offloading computing service to the edge servers or cloud servers is an optimal solution which can yield shorter response times, higher computation efficiency and less power consumption [5]. On the other hand, mobile-edge computing (MEC) is becoming a promising technique to provide more efficient and timely computing service at the mobile edge by offloading the tasks from clouds to the edge [6, 7].

With computation offloading, edge computing can achieve greater effect. But the computing offloading still brings several challenges, such as selecting appropriate applications, accurately estimating power consumption and effective managing the offloading requirements by multiple users at the same time [4, 8]. As we know, energy efficiency of mobile devices, edge servers and cloud servers is different, so the energy consumption is different according to computing place. Improper strategy for offloading strategy would yield more energy which not only generates high electricity bills, but also produces a huge carbon footprint [9]. So, it is significant to make an optimal energy-aware offloading strategy to minimize the energy consumption without degrading performance. Therefore, when we make an offloading decision, firstly, we should consider if the task can be offloaded to servers to process. Then, whose and which task can be offloaded when there are multiple users is a question to be solved. After that, when to implement the offloading and where to offload should be studied.

In this paper, we perform a survey of existing energy-aware computation offloading strategies. We introduce some energy-aware architectures and operating system for edge computing in Sect. 2. Then, aiming to study efficient energy-aware management methods at the edge, we survey some resource managements and scheduling in Sect. 3, and we sort the efforts within the produced data into energy-aware data storage at the edge, data analytics and computing at the edge in Sects. 4 and 5. The main issues of energy-aware computing offloading strategies are discussed in Sect. 6. Finally, we summarize the state-of-the-art of computation offloading approaches and identify the future work in Sect. 7.

2 Energy Aware Architecture and OS for Edge Computing

2.1 Energy Awareness in the Edge OS

By studying previous works, we find that edge computing can achieve maximum performance with minimal energy consumption through some techniques and algorithms. Now, we will introduce some energy aware edge infrastructures.

Ryden et al. [10] propose an edge-based cloud infrastructure, namely Nebula. It is useful in the data-intensive computing scenario because it can leverage the edge resource. It can improve the overall performance by load balancing, locality awareness and fault tolerance with replicating data from these applications. Nebula consists of four components, namely Nebula Central, Datastore, Compute Pool, Nebula Monitor. Besides, Zhang et al. [11] propose a new messaging and collaborating middleware, i.e., *Firework*, which is applied in collaborative edge environment (CEE) for big data processing. Firework is major for data sharing but it can promise end users' data privacy and integrity at the same time. It makes the data processed near the data source so that it can also reduce data movement and response time. For IoT environment, Cao et al. [12] propose the $EdgeOS_H$ for smart home. $EdgeOS_H$ combines the devices, home owners and cloud together, so users can fully enjoy the IoT services. Kuljeet et al. propose the container-as-a-service (CoaaS) [13] framework, to provide a proper task selection and scheduling at the edge of the network. CoaaS uses lightweight containers instead of the conventional virtual machines. CoaaS contains a multi-objective function which can reduce energy consumption by taking various constraints (such as memory, CPU, the user's budget and so on). In addition, Rausch et al. [14] put forward a novel static bridging method to achieve efficient information dissemination in geographical decentralized locations by developing the Message Queue Telemetry Transport (MQTT) systems.

2.2 Energy Savings: Technology and Edge Node Deployment

Different from server systems, most of edge devices can't support large software applications due to the limitation of resources including CPU, memory, and storage. Moreover, the edge devices are heterogeneous, which makes it difficult to deploy applications without modifications. To solve the problem, virtualization technology may be the proper solution. VMs (virtual machines) and containers are both virtualization techniques to gain the resilience of large-scale shared resource, but they can address different problems. Pahl et al. [15] adopt the container technology for edge computing to achieve better performance with less consumption. Ismail et al. [16] deploy Docker containers as an edge platform. Docker is flexible in location movement which requires easy operation, low cost and low storage space. So, it is suitable for fast service deployment and disassembly. In order to improve the communication performance in a virtualized sensors network in edge computing, in our previous work [17], we propose an optimized inter-domain communication approach based on shared memory to improve the inter-domain communication performance of multiple VMs residing in the same sensor hardware. And in [18], the authors propose an optimal policy for the VM migration to minimize the energy cost. The problem can be seen as

Markov decision process (MDP), and if the UE state is limited by a special threshold set, they think the VM migration is always started in one direction. An architecture based on Raspberry Pi Clusters for Container-based edge cloud PaaS has been proposed by Claus and his group [19]. The cluster consists of multiple host nodes, which also contains several containers to provide services.

How to optimally place IoT services on edge resources is an important problem for efficient edge computing. Skarlat *et al.* [20] present Fog Service Placement Problem (FSPP), which allows the virtualized fog resources to perform IoT services, in the meantime, it takes Quality of Service (QoS) limits into consideration. FSPP can provide an optimal mapping between IoT applications and computing resources. The recent work [21] also present their deployment framework for IoT applications, which extend the leverage resource-limited Raspberry Pi devices by leveraging the open-source Kura gateway and docker-based containerization. Meanwhile, Ivan and his group design a framework [22] to guarantee quick response time, they take advantage of service replication based on container-instance at the edge network. Consequently, the framework can exploit the replicas of the services to reduce the overall migration in the context of user movement.

3   Energy Aware Resource Management and Scheduling

3.1   Resources Continuity

Edge computing scheduling strategy is related to resources. Adopting an optimized scheduling strategy, resource utilization can be optimized. In order to provide coordinated resource continuity management, many scholars have proposed strategies that include the Fog to Cloud (F2C) layered model and OpenFog Reference Architecture (OpenFog RA) [23]. Masip-Bruin *et al.* [24] propose a new Fog to Cloud (F2C) layered model, a new architecture that can gain lower services execution time and parallel services operation strategy by exploiting data sharing and data collaboration. Also, Masip-Bruin *et al.* [25] propose a distributed management framework combining the edge and cloud resources to manage resource continuity effectively in hierarchical architecture.

3.2   Energy Aware Resource Scheduling

Resources in the edge computing task scheduling such as data, calculation, storage and network are heterogeneous. Different scheduling strategies should be presented according to different applications. In [26], the authors exploit the Markovian stochastic channel to make an optimal solution for cooperative operation between cloud and edge devices with offloading strategy. And to solve such minimum-energy task scheduling problem, they firstly consider it as a constrained shortest path problem on directed acyclic graphs, then they use the standard "Lagrange Relaxation based Aggregated Cost (LARAC)" algorithm to obtain the solution of this problem. Kwak *et al.* [27] propose a dynamic CPU/network resource and task allocation algorithm in the mobile network environment, which leverage the Lyapunov optimization technique to scale the CPU/network speed. Besides, Kim *et al.* [28] propose traffic flow consolidation to realize energy proportional heterogeneous network. They adopt the opportunity of link power gating in heterodox routers to solve the problem of energy waste, thus saving the power to the greatest extent. The author also proposes traffic consultation, in this way, different traffic flows can be integrated into less links. And Liang et *al.* [29] introduce a new resource allocating method by taking both bandwidth supply and selection of source to deal with the double-decomposition strategy.

4 Energy Aware Data Storage

The size of multi-modal, heterogeneous data known as big data collected through various sensors is growing exponentially. And It is inefficient and impractical in such applications to use traditional architectures and algorithms for storing and processing such data. It demands intelligent data reduction, data storage and analytics at edge devices.

4.1 Storage Infrastructures and Software Defined Storage

How to store the data efficiently is a hot topic in edge computing storage. The existing work [30] proposes Fog Data, which is a service-oriented architecture that can improve the overall performance as well as reduce storage requirements for telemedical. Fog Data has the ability to perform the field data analysis and thereby reducing the data capacity to be stored and transmitted to the cloud. Inspired by the paradigm of Public-Resource Computing (PRC), in order to deal with cloud saturation, the authors of [31] introduce the proposal that if we can deploy the edge computing platform with PRC and storage techniques. Besides, the work by Wu *et al.* [32] present an alternative-cooperative storage algorithm MECCAS based on multiplier, which considers node resource distribution, task scheduling and heterogeneous information of edge and cloud simultaneously. To keep pace with the demand for scale-out storage systems, a wireless-based software defined storage (SDStorage) simulation is proposed [33], in which storage services are co-provided by the nearest MEC nodes with end users.

4.2 Data Caching and Replacement

To develop a new practical system architecture to collect, analyze, and proactively deal with the soaring data, Zeydan *et al.* [34] propose a proactive cache architecture designed for edge caching while can optimize 5G wireless networks. The prediction algorithms at the core site and the cache placement strategy can be processed parallelize. In addition, the iFogStor [35] presented by Mohammed's group provides an optimal data placement strategy. The authors express the Generalized Assignment Problem (GAP) as the related problem of data placement problem. And they put forward two solutions. One is an integer programming solution using the CPLEX MILP and the other is heuristic solution based on the geographical partition to reduce the solution time. To achieve the same goal, Xinga *et al.* [36] employ a multi-factor most commonly used (mLFU) algorithm and a distributed multi-level storage

(DMLS) model to solve the problem. Once the storage capacity runs out of space, mLFU will replace the data with lowest value. Besides, the system can also replicate data in cloud servers in order to avoid important data losing when the system is in idle.

4.3 Data Encryption and Authenticating

In IoT environment, 50B devices estimated to be connected by 2020. And privacy and security are important problem. In [37], the authors propose a method for local difference privacy. Unlike traditional data collection which transfers raw data from users to a cloud server directly, the new mechanism allows pre-processing in the edge devices, encrypting data and reducing the amount of transferred data so as to save energy consumption. In addition, the authors propose two solutions to implement the mechanism, one is thresholding processing and the other is resampling. Out of the same objective, Pang *et al.* [38] adopt a security mechanism whose main idea is that the trusted central database management system (DBMS) maintains a table to preserve and allocate the verifiable B-trees (VB-tree). And then, the edge servers generate result object (it is not modified and always correct), and it generates a verification object (VO) according to the VB-tree. Mollah *et al.* [39] propose a more lightweight and secure data sharing scheme for edge computing and a method for searching the required security data. The scheme consists of four steps: Key generation, Data and keywords uploading, Data sharing and downloading and Data Searching and retrieval. The proposed solution performs well in terms of processing time and data security.

5   Edge Aware Analytics and Computing

Edge computing has the ability to make massive date streams analysis at data collecting and provide actionable information for operational and tactical decisions.

5.1 Data Analytics

In order to serve different users, provide diverse transportation modes and management and make the transportation more intelligent, safer and coordinated. For the edge devices deployed on the transmission bus, Cao *et al.* [40] propose an edge computing platform that can analyze the transmission data flow and monitor abnormal patterns in real time. Nastic *et al.* [41] combine edge computing and cloud computing to propose a unified edge data analysis platform. For security data and time-sensitive data, it can be analyzed at the edge and then transmitted to the cloud. The platform extends the serverless computing to the edge and facilitates edge-cloud federated data analysis.

As a hybrid cloud structure, GigaSight [42] is a distributed cloudlet-cloud computing infrastructure. Cloudlet is a VM-based edge server that is typically deployed on the edge of the network for data edge processing operations. In this architecture, all data are propagated only to the cloudlet in real time, and only results, alone with metadata are further transferred to the cloud.

5.2   Data Computing

For edge devices, it is no doubt that reducing the overall power consumption is a critical issue of power management. There are several solutions to cope with the problem. Li *et al.* [43] propose a middleware layer to manage the functionality of modern multi-core smartphones. The middle layer can schedule the optimal number of online cores and adjust the best frequency for each core dynamically according to the current CPU load to balance energy consumption, performance, and user QoS. In order to leverage the computing capability of the edge devices, JOHN's group [44] describe Mobilouds, a multi-tier management architecture that manages clusters at different levels to save energy. In addition, in order to develop energy-saving mobility management scheme, Sun *et al.* [45] propose a novel energy-aware mobility management (EMM) scheme which is user-centered and based on Lyapunov optimization and multi-armed bandit theories. The QoS-based algorithm can make EMM decision on the base station (BS) association and switcher.

6   Energy Aware Offloading from Edge to Clouds

Computation offloading from edge to cloud is a promising technology that can save battery power while improving the computing capability of edge devices. The cloud computing can save energy for edge devices, however, not all applications are of high efficiency when offloading to the cloud. We should make some decisions when deciding computation offloading: who to offload, when to offload and where to offload. There are many existing works to solve the problems. We explain the computing offloading architecture in Fig. 1 and Table 1. In Fig. 1, it also shows that different offloading strategy should be made according to different situations. And Table 1 explains the terms used in our paper.

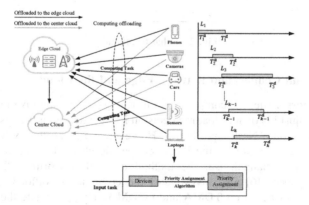

Fig. 1. Computing offloading architecture.

Table 1. Terms and notations

Terms	Explanation
L_k	Device k need to complete a computation task with L_k-bit input data
T_k^a	The data-arrival time instant
T_k^d	The computation deadline

6.1 Computation Partitioning Before Offloading

To determine which task to offload, You *et al.* [46] propose a system model that uses the central controller to select the offloading task by modeling the MEC system. The model has only one edge server, but can serve multiple users while allocating resources using Time-division multiple access (TDMA) and orthogonal frequency-division multiple access (OFDMA). In [47], the authors use a QoE-based utility function to measure the offloading time and energy consumption and calculate the utility ratio to the local execution. To maximize the utility function, the authors firstly divide the problem into two small problems: (1) Optimize communication and computing resources by quasiconvexity and convex optimization and (2) Make the offloading decision according to the submodular set function optimization method, and then they put forward their heuristic offloading decision algorithm (HODA). Also, the paper [48] mainly studies how to realize energy-efficient MEC computation offloading (EECO) mechanisms in 5G heterogeneous networks. They classify different equipment and then assign proper priorities, so as to realize a three-level energy efficiency offloading scheme. Figure 2 shows the model that who should be offloaded.

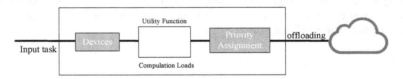

Fig. 2. What to offload.

6.2 Gaming and Cooperation Between Edge and the Cloud

In [49], the authors model the computation offloading as a competitive game, that is to say, each user adjust his own offloading decision independently in the system, so that it always can gain a pure Nash equilibrium. However, the game theory has many constraints, such as the duration of the job, user-specific channel bit rates and the competition on sharing channel. But the method can still perform well after several iterations. The paper [46] also investigates the computation offloading method for mobile-edge devices based on TDMA and OFDMA. They calculate the data arriving time in advance and offload the task with earlier arriving time. And then take the tasks computing time into account if they have same arriving time. They make the offloading sequence by combining the arriving time and computing time. In Fig. 3, we describe the offloading order according to task arriving time instant and latency of devices.

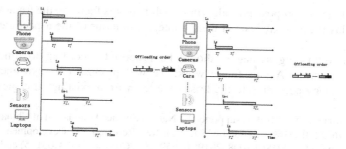

Fig. 3. Mapping between the arriving time and latency.

6.3 Computation Offloading

Considering the environment of multiple cloud providers, Terefe *et al.* [50] proposes a scheme to offload different types of workloads to different servers. Such as, offloading energy-intensive tasks to cloud servers, offloading the computing-intensive (CI) task to an edge server, and offloading the data-intensive (DI) task to a server that is close to the database. Aiming at this three-level hierarchy offloading model, it is critical for us to have a deep understanding of server energy proportionality to provide a reasonable workload placement and save more energy for hybrid cloud architecture [51, 52]. We conclude the above methods with an example in Fig. 4. In virtualized systems, different hypervisor has different energy efficiency even when the same applications are executed and provisioned on top of it [53]. Therefore, energy efficiency of targeted platform must also be considered when deciding where to offloading.

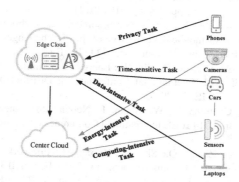

Fig. 4. An example shows where to offload.

7 Conclusions and Future Work

This paper presents a comprehensive survey of the research work conducted on energy aware computation offloading which aims at performance improvement of applications and energy saving executing on the resource constrained edge devices. Some of the offloading strategies propose new algorithms while others focus on the frameworks. We perform a classification analysis of these strategies in terms of the aspect the strategies consider.

Different offloading strategies should be proposed according to different edge computing scenarios. As for future work, we will propose our own energy aware offloading strategy according to the lesson we learn from existing strategies.

Acknowledgments. This work is supported by Natural Science Foundation of China (61472109, 61572163, 61672200, 61602137, and 61802093), Key Research and Development Program of Zhejiang Province (No. 2018C01098, 2019C01059, 2019C03134, 2019C03135) and the Natural Science Foundation of Zhejiang Province (No. LY18F020014).

References

1. Khan, M.A.: A survey of computation offloading strategies for performance improvement of applications running on mobile devices. J. Netw. Comput. Appl. **56**, 28–40 (2015)
2. Shi, W., Dustdar, S.: The promise of edge computing. Computer **49**(5), 78–81 (2016)
3. Shi, W., Cao, J., Zhang, Q., Li, Y., Xu, L.: Edge computing: vision and challenges. IEEE Internet Things J. **3**(5), 637–646 (2016)
4. Mach, P., Becvar, Z.: Mobile edge computing: a survey on architecture and computation offloading. IEEE Commun. Surv. Tutor. **19**(3), 1628–1656 (2017)
5. Chen, X., Jiao, L., Li, W., Fu, X.: Efficient multi-user computation offloading for mobile-edge cloud computing. IEEE/ACM Trans. Netw. **24**(5), 2795–2808 (2016)
6. Tao, X., Ota, K., Dong, M., Qi, H., Li, K.: Performance guaranteed computation offloading for mobile-edge cloud computing. IEEE Wirel. Commun. Lett. **6**(6), 774–777 (2017)
7. Patel, M., Naughton, B., Chan, C., Sprecher, N., Abeta, S., Neal, A.: Mobile-edge computing. ETSI White Paper, pp. 1089–7801 (2014)
8. Jiao, L., Friedman, R., Fu, X., Secci, S., Smoreda, Z., Tschofenig, H.: Cloud-based computation offloading for mobile devices: state of the art, challenges and opportunities. In: 2013 Future Network & Mobile Summit, pp. 1–11. IEEE (2013)
9. Jiang, C., Wang, Y., Ou, D., Luo, B., Shi, W.: Energy proportional servers: where are we in 2016? In: 2017 IEEE 37th International Conference on Distributed Computing Systems (ICDCS), pp. 1649–1660. IEEE (2017)
10. Ryden, M., Oh, K., Chandra, A., Weissman, J.: Nebula: distributed edge cloud for data intensive computing. In: 2014 IEEE International Conference on Cloud Engineering, pp. 57–66. IEEE (2014)
11. Zhang, Q., Zhang, X., Zhang, Q., Shi, W., Zhong, H.: Firework: big data sharing and processing in collaborative edge environment. In: 2016 Fourth IEEE Workshop on Hot Topics in Web Systems and Technologies (HotWeb), pp. 20–25. IEEE (2016)
12. Cao, J., Xu, L., Abdallah, R., Shi, W.: EdgeOSh: a home operating system for Internet of everything. In: 2017 IEEE 37th International Conference on Distributed Computing Systems (ICDCS), pp. 1756–1764. IEEE (2017)
13. Kaur, K., Dhand, T., Kumar, N., Zeadally, S.: Container-as-a-service at the edge: Trade-off between energy efficiency and service availability at Fog nano data centers. IEEE Wirel. Commun. **24**(3), 48–56 (2017)
14. Rausch, T.: Message-oriented middleware for edge computing applications. In: Proceedings of the 18th Doctoral Symposium of the 18th International Middleware Conference, pp. 3–4. ACM (2017)

15. Pahl, C., Lee, B.: Containers and clusters for edge cloud architectures–a technology review. In: 2015 3rd International Conference on Future Internet of Things and Cloud, pp. 379–386. IEEE (2015)
16. Ismail, B.I., et al.: Evaluation of docker as edge computing platform. In: 2015 IEEE Conference on Open Systems (ICOS), pp. 130–135. IEEE (2015)
17. Jiang, C., et al.: Interdomain I/O optimization in virtualized sensor networks. Sensors 18(12), 4395 (2018)
18. Wang, S., Urgaonkar, R., Zafer, M., He, T., Chan, K., Leung, K.K.: Dynamic service migration in mobile edge-clouds. In: 2015 IFIP Networking Conference (IFIP Networking), pp. 1–9. IEEE (2015)
19. Pahl, C., Helmer, S., Miori, L., Sanin, J., Lee, B.: A container-based edge cloud PaaS architecture based on raspberry pi clusters. In: 2016 IEEE 4th International Conference on Future Internet of Things and Cloud Workshops (FiCloudW), pp. 117–124. IEEE (2016)
20. Skarlat, O., Nardelli, M., Schulte, S., Dustdar, S.: Towards QoS-aware fog service placement. In: 2017 IEEE 1st International Conference on Fog and Edge Computing (ICFEC), pp. 89–96. IEEE (2017)
21. Bellavista, P., Zanni, A.: Feasibility of fog computing deployment based on docker containerization over RaspberryPi. In: Proceedings of the 18th International Conference on Distributed Computing and Networking, p. 16. ACM (2017)
22. Farris, I., Taleb, T., Iera, A., Flinck, H.: Lightweight service replication for ultrashort latency applications in mobile edge networks. In: 2017 IEEE International Conference on Communications (ICC), pp. 1–6. IEEE (2017)
23. Open fog consortium working group: OpenFog Reference Architecture for Fog Computing White paper (2017)
24. Masip-Bruin, X., Marín-Tordera, E., Tashakor, G., Jukan, A., Ren, G.J.: Foggy clouds and cloudy fogs: a real need for coordinated management of fog-to-cloud computing systems. IEEE Wirel. Commun. 23(5), 120–128 (2016)
25. Masip-Bruin, X., Marin-Tordera, E., Jukan, A., Ren, G.J.: Managing resources continuity from the edge to the cloud: architecture and performance. Futur. Gener. Comput. Syst. 79, 777–785 (2018)
26. Zhang, W., Wen, Y., Wu, D.O.: Energy-efficient scheduling policy for collaborative execution in mobile cloud computing. In: Proceedings IEEE INFOCOM, Turin, pp. 190–194. IEEE (2013)
27. Kwak, J., Kim, Y., Lee, J., Chong, S.: Dream: Dynamic resource and task allocation for energy minimization in mobile cloud systems. IEEE J. Sel. Areas Commun. 33(12), 2510–2523 (2015)
28. Kim, G., Choi, H., Kim, J.: TCEP: traffic consolidation for energy-proportional high-radix networks. In: Proceedings of the 45th Annual International Symposium on Computer Architecture, pp. 712–725. IEEE Press (2018)
29. Liang, C., He, Y., Yu, F.R., Zhao, N.: Energy-efficient resource allocation in software-defined mobile networks with mobile edge computing and caching. In: 2017 IEEE Conference on Computer Communications Workshops (INFOCOM WKSHPS), pp. 121–126. IEEE (2017)
30. Dubey, H., et al.: Fog data: enhancing telehealth big data through fog computing. In: Proceedings of the ASE BigData & Socialinformatics 2015, p. 14. ACM (2015)
31. Alonso-Monsalve, S., García-Carballeira, F., Calderón, A.: Fog computing through public-resource computing and storage. In: 2017 Second International Conference on Fog and Mobile Edge Computing (FMEC), pp. 81–87. IEEE (2017)

32. Wu, G., et al.: Meccas: collaborative storage algorithm based on alternating direction method of multipliers on mobile edge cloud. In: 2017 IEEE International Conference on Edge Computing (EDGE), pp. 40–46. IEEE (2017)

33. Al-Badarneh, J., Jararweh, Y., Al-Ayyoub, M., Al-Smadi, M., Fontes, R.: Software defined storage for cooperative mobile edge computing systems. In: 2017 Fourth International Conference on Software Defined Systems (SDS), pp. 174–179. IEEE (2017)

34. Zeydan, E., et al.: Big data caching for networking: Moving from cloud to edge. IEEE Commun. Mag. **54**(9), 36–42 (2016)

35. Naas, M.I., Parvedy, P.R., Boukhobza, J., Lemarchand, L.: iFogStor: an IoT data placement strategy for fog infrastructure. In: 2017 IEEE 1st International Conference on Fog and Edge Computing (ICFEC), pp. 97–104. IEEE (2017)

36. Xing, J., Dai, H., Yu, Z.: A distributed multi-level model with dynamic replacement for the storage of smart edge computing. J. Syst. Arch. **83**, 1–11 (2018)

37. Choi, W.S., Tomei, M., Vicarte, J.R.S., Hanumolu, P.K., Kumar, R.: Guaranteeing local differential privacy on ultra-low-power systems. In: 2018 ACM/IEEE 45th Annual International Symposium on Computer Architecture (ISCA), pp. 561–574. IEEE (2018)

38. Pang, H., Tan, K.L.: Authenticating query results in edge computing. In: Proceedings of the 20th International Conference on Data Engineering, pp. 560–571. IEEE (2004)

39. Mollah, M.B., Azad, M.A.K., Vasilakos, A.: Secure data sharing and searching at the edge of cloud-assisted internet of things. IEEE Cloud Comput. **4**(1), 34–42 (2017)

40. Cao, H., Wachowicz, M., Cha, S.: Developing an edge computing platform for realtime descriptive analytics. In: 2017 IEEE International Conference on Big Data (Big Data), pp. 4546–4554. IEEE (2017)

41. Nastic, S., et al.: A serverless real-time data analytics platform for edge computing. IEEE Internet Comput. **21**(4), 64–71 (2017)

42. Satyanarayanan, M., et al.: Edge analytics in the Internet of Things. IEEE Pervasive Comput. **14**(2), 24–31 (2015)

43. Li, S., Mishra, S.: Optimizing power consumption in multicore smartphones. J. Parallel Distrib. Comput. **95**, 124–137 (2016)

44. Panneerselvam, J., Hardy, J., Liu, L., Yuan, B., Antonopoulos, N.: Mobilouds: an energy efficient MCC collaborative framework with extended mobile participation for next generation networks. IEEE Access **4**, 9129–9144 (2016)

45. Sun, Y., Zhou, S., Xu, J.: EMM: Energy-aware mobility management for mobile edge computing in ultra-dense networks. IEEE J. Sel. Areas Commun. **35**(11), 2637–2646 (2017)

46. You, C., Zeng, Y., Zhang, R., Huang, K.: Asynchronous mobile-edge computation offloading: energy-efficient resource management. IEEE Trans. Wirel. Commun. **17**(11), 7590–7605 (2018)

47. Lyu, X., Tian, H., Sengul, C., Zhang, P.: Multiuser joint task offloading and resource optimization in proximate clouds. IEEE Trans. Veh. Technol. **66**(4), 3435–3447 (2017)

48. Zhang, K., et al.: Energy-efficient offloading for mobile edge computing in 5G heterogeneous networks. IEEE Access **4**, 5896–5907 (2016)

49. Zhang, K., Mao, Y., Leng, S., Maharjan, S., Zhang, Y.: Optimal delay constrained offloading for vehicular edge computing networks. In: 2017 IEEE International Conference on Communications (ICC), pp. 1–6. IEEE (2017)

50. Terefe, M.B., Lee, H., Heo, N., Fox, G.C., Oh, S.: Energy-efficient multisite offloading policy using Markov decision process for mobile cloud computing. Pervasive Mob. Comput. **27**, 75–89 (2016)

51. Qiu, Y., Jiang, C., Wang, Y., Ou, D., Li, Y., Wan, J.: Energy aware virtual machine scheduling in data centers. Energies **12**(4), 646 (2019)

52. Jiang, C., Han, G., Lin, J., Jia, G., Shi, W., Wan, J.: Characteristics of co-allocated online services and batch jobs in internet data centers: a case study from Alibaba cloud. IEEE Access **7**, 22495–22508 (2019)
53. Jiang, C., et al.: Energy efficiency comparison of hypervisors. Sustain. Comput. Inform. Syst. **22**, 311–321 (2019)

High Performance Computing for Advanced Modeling and Simulation in Nuclear Energy and Environmental Science

Virtual Reactors Towards the Exascale Supercomputing Era

Xianmeng Wang[1,2], Changjun Hu[1,2], Wen Yang[3], Tiancai Liu[3],
Zhaoshun Wang[1], Xuesong Wang[3], Hongwei Yang[3], Mingyu Wu[3],
Jue Wang[4(✉)], An Wang[1,2], and Zhifeng Zhou[1]

[1] School of Computer and Communication Engineering,
University of Science and Technology, Beijing, China
[2] Beijing Key Laboratory of Knowledge Engineering for Material Science,
Beijing, China
[3] China Institute of Atomic Energy, Beijing, China
[4] Computer Network Information Center, Chinese Academy of Science,
Beijing, China
wangjue@sccas.cn

Abstract. Virtual reactor is an interplanetary research field, which leverages the leading supercomputers to provide a profound understanding of existing reactors and design guidance for future reactors. Virtual reactor is at the cutting-edge of high performance computing and nuclear engineering research fields. The United States, European Union and China have put great effort into virtual reactor research. The research areas of virtual reactors include integrated platform, safety analysis, system analysis, core physics components, database, uncertainty quantification, verification and validation. Typically, core physics consist of thermal-hydraulics, mechanics, neutronics, fuel, and material performance software. Virtual reactor requires enormous computing and storage resource. The computing capabilities of Exascale supercomputers enables realistic models and high-resolution numerical methods come into play. Compared to traditional way, virtual reactor makes simulation more accurate (high-fidelity models are used, such as LES, multi-group transport theory), larger scaled (such as more atoms in molecular dynamics) and tighter coupled. Meanwhile, great challenges have been posed to models, numerical methods, algorithms and programing, especially considering the complicated modern architectures of supercomputers. The paper focuses on the research areas, computing and storage requirements, challenges of virtual reactors.

Keywords: Virtual reactors · High performance computing ·
Exascale supercomputers

1 Introduction

Nuclear energy is an effective way to resolve energy crisis and environmental pollution problems. Safety is critical to the widely use of nuclear energy. Reactor experiments are usually expensive and time consuming, and some important phenomena cannot be obtained through experiments. Virtual reactor plays a significant role in understanding,

© Springer Nature Singapore Pte Ltd. 2019
C. Hu et al. (Eds.): HPCMS 2018/HiDEC 2018, CCIS 913, pp. 95–106, 2019.
https://doi.org/10.1007/978-981-32-9987-0_9

studying and predicting nuclear reactor behaviors. Virtual reactor is a collection of simulating software based on high-fidelity models and ate-of art numerical methods. Virtual reactor is an interplanetary research field, which needs collaborations of researchers and engineers from nuclear engineering, high-performance-computing, software engineering, applied physics, applied mathematics, etc. With the development of high-performance-computing technology, especially the upcoming Exascale super-computers era (with a processing ability of 10^{18} floating-point operations per second), it is possible to solve some currently intractable problems of nuclear energy field. Combing fundamental research and industry application, Virtual Reactors make it possible to achieve reactor power uprates, life extension, safety enhancement, material optimization, waste reducing, and higher fuel burnup for both existing and future reactors.

Some countries and areas have been carrying out research on advanced modeling and simulation of reactors. Supported by DOE (U.S. Department of Energy), CASL (The Consortium for Advanced Simulation of Light Water Reactors) [1] has achieved remarkable achievements. VERA, the main achievement of CASL, consists of four elements: (1) physics components, such as thermal hydraulic and neutronics simulating software; (2) coupling tools; (3) drivers (4) the infrastructure to support collaborative development [2]. The Nuclear Energy Advanced Modeling and Simulation (NEAMS) is also funded by DOE. NEAMS has three produces lines: Fuels Product Line (FPL), Reactors Product Line (RPL) and Integration Product Line (IPL) [3]. MARMOT and BISON are in FPL. SHARP and SAM are in RPL. Some of the packages are intrinsically multi-physical, for example, SHARP couples neutronics, thermal hydraulics and mechanics [4]. Typical modeling and simulation projects in EU are the series of NURESIM research [5]. CESAR (Centre for Exascale Simulation of Advanced Reactors) devotes to the research on advanced simulation on Exascale supercomputers [6]. The CESAR project plans to explore Petascale simulating legacy software to evolve to Exascale software [7].

In this paper, we propose the definition, research areas and core contents of virtual reactors. We discuss enormous computing and storage requirements of virtual reactors. We analyze the research challenges of Virtual Reactors on massive supercomputers, especially the upcoming Exascale supercomputers. The reminder of this pa-per is organized as follows. Section 2 describes the research areas and core contents of virtual reactors. Section 4 discusses the research challenges of virtual reactors. The paper is concluded in Sect. 5.

2   Research Areas of Virtual Reactor

Virtual reactor is a mirror image of a realistic reactor internally and externally. A virtual reactor includes the following research areas, as illustrated in Fig. 1: integrated platform, safety analysis, system analysis, core physics components, database, uncertainty quantification, verification and validation. An integrated platform interacts with users with different purposes. The platform offers user interfaces: input data interface, output data interface, mesh and geometry tools, data analysis tools, visualization tools, and workflow management. Database consist of nuclear data, material data, critical

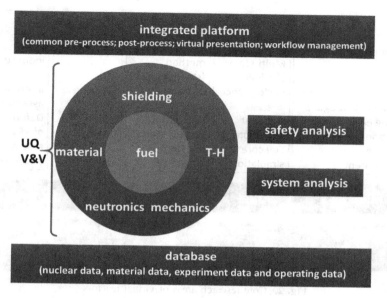

Fig. 1. Research areas of virtual reactors

experiment data and operating data. Database play a fundamental role in the simulation and validation processes.

Core research areas focus on the primary physical components, coupling environment, and an integrated design. Figure 2 represents the core research areas. Thermal-hydraulics, mechanics, neutronics, fuel, material constitute the primary physics components. On some circumstances, chemistry is a part of the primary physics components. Material software researches material performance under strong radiation. Irradiation assisted Stress Corrosion Cracking (IASCC), Stress Corrosion Cracking (SCC), Pellet Clad Interaction (PCI) phenomena, corrosion, fatigue, cladding embrittlement, irradiation swelling, and irradiation embrittlement phenomena are researched in material area. Fuel software is intrinsically multi-physics coupled, in which fission gas production, gas transport, temperature distribution, thermo-mechanical response as considered. Fuel performance software simulates single fuel rod or full core fuels using multi-dimensional methods (such as 3-D or 1.5D). Neutronics analyses the particle transport processes under steady and transient states. Thermal hydraulics studies the flow and heat transfer phenomena of coolant using multi-scale methods, such as molecular dynamics, single/two-phase Computation Fluid Dynamics (CFD), and sub-channel method. Mechanics pays attentions to some critical problems concerning the safety of reactors: flow-induced vibration of internals and assemblies, deformation of reactor pressure vessels (RPV), assemblies and internals.

Some of the components coupled with each other by the coupling tools. Coupling environment provides coupling tools used for multi-physics and multi-scale coupling. The couplings tools include data transfer tool, mesh map tool, and coupling process control tool. Coupling process control environment implements multiple coupling strategies (such as OS, JFNK), controls iteration process and checks convergence.

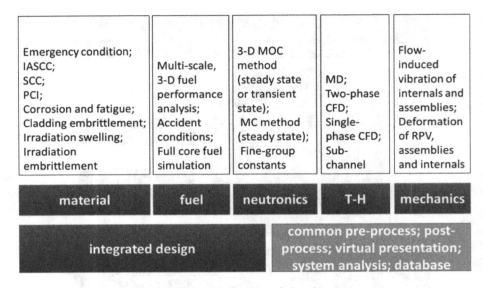

Fig. 2. Core research areas of virtual reactors

3 Computing and Storage Requirements of Some Essential Components in Virtual Reactors

3.1 Material Behavior

Phenomena such as cladding embrittlement and irradiation swelling are of concern to reactor safety. There are a series of multi-scale methods to simulate those important phenomena. Molecular Dynamics (MD) is an atomistic scale method. Adequate number of atoms is necessary to obtain valuable results. Because the memory requirement for MD grows linearly with the amount of atoms, memory is a bottleneck at MD simulating spatial scale. For example, simulating 10^{20} [8] atoms will not only enable material interfaces and heterogeneous regions to be researched, but also improve accuracy in radiation effects simulation. The extremely large number of atoms poses great challenges to supercomputer system memory. Some studies [9, 10] have made progress with reducing memory use. However, the memory requirements for 10^{20} still far exceeded the abilities of the most powerful supercomputers in the world. Let us suppose every atom consumes 100 Bytes memory [9], then 10^{20} atoms will request about 10Z Bytes. Not to mention that extra storage are required, when MD is coupled with other methods such as Kinetic Monte Carlo (KMC). In addition to the enormous memory consumption, MD is computation hungry. In order to accurately describe the movement of atoms and ensure the stability of simulation, the time-step is supposed to be very short. The typical time-step is femtosecond (10^{-15} of a second). A second level simulation demands one thousand trillion time-steps.

3.2   Thermal Hydraulics

Thermal hydraulics analyzes the heat transfer and flow processes of coolant. Multi-scale methods such as molecular dynamics, computational fluid dynamics (single phase and two phases), and sub-channel are included in the thermal-hydraulics software packages.

With the dramatic improvement of supercomputers, CFD has been playing a more and more important role in thermal hydraulics analysis. Kothe predicts the capabilities of thermal hydraulic simulating with the development of HPC [11]: with the Terascale computing capability, full-core simulation can be accomplished using lumped parameter models; on Petascale supercomputers, high-fidelity LES simulation can be carried out on localized regions (such as steam generator, upper plenum); at the Exascale era, LES model has the chance to come into play for the entire reactor core. Simulating based on Direct Numerical Simulation (DNS) is far beyond the capability of the most powerful supercomputers in the world. Jamshed [11] computes that over 160 years are required to simulate a simple flow in a box using DNS on Tianhe-2 under a Reynolds number of 96,000.

Full-core CFD simulation is extremely computing resource hungry for all the models. Igor A. estimates that 300 Zetta-scale (10^{21} Flops/s) supercenters are required to full resolve the reactor core at a realist Reynold number using DNS [13]. Large Eddy Simulation (LES) model demands less computing capability compared to DNS. However, adopting LES models also stretches the limits of the available leadership-class supercomputers. Fischer [14] analyses one assembly with 524,288 cores of IBM Blue Gene/Q supercomputer using LES model. As far as the full core simulation is concerned, more computation resource is required. Chen et al. estimate that more than 60 billion meshes are required in the RANS model based CFD simulation of the whole PWR core [17] (Fig. 3).

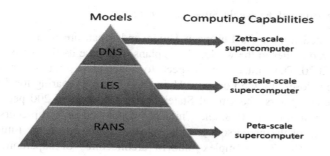

Fig. 3. More powerful computing capabilities support more accurate models.

3.3   Neutronics

Monte Carlo method and deterministic method can be used to research neutronics transport problem. Both Monte Carlo simulation and deterministic are computing resource hungry. Let us take using Method of Characteristic method (MOC, a deterministic method) to simulate a CFR600 [15] as an example. The computation requirement of steady-state simulation can be estimated as follows: energy group (1028) * scatter source iteration (50) * fission source iteration (200) * floating point operations per energy group per iteration (4.96 * 10^{13}). The total calculation is about 5.1 * 10^{20}. As far as MC method is concerned, it takes Deng [16] one hour to simulate more than 1.5 million depletion region with 120 thousand cores on Tianhe-II super-computer (Tianhe-II has a performance of 33 PetaFlops).

3.4 Fuel Performance

Fuel performance simulating software analyzes the temperature, stress-strain, fission product release, internal pressure of fuels through the entire life cycle. Simulation of the full core fuel rods demands hundreds of millions of meshes. The meshes vary according different reactor types and simulation cases. A rough estimate of full-core fuel simulation of Daya Bay nuclear plant is presented in Table 1. There are 157 assemblies in Daya Bay nuclear plant. Each assembly consists of 264 rods, and each rod comprises of 217 pellets.

Table 1. A rough estimate of simulation meshes of full-core fuel performance of Daya Bay nuclear plant

Element	Each pellet	Each rod	Each assembly	Full core
Radial	50	50	50 * 264	50 * 264 * 157
Axial	1	1 * 271	1 * 271	1 * 271
Meshes	50	13550	3577200	5.6 * 10^8

4   Research Challenges of Virtual Reactors

4.1   Architectures of Exascale Supercomputers

China, the United States, the European Union and Japan are in a race for the first Exascale supercomputer in the world. China plans to release its first Exascale machine by the end of 2020. The United States expects to launch at least one supercomputers by 2021, followed closely by the European Union and Japan. Preparing for the ambitious Exascale supercomputers, the United States is due to deliver a 200 petaflops super-computer called Summit in 2018, and China has developed several precursor systems. The architectures of the precursors are likely to be continued on the future Exascale supercomputers [18]. The complex modern architectures of supercomputers pose challenges for virtual reactors. As an example, a Sunway processor comprises four core groups (CGs) [19]. As shown in Fig. 4, each CG comes with one management processing element (MPE), and one computing processing element (CPE) cluster of 64 CPEs. As far as the memory hierarchy is concerned, each CPE has a 64 KB Scratch Pad Memory (SPM), and data can be transported across the SPM and main memory using a memory controller. The architecture features pose challenges to the development of some simulating software in virtual reactors. For example, the most compute intensive part of MD is to calculate interaction force among atoms. Typically, Embedded-Atom Method (EAM) potential is used in the force calculation of metal material, which involves accessing to three interpolation tables. Table queries are necessary at each time-step and for every atom. Each interpolation table is (used in LAMMPS and CoMD) about 270 KB. The memory requirements of interpolation tables exceed the local store of each CPE. Therefore, CPEs have to frequently access data from main memory, which severely hinders the overall performance. The frequently memory access between CPEs and main memory is also a bottleneck of other simulation software such as CFD [20].

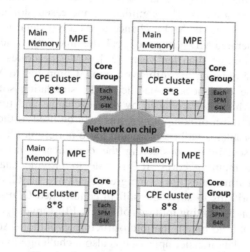

Fig. 4. Sunway processor architecture

Hybrid architecture has been the trend in supercomputers recently. In addition to the Sunway supercomputer, many other supercomputers adopt hybrid architectures. Tianhe-2 is powered by Intel Xeon E5 processors and Intel Xeon Phi coprocessors. The expecting supercomputer Summit will have a heterogeneous architecture with IBM CPUs and NVIDIA GPUs. Hybrid architecture increases difficulties in programming, and require algorithms to be more aware of the hybrid system hierarchy. Parallel algorithms for different problems should be designed at fine granularity according to the features of the problem and computing system. However, specialized design may hinder the portability of software.

4.2 Material Behavior

The research on radiation damage of some reactor critical materials, such as RPV and fuel cladding, plays a critical role in ensuring safe operation of reactors. The radiation damage phenomena are inherently multi-scale processes, which scales from atomic to meters spatially and picosecond to years temporally [21]. The hierarchical multi-scale approach to materials degradation under irradiation conditions involving the following methodologies: ab initio, MD, KMC, field equations, rate theory (RT) and Finite element method (FEM). To leveraging those methodologies in a tightly coupled manner and exploit the ability of each method is the major challenge of material behavior software.

Each of the method aims at specific time and length scales. There are different challenges to take advantage of those methods at Exascale supercomputing era according to the different models features. MD method provides accurate trajectories of atoms. As described in part 2.3, the memory requirement of MD limits the spatial scale, and computation for the huge number of time-steps hinders the time reach. As a consequence, the simulating length scale of MD is very small (characteristic nm) and time is short (characteristic μs). The significantly increased storage ability of super-computers at exascale era gives MD a chance to largely extend length scale, but not time scale [22]. Accelerated MD is hope to break the time limit which has been stuck at the same position for more than ten years [22]. KMC describes the evolution of a dynamic system by simulating the diffusive jumps. Compared to MD, KMC reaches larger time scale. The bottleneck of parallel KMC simulating software is the com-mutation overhead, which is introduced by data exchange and time synchronization [23]. More than ten million of computing cores may be used in the Exascale era, and the communication problems will be more and more noticeable. It is a great challenge to purse satisfying scalability considering the complicated network topology and extremely massive computing cores. RT is able to provide analysis of high-dose irradiation on reactor timescales [24]. One great challenge of RT method is to design efficient parallel algorithms to solve the stiff ill-conditioned ODEs [24]. RT analyses the defects distribution by solving millions of ODEs. FEM investigates the macro-scale process, which is unable to obtain the microstructure evolution. Adopting appropriate coupling strategy and data transfer approach is also a challenge to explore the material degradation process.

4.3   Thermal Hydraulics

Thermal hydraulics software simulates the coolant behavior, which plays a funda-mental role in evaluating reactor safety and optimizing design. Both sub-channel and CFD methods are of concern to thermal hydraulics research in virtual reactor. Sub-channel uses simplified models, and thus do not need vast computational resource. Sub-channel method is widely used thanks to its high efficiency. On the other hand, three-dimensional CFD method accurately analyze the realistic phenomena and thus extre-mely computationally intensive.

Sub-channel is a coarse-grained method. Small clusters are able to carry out full-core pin-cell-resolved analysis. CASL has made great efforts to parallel and optimize sub-channel software COBRA-TF [26]. Utilizing domain-decomposition parallel strategy, COBRA-TF has performed full-core analysis on less than 500 cores [27]. One challenge to full-core sub-channel software is to make its pre-processor practical for various reactor types. Generating input files is extremely laborious and error prone for full-core pin-cell-resolved simulation [28]. For example, a PWR may contain about 60,000 sub-channels and 200,000 lines of inputs for a quarter-core model are required [28]. As a result, a pre-processor to automatic generate input file is very critical.

COBRA-TF has developed a specific pre-processor for PWR. A commonly-used pre-processor for various reactor types (such as PWR, fast reactor) is worthy of research.

The development of high performance computing gives CFD a tremendous opportunity to play a more important role in thermal hydraulic research. At the Exascale era, LES model has the chance to come into play for the entire core [11, 29]. High-fidelity model requests high-order numerical solution method, which gives rise to the wide attention to spectral element method (SEM). SEM shares the advantage of very high-order accuracy with spectral techniques [30]. Nek5000 [31], based on SEM, has achieved great parallel efficiency and has been successfully applied to nuclear reactor flows [32]. One limitation of SEM is that it only supports quadrilateral or hexahedral meshes. It is a great challenge to use quadrilateral/ hexahedral meshes to simulate some complex structures such as grid spacer in reactors. Another challenge of CFD is to analyze multi-phase processes. Typically, multi-phase simulating heavily depend on empirical parameters [33]. Exascale and more powerful supercomputers in the future will give promise to science-based models and precisely simulation of multi-phase phenomena.

4.4 Neutronics

There are two different ways to perform nuclear reactor physics simulation: stochastic and deterministic methods. Monte Carlo belongs to stochastic models. Monte Carlo method solves the Boltzmann transport equation (BTE) and provides detailed information of nuclear system. There are several deterministic methods: MOC, S_N, P_N, and CP. Both stochastic and deterministic are storage expensive. Kothe [11] analyses the neutronics simulating capability: few-group diffusion theory is used and fuel assemblies are homogenized on Terascale supercomputers, multi-group transport method is used and fuel pin-cells are homogenized with Petascale supercomputers, continuous energy Monte Carlo method is used and realistic is obtained with Exascale supercomputers [11]. One huge challenge deterministic method facing is to design high scalable parallel algorithms, considering that it's extremely slow to converge using source iteration technology to solve transport problem [33]. Since Kord Smith put forward the full-core pin-by-pin modeling challenge, considerable efforts have be made to solve the problem. As the geometries become finer and physical models become more accurate, the storage demand of geometry information and tally data grow gradually.

4.5 Multi-physics and Multi-scale Coupling

Nuclear energy systems are extremely complicated, because the operating conditions are changeable and the internal phenomena are intrinsically strongly multi-physics coupled. Traditionally, research on the nuclear energy systems is divided into some isolated parts, such as neutronics, thermal-hydraulics, mechanics, material, etc. Feedbacks among those single physics parts are very limited in a traditional simulating manner. There are some multi-scale methods of researching a single physics process. For example, MD, KMC, RT and FEM are used to simulate different time and spatial phenomena of material performance. To accurately and effectively simulating the phenomena in reactors, multi-physics coupling and multi-scale coupling are supposed to be introduced.

Coupling can be implemented in a loose or tight way. In a tight coupling manner, it is vital to accurate model different physical aspects at the same time. Solving the tightly coupled models poses great challenges to both numerical method and computing power of supercomputers. Jacobian-Free Newton-Krylov (JFNK) method is at the frontier of tight coupling research field. In a loose coupling manner, Operator Splitting, Picard iteration strategies are usually used. Single physics parts are treated separately and information is transferred as boundary conditions among them. Some tools are essential in loose coupling: data transfer tools, mesh map tools, coupling process control tools (which implement coupling strategies, control iterations, check converge, etc.).

4.6   V&V and UQ

Experimentalists and computational scientists cooperate together to validate software. By analyzing accuracy, verification process determines if the algorithms implements the models at a required fidelity and if the computer software implement the algorithms correctly. Validation assesses that to which degree can virtual reactors reflect the realistic phenomena. On most of the occasions, experiment results are compared with the simulation results. Uncertainty Quantification analyzes and quantifies characterization in order to reduce uncertainties. Uncertainty Quantification plays a growing important role in V&V and UQ of virtual reactors.

V&V are indispensable in nuclear energy research, considering nuclear energy is a classic high-consequence research field. V&V and UQ for virtual reactors face some challenges which need to be addressed. *Multiple sources of data* increase the difficulties in validation. Data used in the V&V process are various, which may come from operating data or experiment data, PWR or fast reactor. *Testing software* is one fundamental step in verification. The test process will become extremely complicated on massively parallel software, especially when running supercomputers which are not very stable. *Complex nonlinear multi-physics and multi-scale systems of reactors* make the V&V process excessive difficult. V&V methodologies for individual physical process and coupled complicated systems are supposed to vary from application to application.

5   Conclusions

The increasingly improvements of supercomputers, especially the upcoming of Exascale supercomputing era, offer opportunities to predict the reactor systems in an accurate and effective way ever than before. It is possible that some intricate problems which hinder the efficient use of nuclear energy will be solved. Leveraging the leadership class supercomputers to analyze complicated reactor systems, virtual reactor is at the cutting edge of high performance computing and nuclear energy research fields. A virtual reactor includes the following research areas: safety analysis, system analysis, core physics components, database, uncertainty quantification, verification and validation. Core research areas focus on an integrated design, and primary physical components which typically consist of thermal-hydraulics, mechanics, neutronics, fuel, and material performance. The computing capabilities of Exascale supercomputers enable realistic models and high-resolution numerical methods to come into play, which results in the enormous computing and storage demand of virtual reactors. As far as some simulations in virtual reactors are concerned, the most powerful supercomputers are unable to meet the requirements. Meanwhile, great challenges have been posed to some essential physical research software (such as material, thermal hydraulics and neutronics), multi-physics coupling, multi-scale coupling, and V&V of virtual reactors. Engineers and researchers from nuclear engineering, software engineering, physics, mathematics, and high performance computing research fields will meet the challenges together.

Acknowledgement. The research is supported by National Key R&D Program of China No. 2017YFB0202303.

References

1. http://www.casl.gov/
2. Turner, J.A., Clarno, K., Sieger, M., et al.: The Virtual environment for reactor applications (vera): design and architecture. J. Comput. Phys. **326**, 544–568 (2016)
3. Rearden, B.T.: An overview of NEAMS 2017 (2017)
4. Merzari, E., Shemon, E.R., Yu, Y.Q, et al.: Multi-physics demonstration problem with the SHARP reactor simulation toolkit (2014)
5. Chauliac, C., Aragonés, J.M., Bestion, D., et al.: NURESIM – a European simulation platform for nuclear reactor safety: multi-scale and multi-physics calculations, sensitivity and uncertainty analysis. Nucl. Eng. Des. **241**(9), 3416–3426 (2011)
6. CESAR Homepage. https://cesar.mcs.anl.gov/
7. Team The-CESAR: The CESAR Codesign Center: Early Results
8. Stan, M., Yip, S.: Science based nuclear energy systems enabled by advanced modeling and simulation at the extreme scale. White Paper on Advanced Materials for Nuclear Energy Systems, Design and Evaluation of Nuclear Fuels and Structural Materials: Predictive Modeling and High-Performance Simulations
9. Hu, C., Bai, H., He, X., et al.: Crystal MD: the massively parallel molecular dynamics software for metal with BCC structure. Comput. Phys. Commun. **211**, 73–78 (2017)
10. Hu, C., Wang, X., Li, J., et al.: Kernel optimization for short-range molecular dynamics. Comput. Phys. Commun. **211**, 31–40 (2017)
11. Kothe, D.: Toward predictive modeling of nuclear reactor performance: application development experience, challenges, and plans in CASL, CASI-U-2014-0359-000 (2014)
12. Jamshed, S.: High reynolds number flows. In: Using HPC for Computational Fluid Dynamics. Academic Press, Oxford, pp. 81–100 (2015). ISBN 9780128015674. Chapter 4
13. Bolotnov, I.A.: Exascale applications for nuclear reactor thermal-hydraulics: fully resolved bubbly flow in realistic reactor core fuel assembly
14. Fischer, P.: Path to high-order unstructured-grid exascale CFD. https://www.orau.gov/turbulentflow2015/plenary-talks/Fischer_Paul.pdf
15. Hong-yi, Y., et al.: Technical Progress of 600 MW demonstration fast reactor (CFR600). Annu. Rep. China Inst. Atomic Energy, 42–45 (2016)

16. Li, D., Gang, L., Zhang, B, et al.: JMCT Monte Carlo simulation analysis of BEAVRS and SG-III Shielding, p. 06017 (2017)
17. Chen, G., Zhang, Z., et al.: Research on high efficient CFD schemes for PWRs. Nucl. Power Eng. **37**, 15–18 (2016)
18. Bourzac, K.: Stretching supercomputers to the limit. Nature **551**, 554–556 (2017)
19. Fu, H., Liao, J., Yang, J., et al.: The Sunway TaihuLight supercomputer: system and applications. Sci. China Inf. Sci. **59**(7), 072001 (2016)
20. Meng, D., Wen, M., Wei, J., et al.: Hybrid implementation and optimization of OpenFOAM on the SW26010 many-core processor (2016)
21. Wirth, B.D., Odette, G.R., Marian, J., et al.: Multiscale modeling of radiation damage in Fe-based alloys in the fusion environment. J. Nucl. Mater. **329**(8), 103–111 (2004)
22. Extending the Reach of Molecular Dynamics Simulations by Leveraging Exascale, A conversation with Danny Perez of Los Alamos National Laboratory (2018). https://www.exascaleproject.org/extending-reach-molecular-dynamics-simulations-leveraging-exascale/
23. Wu, B., Li, S., Zhang, Y., et al.: Hybrid-optimization strategy for the communication of large-scale Kinetic Monte Carlo simulation. Comput. Phys. Commun. **211**, 113–123 (2017)
24. Odette, G.R., Wirth, B.D., Bacon, D.J., et al.: Multiscale-multiphysics modeling of radiation-damaged materials: embrittlement of pressure-vessel steels. MRS Bull. **26**(3), 176–181 (2001)
25. D'Agostino, D., Pasquale, G., Clematis, A., et al.: Parallel solutions for voxel-based simulations of reaction-diffusion systems. Biomed. Res. Int. **2014**(3), 980501 (2014)
26. Salko, R., Lange, T., Kucukboyaci, V., et al.: Development of COBRA-TF for modeling full-core, reactor operating cycles. In: Advances in Nuclear Fuel Management V (ANFM 2015) (2015)
27. Salko, R.K., Avramova, M.N., Schmidt, R.C.: Suggestions for COBRA-TF parallelization and optimization (2012)
28. Kucukboyaci, V., Sung, Y., Salko, R.: COBRA-TF parallelization and application to PWR reactor core subchannel DNB analysis. In: ANS MC2015 - Joint International Conference on Mathematics and Computation (2015)
29. Tom Evans (PI): Coupled Monte Carlo Neutronics and Fluid Flow Simulation of Small Modular Reactors (ExaSMR), ECP Application Development, HPC Users Forum (2017)
30. Patera, A.T.: A spectral element method for fluid dynamics: laminar flow in a channel expansion. J. Comput. Phys. **54**(3), 468–488 (1984)
31. https://nek5000.mcs.anl.gov/
32. Merzari, E., Obabko, A., Fischer, P., et al.: Large-scale large eddy simulation of nuclear reactor flows: issues and perspectives. Nucl. Eng. Des. **312**, 86–98 (2017)
33. Moniz, E., Rosner, R.: Science based nuclear energy systems enabled by advanced modeling and simulation at the extreme scale. In: ASCR Scientific Grand Challenges Workshop Series, Technical report (2009)
34. Ligang: PhD dissertation, China Academy of Engineering Physics (2014)
35. Short, M.P., Hussey, D., Kendrick, B.K., et al.: Multiphysics modeling of porous CRUD deposits in nuclear reactors. J. Nucl. Mater. **443**(1–3), 579–587 (2013)

Prospects for CVR-0: A Prototype of China Virtual Reactor

An Wang[1,2], Changjun Hu[1,2], Wen Yang[3(✉)], Jue Wang[4],
Zhaoshun Wang[1], Tiancai Liu[3], Xuesong Wang[3], Hongwei Yang[3],
Mingyu Wu[3], Xianmeng Wang[1,2], Lingyu Yang[1,2],
and Dandan Chen[1,2]

[1] University of Science and Technology Beijing, Beijing, China
[2] Beijing Key Laboratory of Knowledge Engineering for Material Science,
Beijing, China
[3] China Institute of Atomic Energy, Beijing 102413, China
ywhyangwen@163.com
[4] Computer Network Information Center of Chinese Academy of Sciences,
Beijing, China

Abstract. A virtual nuclear reactor is a simulation environment, which has lately received great attention due to its contributions to improving nuclear safety and extending the life of the world's aging nuclear fleet at low cost. CVR-0, the prototype of China Virtual Reactor, is a virtual nuclear reactor being developed for Generation-III and Generation-IV reactors. The CVR program was established for the purpose of performing multi-physics simulations on high-fidelity geometry at large spatial and temporal scales and leveraging the next-generation supercomputers under development in China. Recent efforts to develop the simulation capabilities of CVR-0 has been made to achieve the near-term goal. In this work, we propose the main focuses and preliminary architecture of CVR-0. The overall goals and milestones of the CVR program are given in brief, as well as the estimated computational resources required for high-fidelity simulations. The estimates indicate that improving parallel efficiency on supercomputers remains an ongoing challenge due to the large scale of full-core calculations.

Keywords: Nuclear reactor · High performance computing ·
Modeling and simulation

1 Introduction

Nuclear power has become an effective solution to the world's energy and environmental problems, along with the increasing amount of electricity consumption. Existing nuclear reactors, such as light water reactors (LWRs), very-high-temperature reactors (VHTR), and fast breeder reactors (FBR) [1], have been running for decades. FBRs were estimated to reach at the most 30% of the total nuclear capacity in China by 2050 [2]. Both the observation of in-pile phenomena and the measurement of physical parameters are limited by extreme hazard conditions in a reactor pressure vessel (RPV).

© Springer Nature Singapore Pte Ltd. 2019
C. Hu et al. (Eds.): HPCMS 2018/HiDEC 2018, CCIS 913, pp. 107–125, 2019.
https://doi.org/10.1007/978-981-32-9987-0_10

Computer simulation is a scientific approach to solve physical problems with computers, commonly referred to as a peer to theory and experiment. Physical processes in a nuclear reactor are usually represented as partial differential equations (PDEs), which can be deformed into linear systems or stochastic systems necessary for programming. Except for the accuracy, the precision of the solution to PDEs is of great importance to reactor operation. It depends on both mathematical and computational models of reactors with different, complicated geometries. Therefore, a significant amount of computational resources is required to perform high-fidelity simulations, especially of nuclear reactors. China is now the biggest supercomputer holder in the world [3]. As of June 2016, the Sunway Taihulight supercomputer is entitled the world's fastest supercomputer with a peak performance greater than 100 petaflops (10^{17} floating-point operations per second) [4], almost tripling its nearest rival, Tianhe-2 [5]. Recently, considerable effort has been devoted to build 'exascale' machines capable of running at over 1,000 petaflops. Based on the Tianhe-2 and Sunway Taihulight, two of China's three exascale supercomputer prototypes are being developed, supported by China's 13th Five-Year Plan.

A virtual nuclear reactor (or virtual reactor) is a simulation environment (or toolkit) consisting of advanced computational tools on the basis of advanced modeling, advanced coupling methods, and large-scale parallel computing. It can improve reactor safety and lower the costs of experiments. The primary aim of a virtual reactor is, in general, to predict the performance of nuclear reactors during its entire lifecycle in support of a range of engineering applications covering reactor design optimization, lifetime extension, simulations under various operating conditions, analysis of severe accident scenarios, research and development (R&D) of advanced nuclear fuels and materials, etc. Computational components built to solve the problems of neutronics, thermal-hydraulics, mechanics, and fuel performance are indispensable to a virtual reactor, as well as their integration and uncertainty quantification.

Recently, there has been growing interest in the development of virtual reactors. In China, studies on virtual reactors are mainly led by China's three nuclear power corporations: the China National Nuclear Corporation (CNNC), China General Nuclear Power Corporation (CGN), and State Power Investment Corporation Limited (SPIC). In 2016, China Institute of Atomic Energy (CIAE), the main research organization of CNNC, released a software for the simulation of the Chinese-built Miniature Neutron Source Reactors (MNSR) [6], namely the Digital MNSR. The Digital MNSR can simulate and visualize a variety of processes such as the first criticality, reactor operation, demonstration, and decommissioning.

To leverage the architecture of exascale machines, we propose a prototype of China Virtual Reactor (CVR-0) for the simulation of nuclear reactors in this work. The current goal of CVR-0 is to provide a cost-effective simulation environment for a demonstration of the simulation of Gen-IV reactors.

The rest of the paper is organized as follows: Sect. 2 discusses the related work on virtual reactors, especially the CASL and NEAMS programs. Then we describe the architecture and objectives of CVR-0 in Sect. 3. In Sect. 4, a brief summary of the recent progress of the CVR program is given. Subsequently, the conclusion is made in Sect. 5.

2   Related Work

2.1   Existing Virtual Reactors

In recent years, several state-of-the-art multi-physics simulation toolkits have been developed for both existing and next-generation reactors. Some of them have capabilities of modeling and simulating a complete reactor. Studies over the past two decades, mainly from Europe, the United States and China, have provided important information on virtual reactor development.

The NURESIM platform is a set of codes designed for the simulation of normal operation and design basis accidents of LWRs, developed by the NURESAFE European consortium [7]. The platform aims to be a reference for multi-scale and multi-physics simulations through three successive projects named NURESIM, NURISP, and NURESAFE, starting in 2005. Based upon the open-source simulation platform SALOME [8], the NURISIM project (2005–2008) established a prototype of an integrated multi-physics environment comprising of a range of simulation capabilities including core physics, thermal-hydraulics, and S&U (sensitivity and uncertainty). Then, the NURISP project (2009–2011) was launched to improve and extend the simulation capabilities of the platform to achieve a higher precision both in space and time [9]. A fuel thermo-mechanics code was added during this project. The third project, NURESAFE (2013–2015), carried out six sub-projects to expand the use of the NURESIM platform to meet the needs of the European nuclear industry [10]. Up to now, the NURESIM simulation platform has been tested for Gen-II and Gen-III reactors and intended to provide extensibility to Gen-IV reactors. In addition to the NURESIM platform, there are a large number of simulation tools integrated into SALOME, especially Code_Aster and Code_Saturne built by EDF Energy [11].

VERA [12], the Virtual Environment for Reactor Applications, is a simulation environment developed by the Consortium for Advanced Simulation of Light Water Reactors (CASL) [13, 14] which is led by the U.S. Department of Energy (the U.S. DOE) in 2010. VERA mainly consists of existing computational codes and open-source frameworks for the modeling and simulation of LWRs. These tools helped to build a fully-integrated core simulator (VERA-CS) and to leverage a fuel performance code (BISON) [15] with the support of MOOSE [16] during the development. In addition, a multi-physics coupling tool, namely LIME [17], was incorporated into VERA to provide interfaces between codes. Then, to address some of the shortcomings of LIME, PIKE was designed with the Trilinos framework [18]. The coupling tools enable VERA to solve multi-physics problems with various coupling methods such as the Picard iteration and JFNK [19]. The primary objective of the CASL project is to enhance safety and performance of the existing reactors to lower costs. Recently, VERA has been used to simulate the startup of the AP1000 PWR [20] and Watts Bar Nuclear Unit 2 (WBN2) [21], proving its striking capabilities of core calculations and multi-physics simulations.

When the CASL project was in progress, the NEAMS ToolKit was under development by the Nuclear Energy Advanced Modeling and Simulation (NEAMS) Program of the U.S. DOE. The overarching objective of the NEAMS Program is to provide a "pellet-to-plant" simulation capability for the simulation and prediction of a variety of reactor systems [22]. The analysis on sodium-cooled fast reactors (SFR) is taken as the starting point at present. Since 2009, the NEAMS program has proposed three modular product lines to achieve its goals: the Fuels Product Line (FPL), the Reactors Product Line (RPL), and the Integration Product Line (IPL). The FPL and the RPL are aimed at the development of separate physics components, whereas the IPL focuses on the integration of computational capabilities to facilitate high-fidelity simulations by providing users a common platform [23, 24]. Within the context of the three lines, many simulation tools were incorporated into the NEAMS ToolKit, such as the BISON and MARMOT [25] fuel performance software and the Simulation-based High-efficiency Advanced Reactor Prototyping (SHARP) [26]. The three key simulation codes integrated into SHARP are the neutronics code PROTEUS, the thermal-hydraulics code Nek5000, and the structural mechanics code Diablo, each of which was designed to leverage the existing leadership supercomputers. Moreover, the performance improvements to PROTEUS and Nek5000 towards the next-generation supercomputer architectures are central to the Center for Exascale Simulation of Advanced Reactors (CESAR) [27].

As the Research and Development (R&D) on reactor simulations went further, the NEAMS Workbench was established to provide a common user interface for the modeling and simulation of reactors [24]. Simulation tools such as MOOSE, BISON, Dakota, Argonne Reactor Codes (ARC), and SCALE were integrated into the NEAMS Workbench Beta 1.0 release. The integration of the rest of the tools of both VERA and NEAMS ToolKit is ongoing. The U.S. Department of Energy Office of Nuclear Energy (the U.S. DOE-NE) has been working on the Gateway for Accelerated Innovation in Nuclear (GAIN) to advance commercialization of innovative nuclear energy technology [28] for months.

Aiming to the full-core simulation of reactors, especially the existing PWRs, the J Particle Transport System (JPTS) was developed by Institute of Applied Physics and Computational Mathematics (IAPCM) in China. The JPTS package is comprised of four computational tools JNuDa, JSNT, JMCT, JBURN and a data library NuDa [29]. In 2017, IAPCM claimed a successful simulation of the BEAVRS with up to 1.5 million depletion regions by using JMCT Monte Carlo code deployed on the Tianhe-2 computer [30].

A set of reactor simulation tools built by Nuclear Engineering Computational Physics Laboratory (NECP) of Xi'an Jiaotong University focuses on core calculations as well. The NECP package contains a couple of simulation capabilities mainly supported by NECP-X [31] (a neutronics code), NECP-Bamboo [32] (a nuclear fuel management toolkit), NECP-ONION [33] (a power-distribution monitoring code), and NECP-Atlas (a nuclear data processing code). These tools has been exploited by research institutions and nuclear power plants in China for the purpose of analysis and monitoring of nuclear reactors, especially PWRs.

2.2   Capabilities of VERA and the NEAMS ToolKit

As mentioned above, VERA has been applied to commercial PWRs after several years of development. The computational codes it contains have been verified to some extent. Meanwhile, making full use of the performance of exascale machines is not the primary goal of the NEAMS program, unlike CESAR, which focuses on the scalability of neutronics and computational fluid dynamics (CFD) codes, on supercomputers [34]. In Tables 1 and 2, we list the capabilities and problem sizes of the core computing components in VERA and the NEAMS ToolKit respectively.

Table 1. Capabilities and problem sizes of the codes in VERA.

Components	Capabilities	Codes
Neutronics	Numerical methods – 2D/1D Method of characteristics (MOC) – Monte Carlo (MC)	MOC: MPACT [35] – Verified with Watts Bar Nuclear Unit1 – Processors: >4700 MC: Shift [36] – Verified with C5G7 Rodded B – Particles: >500 thousand – Processors: >240 thousand
Thermal hydraulics	Problems of interest – DNB – GTRF/FAD Numerical methods – Subchannel thermal-hydraulics – Single-phase CFD with RANS, URANS, LES, and DNS – Multi-phase CFD	Subchannel: COBRA-TF [37] – Full-core simulations CFD: Hydra-TH [38] Single-phase – Meshes: 47 million – Processors: 100 thousand Multi-phase – Meshes: 200 million – Processors: 36 thousand
Fuel performance	Problems of interest – Thermal behavior – Fission gas behavior – Mechanical behavior	2-D analysis: Peregrine2D 3-D analysis: BISON [39]
Chemistry	Problems of interest – CRUD	MAMBA [40, 41]

Table 2. Capabilities and problem sizes of the codes in the NEAMS ToolKit.

Components	Capabilities	Codes
Neutronics	Numerical methods – Method of characteristics – SN method – SPN method	MOC: PROTEUS-MOCEX [42] – C5G7: >10 billion per group – Processors: 2048 on Blue Gene/Q SN: PROTEUS-SN [43] Strong spatial scalability – Processors: 32,768 – Scaling: 94% Weak angle scalability – Processors: 294,912 – Scaling: 76%
Thermal-hydraulics	Problems of interest – Coupling with neutronics and mechanics – Fuel performance Numerical methods – Single-phase CFD with DNS and LES.	CFD: Nek5000 [44] – Pins: 217 – Meshes: 2 billion – Processors: 520 thousand
Structural mechanics	Problems of interest – Coupling with neutronics and thermal-hydraulics – Fuel performance	SHARP-Diablo [45]
Fuel performance	Problems of interest – Steady state and slowly transient phenomena	3-D analysis: BISON
Materials simulation	Problems of interest – The irradiation performance of oxide and metallic fuels in three dimensions for both thermal and fast-spectrum reactors Numerical Methods – Density functional theory – Phase field	MARMOT [25] Mesoscale simulations

3   Architecture and Objectives of CVR-0

3.1   CVR-0 Architecture

As shown in Fig. 1, CVR-0 has a four-layer hierarchy. The long-term goal of CVR-0 is to be deployed on the exascale machines in China for use.

Libraries. A lot of libraries have been developed to facilitate the solution of scientific problems. For example, Trilinos [46] is an open source library containing a variety of capabilities including meshing, load balancing, linear solvers, etc.

– Several state-of-the-art solver libraries such as PETSc [47] may be incorporated into CVR-0 to enhance the efficiency of the numerical codes. The existing solver libraries, however, may be effective when running on existing computer architectures instead of the next-generation ones.

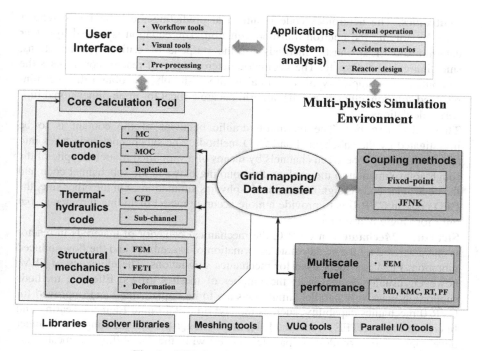

Fig. 1. CVR-0 architecture and capabilities.

- Meshing tools provide mesh-based simulations, such as the finite element method (FEM) and the finite volume method (FVM), with the abilities of mesh generation, storage, and grid mapping. The parallel efficiency is strongly affected by meshing tools. For example, PUMI is an effective system for mesh data management [48].
- VUQ tools or testing frameworks are part of the Verification and Validation (V&V) plan, which play a significant role in ensuring the correctness and accuracy of simulation results. For example, Dakota 5 is an open source toolkit containing algorithms for uncertainty quantification [49]. It is a well-structured software, but further optimized VUQ algorithms are required by CVR-0 due to the architecture of exascale machines.
- Considering that several commonly used file formats such as hdf5 are required by many codes in CVR-0, it is necessary to build tools to read and write these data files. Parallel I/O tools can improve the I/O performance of CVR-0 on different architectures [50].

Multi-physics simulation environment. It is comprised of a range of fundamental capabilities covering neutronics, thermal-hydraulics, mechanics, fuel performance, and microstructure evolution of nuclear materials. In the first place, all of them will be implemented respectively to be used alone. Then, separated codes will be integrated into the environment in support of applications.

- **Neutronics.** The neutronics code is aimed at predicting the behavior of reactor cores by solving the neutron transport equation. The equation is solved by either deterministic or stochastic methods for the purpose of criticality calculations, shielding calculations, etc. The geometric heterogeneity of reactor cores raises the computational complexity of numerical methods sharply. To obtain the fuel pin-resolved solution, efficient parallel algorithms are critical for three-dimensional full-core calculations.

- **Thermal-Hydraulics.** The thermal-hydraulic behavior of the coolant is to be investigated by the subchannel and CFD methods. The subchannel code takes into account cross-flow between channels by means of a simplified model. In spite of the rough approximation to the coolant, the coupling between the subchannel code and the neutronics code is significant in multi-physics simulations. On the other side, the CFD code in CVR-0 is to provide a more accurate model including turbulence, but only for single-phase fluid flow.

- **Structural Mechanics.** In CVR-0, the mechanical behavior of materials in reactor is characterized by the steady-state deformation of assemblies and the flow-induced vibration. FEM is widely used for mechanics simulations. The efficiency of FEM, however, usually decreases as the number of meshes grows. Effective methods supporting massively parallel simulations are to be implemented and improved for CVR-0 mechanics capability, such as the Hybrid Total Finite Element Tearing and Interconnection (HTFETI) method [51]. In addition, a parallel meshing tool is under development to provide the parallel solver with the capability of mesh data management.

- **Fuel Performance.** The fuel performance is observed in a very complicated environment with various factors including coolant temperature, pressure, corrosion, radiation, etc. The analysis tool focuses on four physical processes: (1) the heat transfer in the pellet and between the pellet and the coolant, (2) the deformation of the pellet and the cladding, (3) the production and release behavior of fission gases, and (4) the corrosion behavior of Zr alloy cladding.

- **Materials Simulation.** The materials simulation codes are under development aiming to study the radiation effects, such as embrittlement and swelling, of RPV steel, reactor internals, and fuel cladding materials. The multiscale modeling [52] is to be used to gain a detailed understanding of radiation damage in materials. This approach is considered an accurate prediction of the microstructure evolution in materials under radiation.

- **Multi-physics couplings.** For some specific physical phenomena in a reactor, loosely coupled models such as neutronics and thermal-hydraulics are required. In this case, the focus of the adopted coupling strategy is about data transfers. Fixed-point iteration is a widely used strategy to address the problem. For example, physical parameters such as coolant temperature are passed by interfaces between the thermal-hydraulics code and the neutronics code when they are loosely coupled. Another commonly used coupling strategy, namely "tight coupling", allows for simultaneous value update of multiple variables in a nonlinear system of differential equations deduced from multi-physics models. Thermomechanical problem is one of the models to be solved in a tightly coupled manner such as the Jacobian-free Newton Krylov (JFNK) method [19].

User Interface and applications. The User Interface (UI) is comprised of components that interact directly with users, including workflow management, visualization, pre-processing, etc. It can also manage applications supported by CVR-0. An application is directed toward a bundle of simulation capabilities, such as system analysis.

3.2   Primary Objectives

The prospects for simulation capabilities of the computational tools in CVR-0 are listed in Table 3. To simulate a Gen-IV reactor at an extremely high precision, cells of the geometry may be over tens of billions and particles to count could exceed hundreds of billions. However, no computer has yet been able to complete the calculation within the time required by reactor engineers.

Table 3. Capabilities and intended problem sizes of the codes in CVR-0 (2017–2021).

Components	Capabilities	Problem sizes
Neutronics	Numerical methods – Method of characteristics – Monte Carlo	MOC – Tracks: >100 billion – Criticality calculation: >2.04×10^{20} floating-point operations MC – Depletion regions: >1 million – Tallies: >100 billion – ≤ 1 standard deviation for 95% fuel pin-powers
Thermal-hydraulics	Physical problems – Heat transfer – Flow-induced vibration Numerical methods – Subchannel TH – Single-phase CFD with RANS, LES, etc.	Subchannel: Full-core simulations CFD meshes: >10 billion
Structural mechanics	Physical Problems – Statics – Flow-induced vibration	FEM meshes: >10 billion
Fuel performance	Physical Problems – Full-core fuel performance model	Single fuel rod Multiple fuel rods
Materials simulation	Physical Problems – Irradiation embrittlement – Irradiation swelling – Zirconium-hydrogen Numerical Methods – Molecular dynamics [53] – Kinetic Monte Carlo [54] – Rate theory – Phase field	Particles: >100 billion Degrees of freedom: >1,000 billion

The development of the computational components in CVR-0 is to be done by mid-2020. Multi-physics coupling capabilities will be finished around September 2020. Upon optimizing the parallel algorithms, all of the components will be integrated into the CVR-0 system to be tested and verified. It is expected that CVR-0 will be put into use for Gen-IV reactors in mid-2021.

The near-term goals of CVR-0 development are to couple a neutronics code with a subchannel code in support of the preliminary multi-physics capability and to provide a multi-scale simulation capability of nuclear fuels and materials. Recently, we have modeled and developed several modules of the fuel performance analysis code. We are now working on the improvement of a molecular dynamics (MD) code, a kinetic Monte Carlo (KMC) code, and a mean-field rate theory (RT) model.

There are some similarities and differences between CVR-0, VERA, and the NEAMS toolkit.

Neutronics. Both of the SN and Monte Carlo (MC) methods are able to solve the full-core problem, while the performance of the method of characteristics (MOC) on large-scale problems is not good enough. In general, the goal of neutronics codes is solving full-core transport problem with structured and unstructured geometry. The MOC solver in CVR-0 is expected to be optimized to achieve a higher efficiency.

Thermal-Hydraulics. Both VERA and CVR-0 are designed to perform full-core simulations by the subchannel method. Compared to VERA, CVR-0 is a prototype system which intends to complete a full-core simulation with the single-phase CFD code.

Structural Mechanics. The capabilities of the mechanics codes of the three toolkits are quite similar to each other.

Fuel Performance. Each of the three toolkits is devoted to performing full-core fuel performance analysis. In the NEAMS ToolKit, the multiscale fuel performance capability was reached by integration of MARMOT and BISON based on MOOSE. BISON can be used for both normal and accident scenarios while CVR-0 focuses on steady-state analysis.

Materials Simulation. MARMOT from the NEAMS ToolKit is used for observation of the microstructure evolution at the mesoscopic scale. CVR-0 aims to couple an MD code with a KMC code tightly to investigate materials behavior at mesoscale. In the future, the rate theory will be added into CVR-0 for simulation at larger spatial scales.

4   Progress in CVR-0

It is a challenge to perform a multiscale simulation of fuel performance from microscale to macroscale. The physical phenomena in a reactor are described by nonlinear systems, causing the simulation to be time-consuming and memory-consuming for computers. Our recent studies on physical models, parallel algorithms, and the verification and validation of CVR-0 are as listed below.

4.1   Physical Models and Multi-physics Couplings

We are working on establishing the physical models of each of the computational tools, as well as the relations among these models. Data transfers between the models are shown in Fig. 2. In CVR-0, the fuel performance model is one-way coupled with the neutronics model or with the CFD model whereas the other models are primarily coupled in a two-way manner.

4.2   Parallel Algorithms

Considering that the architecture of the next-generation exascale machines in China is being built on the basis of the Tianhe-2 and Sunway Taihulight supercomputers, a set of techniques may help to accelerate the computation of reactor simulation. Multi-level communication is a commonly used approach to leverage co-processors and their small local caches on a supercomputer. Besides, many other techniques proved to be effective in our previous studies [54, 55], such as data prefetching, automatic tuning, and cache-oblivious algorithms [56].

Materials Simulation

Materials simulation plays a fundamental role in predicting the microstructure evolution in materials. In CVR-0, The technology roadmap for multiscale simulations is shown in Fig. 3. The MD code is used to simulate the cascade collision to obtain the distribution of initial defects, which is then used as part of the input for the KMC code. Then, the process of defects annealing is performed by the KMC code to calculate the survival rate, ratio of clusters, and distribution of remaining defects. These are the necessary information to drive the rate theory (RT) code and phase field (PF) code to predict long-term defect evolution. One of the aims of CVR-0 is to provide a multiscale simulation code that combines MD, KMC, and RT.

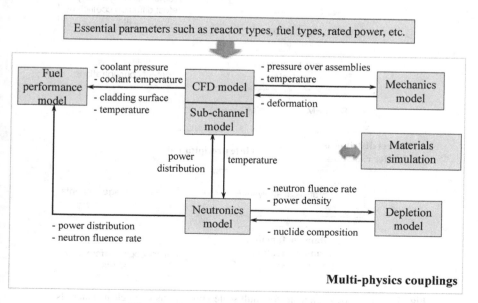

Fig. 2. Multi-physics couplings in CVR-0.

The most time-consuming part of an MD code is usually the calculation of inter-molecular forces. The number of atoms in a system increases rapidly as the problem size grows. To observe the microstructure evolution over a long period of time (seconds or longer) with a rather small time step (femtoseconds), the hot spots in MD codes of today are usually executed in parallel.

For this reason, we developed a massively parallel MD code, Crystal-MD [55]. The initial goal of the code is to investigate the behavior of Body-Centered Cubic (BCC) structured metals under radiation. Crystal-MD uses a special data structure, namely the lattice neighbor list, to reduce the memory usage of the data structure for BCC. The parallel algorithm of Crystal-MD also has been improved by a multi-threading optimization method, the Partition-and-Separate-Calculation method (PSC), for the calculation of short-range forces [53]. Hence, Crystal-MD is now able to simulate a system of 2×10^{12} Fe atoms with more than 80 thousand processors with the parallel efficiency over 90% on the Tianhe-2 supercomputer [55].

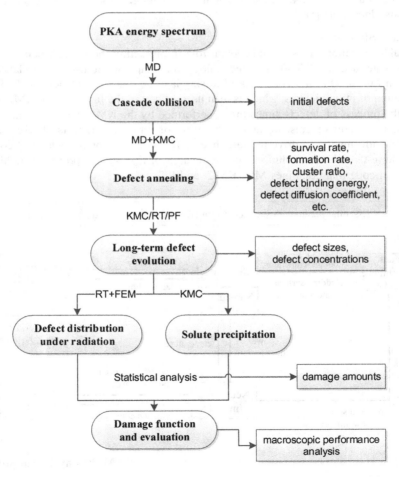

Fig. 3. Technology roadmap for multiscale simulations of nuclear materials.

Recently, we have made some improvements to Crystal-MD. A statistics module was added to analyze the results obtained with different initial inputs such as PKAs and temperatures. Another essential feature we are working on is the effects of alloying elements on initial defects. It will lead to an increasing amount of memory usage and communication overhead. The knowledge of next-generation heterogeneous super-computers plays a crucial role in addressing these issues.

Compared to MD, the KMC method performs the simulation at larger spatial and temporal scales. But a parallel implementation of KMC, especially the domain decomposition, are believed to impact on the stochastic process underlying the serial algorithm [57]. Consequently, the parallel algorithm requires some methods to guarantee the correctness of simulation results. It will take more iterations to converge and lead to a considerable amount of message passing.

Based on SPPARKS [57], we developed a massively parallel simulation code, Crystal-KMC [54], which is optimized to leverage the Sunway Taihulight supercomputer. Three main techniques were used to achieve a high efficiency: the communication aggregation, the shared-memory method, and the neighborhood collective operations [54, 58]. In the case of diffusion in erbium hydrides, the communication time of Crystal-KMC, compared with SPPARKS, is reduced by 28.5% using 768 processors on Tianhe-2 [54].

In order to study the effects of different alloy/impurity elements on radiation defects, we intend to add a few new elements (Fe-Cu-Mn-Ni) to the model of Crystal-KMC (Fe-Cu only). However, a more complicated model will cause a sharp increase in the amount of communication.

Mean-field RT method has advantages in computational speed and efficiency. It can also simulate defect evolution without the limits of spatial and temporal scales. A compact exponential time differencing (ETD) method [59] has been implemented in the RT code to solve the system of ordinary differential equations (ODEs). The RT code is now able to obtain the first-order and fourth-order ETD solution of the evolution problem of vacancy clusters. The results of the code are in good agreement with the exact solution in [60]. But the massively parallel capability (solving up to $\sim 10^6$ ODEs) of the RT code still needs to be improved. Moreover, there will be an increasing number of ODEs when other defect types (interstitial atoms, multiple solute-vacancy, etc.) are added to the model. It will cause a significant increase in the amount of communication and computation, which remains an ongoing challenge.

Fuel Performance

As depicted in Fig. 4, the fuel performance code mainly consists of six models used to simulate the behavior of the fuel elements during reactor operation: the neutronics model, the temperature model, the mechanics model, the fission gas release (FGR) model, the rod internal pressure (RIP) model, and the cladding corrosion model. In the temperature model, a fuel rod is regarded as separate axial segments. For every segment, the one-dimensional heat conduction equation is solved in the radial direction to provide the temperature distribution in the pellet and in the cladding. The temperature model has been implemented for the parallel simulation of multiple fuel rods and is being tested.

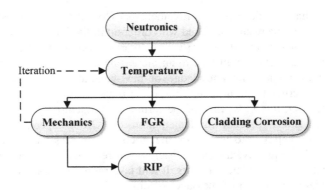

Fig. 4. Interactions between the models implemented in the fuel performance code.

Neutronics

The goal of the neutronics codes in CVR-0 is to perform the full-core calculation of Generation IV reactors at a pin-by-pin precision. There are two methods to be implemented: the method of characteristics (MOC) and the Monte Carlo (MC) method.

MOC is a form of the discrete neutron transport equation, which allows us to overlap the problem domain with tracks and solve the transport equation along each of the tracks. Constructive solid geometry (CSG) is a commonly used approach which an MOC code could use for modeling a reactor core. Modular ray tracing remains an effective technique for preprocessing to massively reduce the memory consumption and improve the computational efficiency. A serial MOC code is now under test and has passed several benchmarks including C5G7. However, a large number of assemblies for full-core calculations render it memory-consuming, which forces us to design a multi-level parallel scheme for MOC.

We analyzed the characteristics of the CSG implementation, which uses Universe, Lattice, Cell, Surface, Plane, and other data structures to construct assemblies or rods within a reactor. They are nested and can be thought of as a tree logically. Naturally, it is possible to design an algorithm for domain decomposition at a certain depth of the tree and then distribute the subtrees to different processes [61]. Difficulties arise, however, when an attempt is made to determine the depth and to make use of co-processors on supercomputers such as the Tianhe and Sunway series. In addition, a 3-D MOC procedure will leave us with a huge number of tracks, which is too many to be handled by a single thread or even a process. Tracks are supposed to be distributed to processes on different compute nodes. However, it leads to a sharp increase in communication overhead and remains a problem to be solved allowing for the heterogeneous architecture of leadership-class computers.

Thermal-Hydraulics

The CFD code in CVR-0 is designed to give a prediction for equilibrium and non-equilibrium flows, which is based on the Reynolds-averaged Navier-Stokes (RANS) equations and large eddy simulation (LES) respectively. FEM and FVM are currently the most popular methods for numerically solving the equations. Nevertheless, several studies have revealed that spectral element methods are particularly useful in the numerical solution of the incompressible Navier-Stokes equations [62, 63]. It has been found that the combination of finite element and spectral techniques could guarantee both the geometric flexibility and the accuracy of spectral element methods. A lightweight spectral element code is being developed on the Sunway Taihulight supercomputer. Being limited to the architecture of the computer, especially in terms of the local memory size of CPEs [64], there are obvious difficulties in the implementation of dense matrix multiplication, which is time-consuming in the spectral element code.

Structural Mechanics

The main purpose of the mechanics code is to simulate the wear behavior of fuel assemblies which is mainly caused by the deformation of fuel assemblies and flow-induced vibration. A huge number of meshes are required for FEM to produce high-accuracy numerical solutions. Commonly-used meshing tools are usually able to generate structured or unstructured meshes efficiently, as well as to support techniques like load balancing and adaptive mesh refinement. In order to test current open-source codes on SW26010 many-core processors [64], we have made some modifications to PUMI [48] and OOFEM [65]. Our short-term goal is to develop a Finite Element Tearing and Interconnection (FETI) solver in support of efficient meshing tools.

4.3   Verification and Validation

The V&V for CVR-0 faces many difficulties. We must take into account not only the diversity of the physical processes inside a reactor but also the accuracy and validity of each code. Furthermore, we have to analyze the errors introduced by parallelism and the computer itself. The V&V for CVR-0 is a group of activities for verifying multi-physics coupling simulation software, underlying the features of V&V in scientific computing [66–68]. One of the greatest challenges is the Oracle Problem in software testing [69]. At present, a preliminary V&V framework has been designed for CVR-0.

5   Conclusion

Virtual reactors have attracted considerable attention due to its capability to meet the demand of high-fidelity full-core simulations. It is able to achieve several significant objectives both in engineering and science. Therefore, virtual reactors are considered a great contributor to existing commercial reactors and next-generation reactors. Existing virtual reactors can be differentiated by the degree of integration and fidelity. Most of them are designed for the analysis of operating commercial PWRs and expected to be deployed on PCs or small clusters. To obtain a high-speed response time, each of the computational components can only handle physical problems with fairly homogenized geometries and be integrated together in a loosely coupled manner. Previous studies of virtual reactors such as the NURISM platform, the VERA environment, and the NEAMS ToolKit have revealed a huge demand for computational resources.

In this paper we point out that the computational tools in CVR-0 are aiming at the exascale machines under development. The goals of each tool are described briefly.

We present a four-layer hierarchy is established for CVR-0. The development process is full of challenges, especially in terms of the multi-scale, multi-physics simulations of fluid-thermal-structural problems.

In order to design scalable parallel algorithms for exascale computers, we have to exploit numerous programming techniques such as the multi-level communication, load balancing, and automatic tuning. Thus far, we have made some progress in the development of physical models and parallel algorithms. However, the efficiency of high-fidelity simulations and performance of computer hardware are two of the critical bottlenecks to be addressed.

Acknowledgements. This work was supported by the National Key Research and Development Program of China (No. 2017YFB0202303 and No. 2017YFB0202300).

References

1. Hong-yi, Y., et al..: Technical progress of 600 MW demonstration fast reactor (CFR600). Annual Report of China Institute of Atomic Energy (00), pp. 42–45 (2016)
2. Chen, Y., Martin, G., Chabert, C., Eschbach, R., He, H., Ye, G.-a.: Prospects in China for nuclear development up to 2050. Prog. Nucl. Energy **103**, 81–90 (2018)
3. TOP500 List Statistics. https://www.top500.org/statistics/list/. Accessed 5 Mar 2018
4. Fu, H., et al.: The Sunway TaihuLight supercomputer: system and applications. Sci. China Inf. Sci. **59**(7), 072001 (2016)
5. Liao, X., Xiao, L., Yang, C., Lu, Y.: MilkyWay-2 supercomputer: system and application. Front. Comput. Sci. **8**(3), 345–356 (2014)
6. IAEA Homepage. https://www.iaea.org/. Accessed 25 Apr 2018
7. Chauliac, C., et al.: NURESIM – a European simulation platform for nuclear reactor safety: Multi-scale and multi-physics calculations, sensitivity and uncertainty analysis. Nucl. Eng. Des. **241**(9), 3416–3426 (2011)
8. SALOME platform. https://www.salome-platform.org/. Accessed 5 Mar 2018
9. Chanaron, B., et al.: Advanced multi-physics simulation for reactor safety in the framework of the NURESAFE project. Ann. Nucl. Energy **84**, 166–177 (2015)
10. NURESAFE Homepage. http://www.nuresafe.eu/. Accessed 5 Mar 2018
11. Simulation Softwares - EDF R&D. https://www.edf.fr/en/the-edf-group/world-s-largest-power-company/activities/research-and-development/scientific-communities/simulation-softwares. Accessed 5 Mar 2018
12. Turner, J.A., et al.: The virtual environment for reactor applications (VERA): design and architecture. J. Comput. Phys. **326**, 544–568 (2016)
13. CASL Homepage. https://www.casl.gov/. Accessed 5 Mar 2018
14. Kothe, D.B.: CASL: the consortium for advanced simulation of light water reactors. Bull. Am. Phys. Soc. 55 (2010)
15. Newman, C., Hansen, G., Gaston, D.: Three dimensional coupled simulation of thermo-mechanics, heat, and oxygen diffusion in UO2 nuclear fuel rods. J. Nucl. Mater. **392**(1), 6–15 (2009)
16. Gaston, D., Newman, C., Hansen, G., Lebrun-Grandié, D.: MOOSE: a parallel computational framework for coupled systems of nonlinear equations. Nucl. Eng. Des. **239**(10), 1768–1778 (2009)

17. Schmidt, R.: Introduction to LIME: a lightweight integrating multi-physics environment for coupling codes. Technical report, Sandia National Laboratories (2010)
18. Heroux, M.A., Willenbring, J.M.: A new overview of the Trilinos project. Sci. Program. **20** (2), 83–88 (2012)
19. Knoll, D.A., Keyes, D.E.: Jacobian-free Newton-Krylov methods: a survey of approaches and applications. J. Comput. Phys. **193**(2), 357–397 (2004)
20. Franceschini, F., et al.: AP1000 PWR Startup core modeling and simulation with VERA-CS. In: Advances in Nuclear Fuel Management V. ANS, Illinois, USA (2015)
21. Godfrey, A.T., Collins, B.S., Gentry, C.A., Stimpson, S.G., Ritchie, J.A.: Watts Bar Unit 2 Startup Results with VERA. Technical report, Oak Ridge National Laboratory (2017)
22. Bradley, K.: NEAMS: the nuclear energy advanced modeling and simulation program. Technical report, Argonne National Laboratory (2013)
23. Sofu, T., Thomas, J.: U.S. DOE NEAMS program and SHARP multi-physics toolkit for high-fidelity SFR core design and analysis. In: International Conference on Fast Reactors and Related Fuel Cycles: Next Generation Nuclear Systems for Sustainable Development. IAEA, Vienna (2017)
24. Rearden, B.T., Lefebvre, R.A., Thompson, A.B., Langley, B.R., Stauff, N.E.: Introduction to the nuclear energy advanced modeling and simulation workbench. In: International Conference on Mathematics and Computational Methods Applied to Nuclear Science and Engineering, pp. 16–20. ANS, Illinois (2017)
25. Nuclear Fuels. https://www.energy.gov/ne/advanced-modeling-simulation/nuclear-fuels. Accessed 25 Apr 2018
26. Siegel, A., et al.: Software design of SHARP. In: Joint International Topical Meeting on Mathematics and Computation and Supercomputing in Nuclear Applications. ANS, Illinois (2007)
27. CESAR Homepage. https://cesar.mcs.anl.gov/. Accessed 5 Mar 2018
28. GAIN Homepage. https://gain.inl.gov/. Accessed 5 Mar 2018
29. Li, G., Zhang, B., Deng, L., Hu, Z., Ma, Y.: Development of Monte Carlo particle transport code JMCT. High Power Laser Part. Beams **25**(1), 158–162 (2013)
30. Li, D., et al.: JMCT Monte Carlo simulation analysis of BEAVRS and SG-III shielding. EPJ Web Conf. **153**, 06017 (2017)
31. Chen, J., et al.: A new high-fidelity neutronics code NECP-X. Ann. Nucl. Energy **116**, 417–428 (2018)
32. NECP-Bamboo Homepage. http://bamboo.xjtu.edu.cn/page/introduction. Accessed 5 Mar 2018
33. Li, Z., et al.: Development and validation of a PWR on-line power-distribution monitoring system NECP-ONION. Nucl. Eng. Des. **322**, 104–115 (2017)
34. Smith, K., Forget, B.: Challenges in the development of high-fidelity LWR core neutronics tools. In: International Conference on Mathematics and Computational Methods Applied to Nuclear Science and Engineering. ANS, Illinois (2013)
35. Downar, T., Kochunas, B., Collins, B.: MPACT verification and validation: status and plans. Technical report, Oak Ridge National Laboratory (2015)
36. Sly, N.C.: Verification of the shift Monte Carlo code using the C5G7 and CASL benchmark Problems. Master's thesis, University of Tennessee (2014)
37. Kucukboyaci, V., Sung, Y., Salko, R.: COBRA-TF parallelization and application to PWR reactor core subchannel DNB analysis. In: Joint International Conference on Mathematics and Computation, Supercomputing in Nuclear Applications and the Monte Carlo Method, pp. 1–18. ANS, Illinois (2015)
38. Christon, M.A.: Overview of thermal hydraulics and hydra-TH capabilities. Technical report, Los Alamos National Laboratory (2014)

39. Perez, D.M., Williamson, R., Novascone, S., Pastore, G., Hales, J., Spencer, B.: Assessment of BISON: a nuclear fuel performance analysis code. Technical report, Idaho National Laboratory (2013)
40. Deshon, J., Hussey, D., Kendrick, B., McGurk, J., Secker, J., Short, M.: Pressurized water reactor fuel crud and corrosion modeling. JOM **63**(8), 64 (2011)
41. Short, M.P., Hussey, D., Kendrick, B.K., Besmann, T.M., Stanek, C.R., Yip, S.: Multiphysics modeling of porous CRUD deposits in nuclear reactors. J. Nucl. Mater. **443** (1), 579–587 (2013)
42. Jung, Y., Lee, C., Smith, M.: Verification of high-fidelity neutronics code PROTEUS for C5G7 benchmark problems. Trans. Am. Nucl. Soc. **116**, 1042–1044 (2017)
43. Shemon, E., Yu, Y., Kim, T.: Application of the SHARP toolkit to Sodium-cooled fast reactor challenge problems. Technical report, Argonne National Lab (2017)
44. Scalable Spectral Element Methods. http://www.mcs.anl.gov/~fischer/sem1b/. Accessed 25 Apr 2018
45. Yu, Y., Shemon, E., Thomas, J., Mahadevan, V.S., Rahaman, R.O., Solberg, J.: SHARP user manual. Technical report, Argonne National Lab (2016)
46. Trilinos. https://trilinos.org/. Accessed 5 Mar 2018
47. PETSc. https://www.mcs.anl.gov/petsc/. Accessed 5 Mar 2018
48. Ibanez, D.A., Seol, E.S., Smith, C.W., Shephard, M.S.: PUMI: parallel unstructured mesh infrastructure. ACM Trans. Math. Softw. (TOMS) **42**(3), 17 (2016)
49. Adams, B.M., et al.: Dakota, a multilevel parallel object-oriented framework for design optimization, parameter estimation, uncertainty quantification, and sensitivity analysis: Version 5.0 user's manual. Technical report, Sandia National Laboratories (2009)
50. Li, S., Hu, C., Zhang, J., Zhang, Y.: Automatic tuning of sparse matrix-vector multiplication on multicore clusters. Sci. China Inf. Sci. **58**(9), 1–14 (2015)
51. Říha, L., Brzobohatý, T., Markopoulos, A., Meca, O., Kozubek, T.: Massively parallel hybrid total FETI (HTFETI) solver. In: Platform for Advanced Scientific Computing Conference (PASC 2016), Artical No. 7. ACM, New York (2016)
52. Wirth, B., Odette, G., Marian, J., Ventelon, L., Young-Vandersall, J., Zepeda-Ruiz, L.: Multiscale modeling of radiation damage in Fe-based alloys in the fusion environment. J. Nucl. Mater. **329**, 103–111 (2004)
53. Hu, C., et al.: Kernel optimization for short-range molecular dynamics. Comput. Phys. Commun. **211**, 31–40 (2017)
54. Wu, B., Li, S., Zhang, Y., Nie, N.: Hybrid-optimization strategy for the communication of large-scale Kinetic Monte Carlo simulation. Comput. Phys. Commun. **211**, 113–123 (2017)
55. Hu, C., et al.: Crystal MD: The massively parallel molecular dynamics software for metal with BCC structure. Comput. Phys. Commun. **211**, 73–78 (2017)
56. Li, S., Zhang, Y., Hoefler, T.: Cache-oblivious MPI all-to-all communications based on Morton order. IEEE Trans. Parallel Distrib. Syst. **29**(3), 542–555 (2018)
57. Plimpton, S., et al.: Crossing the mesoscale no-man's land via parallel kinetic Monte Carlo. Technical report, Sandia National Laboratories (2009)
58. Li, S., Hoefler, T., Hu, C., Snir, M.: Improved MPI collectives for MPI processes in shared address spaces. Cluster Comput. **17**(4), 1139–1155 (2014)
59. Ashi, H.: Numerical methods for stiff systems. Master's thesis, University of Nottingham (2008)
60. Terrier, P., Athènes, M., Jourdan, T., Adjanor, G., Stoltz, G.: Cluster dynamics modelling of materials: a new hybrid deterministic/stochastic coupling approach. J. Comput. Phys. **350**, 280–295 (2017)

61. Kochunas, B.M.: A hybrid parallel algorithm for the 3-d method of characteristics solution of the boltzmann transport equation on high performance compute clusters. Ph.D. thesis, University of Michigan (2013)

62. Patera, A.T.: A spectral element method for fluid dynamics: laminar flow in a channel expansion. J. Comput. Phys. **54**(3), 468–488 (1984)

63. NEK5000 Homepage, https://nek5000.mcs.anl.gov/, last accessed 2018/4/25

64. Zheng, F., Li, H.-L., Lv, H., Guo, F., Xu, X.-H., Xie, X.-H.: Cooperative computing techniques for a deeply fused and heterogeneous many-core processor architecture. J. Comput. Sci. Technol. **30**(1), 145–162 (2015)

65. Patzák, B., Bittnar, Z.: Design of object oriented finite element code. Adv. Eng. Softw. **32** (10–11), 759–767 (2001)

66. Radatz, J., Geraci, A., Katki, F.: IEEE standard glossary of software engineering terminology. IEEE Std 610121990(121990), 3 (1990)

67. Oberkampf, W.L., Sindir, M., Conlisk, A.: Guide for the verification and validation of computational fluid dynamics simulations. Standard, American Institute of Aeronautics and Astronautics (1998)

68. Schwer, L.E.: An overview of the PTC 60/V&V 10: guide for verification and validation in computational solid mechanics. Eng. Comput. **23**(4), 245–252 (2007)

69. Kanewala, U., Bieman, J.M.: Testing scientific software: a systematic literature review. Inf. Softw. Technol. **56**(10), 1219–1232 (2014)

Diffusion Mechanism of Small Helium-Vacancy Clusters in BCC Fe and Fe-10%Cr Alloy

Xueyuan Liang[1] and Xinfu He[1,2(✉)]

[1] Institute for Standardization of Nuclear Industry, Beijing, China
hexinfu@ciae.ac.cn
[2] China Institute of Atomic Energy, Beijing 102413, People's Republic of China

Abstract. In this work, we studied the migration of Helium-Vacancy (He-Vac) clusters in several <110> tilt grain boundaries (GBs) in pure Fe and Fe-10%Cr random alloy, with the misorientation angle varying in the range of 26°–141°. We performed systematic molecular statics and molecular dynamics simulations to characterize the stability of He-Vac clusters in bulk and GBs and to estimate the diffusion coefficient, migration mechanism, and effective core migration energy. The simulations were performed in the temperature range 800–1400 K, applying a recent set of interatomic potentials, specially fitted to the properties of He in bulk Fe. We found that the addition of Cr has no effects on the binding energies of He to the He-Vac clusters in bulk and GBs. He-Vac clusters are stable on MD time scale and diffuse on the GB plane performing one- or two-dimensional migration, depending on the GB structure. The results clearly demonstrate that the accommodation, migration mechanism, and diffusivity of He-Vac clusters are extremely sensitive to variations in atomic structure of a particular GB. Dissociation and re-combination of He-Vac clusters also contributes to the mechanism of He-Vac cluster diffusion. Alloying with Cr was found to enhance the mobility of He-Vac clusters in the GB region.

Keywords: Helium-vacancy clusters · Molecular dynamics · Diffusion mechanism · Fe-Cr alloy

1 Introduction

Reduced-activation Ferritic/Martensitic (RAFM) steels are one of attractive candidate structure materials for fusion reactor. Insoluble Helium (He), produced by transmutation, plays an important role in the microstructural evolution of these steels under prolonged neutron irradiation [1]. He atoms are strongly trapped at open volume lattice defects and tend to gather into bubbles. Accumulation of He at grain boundaries (GBs) will lead to the formation of He bubbles leading to inter-granular embrittlement. Hence, accumulation of He can have major implications for the integrity of fusion components & structures such as: (1) loss of high-temperature creep strength; (2) increased swelling and irradiation creep at intermediate temperatures; (3) potential for loss of ductility and fracture toughness at low temperatures [2]. Rationalization of these phenomena requires an understanding of the basic processes contributing to the microstructural evolution, such as He diffusion, trapping, nucleation, and growth of

© Springer Nature Singapore Pte Ltd. 2019
C. Hu et al. (Eds.): HPCMS 2018/HiDEC 2018, CCIS 913, pp. 126–134, 2019.
https://doi.org/10.1007/978-981-32-9987-0_11

He-vacancy (He-Vac) clusters, as well as their relation with the change in mechanical properties. The mechanisms and processes of Helium bubble nucleation and growth are still not completely understood and research in this field is ongoing [3].

He-Vac clusters behavior has been investigated in various types of GBs in BCC Fe by atomistic simulations including ab initio [4, 5], Molecular Dynamics [6–8] and Kinetic Monte Carlo methods [9]. The migration mechanism and corresponding diffusional characteristics of He-Vac clusters were found to depend on the GB types. Mono-vacancy, small vacancy clusters and open volume sites at GBs are efficient traps for He atoms. Most of these studies were performed in pure Fe. It should be however noted that alloying of Fe by Cr affects the kinetics of He bubble nucleation and growth, as well as the diffusivity of nanometric bubbles, as directly observed using transmission electron microscopy [10]. Therefore, a possible role of Cr as the main alloying element in ferritic/martensitic steels needs to be assessed. In this work, we perform a comparative study of the diffusivity of He-Vac clusters at GBs in BCC Fe and Fe-10Cr alloy.

2 Methodology

The following <110> tilt GBs were considered: $\sum19\{331\}$, $\sum9\{221\}$, $\sum3\{111\}$, $\sum3\{112\}$, $\sum11\{113\}$, and $\sum9\{114\}$. The sizes of the crystallite used in Molecular Dynamics (MD) simulations are listed in Table 1. In Table 1, we also report the GB width, obtained by Molecular Statics (MS) relaxations, which is a crucial parameter for the definition of migration mode, as will be shown later. MD and MS calculations were performed to investigate the energetic and thermal stability of He-Vac clusters in bulk and at GBs. Several small He-Vac clusters (HeV2, HeV, He2V, He2V3, He3V4, He4V) with He-to-Vacancy ratio varied from 0.5 to 4 were considered in the present work.

Table 1. Characteristics of <110> tilt grain boundaries in pure Fe and Fe-10%Cr random alloys. The GB energy, width of GBs are given.

GB type	Crystal size, $a_0 \times a_0 \times a_0$	γ_{GB}, J/m^2		w_{GB}, nm
		Pure Fe	Fe-10%Cr	
$\Sigma9\{221\}$	$5.6 \times 9.0 \times 25.4$	1.1467	1.1932	1.62
$\Sigma19\{331\}$	$5.6 \times 13.0 \times 37.0$	1.1383	1.3382	2.22
$\Sigma3\{111\}$	$9.89 \times 9.79 \times 31.0$	1.2924	1.2802	1.32
$\Sigma3\{112\}$	$7.0 \times 6.92 \times 29.39$	0.2619	0.3205	1.40
$\Sigma11\{113\}$	$5.65 \times 9.94 \times 28.1$	1.5613	1.5867	2.20
$\Sigma9\{114\}$	$5.65 \times 12.72 \times 18.$	1.2798	1.2581	2.28

Estimation of the binding and dissociation energies for He-Vac clusters (henceforth He$_n$V$_m$, where n and m denote the number of He atoms and vacancies forming a cluster) are defined as the energy difference between the situations where the defects is infinitely separated from the complex and where it is added to the complex, making respectively a $He_{n+1}V_m$ and He_nV_{m+1} complex. The corresponding binding energy of a vacancy and interstitial He to a He-Vac cluster was then estimated as:

$$E_b(V) = E_f(V) + E_f(He_nV_{m-1}) - E_f(He_nV_m) \qquad (1)$$

$$E_b(He) = E_f(He) + E_f(He_{n-1}V_m) - E_f(He_nV_m) \qquad (2)$$

The formation energies of an isolated vacancy and He in the tetrahedral position were estimated to be 1.72 and 4.39 eV in pure Fe. In the case of Fe–10Cr alloys, again a set of calculations when He-Vac cluster was introduced in different positions in the Fe–10Cr crystallite was performed to estimate the mean values, for details see our previous paper [11].

MD simulations were applied to study the stability and mobility of He-Vac clusters at finite temperature, varied from 800 to 1400 K and each run lasted up to 50 ns. Visualization techniques were employed to follow configurations of He-Vac clusters during MD runs, and their positions were determined based on the coordinates of He atoms by computing center mass at each step. Details on computation of diffusional characteristics are reported in our previous works [8, 11].

Table 2. Estimated migration energy and diffusion coefficient prefactor of He-Vac clusters in each GB in Fe-10%Cr random alloys

	HeV_2		HeV		He_2V	
	D_0 cm^2/s	E_m(eV)	D_0 cm^2/s	E_m(eV)	D_0 (cm^2/s)	E_m(eV)
$\Sigma9\{221\}$			2.75E-06	0.31±0.05		
$\Sigma19\{331\}$	2.78E-05	1.01±0.08	2.39E-05	0.63±0.05		
$\Sigma3\{111\}$	1.44E-03	0.95±0.14	3.90E-04	0.80±0.11	4.62E-04	0.75±0.11
$\Sigma3\{112\}$	1.40E-03	0.94±0.14	1.43E-03	1.00±0.06	6.02E-06	0.30±0.05
$\Sigma11\{113\}$						
$\Sigma9\{114\}$			3.99E-04	0.91±0.16	6.38E-05	0.52±0.06
	He_2V_3		He_3V_4		He_4V	
	D_0 cm^2/s	E_m(eV)	D_0 cm^2/s	E_m(eV)	D_0 (cm^2/s)	E_m(eV)
$\Sigma9\{221\}$					3.13E-06	0.29±0.04
$\Sigma19\{331\}$	4.58E-06	1.11±0.10	1.20E-08	0.68±0.14	1.28E-04	0.72±0.15
$\Sigma3\{111\}$					3.43E-05	0.54±0.08
$\Sigma3\{112\}$	4.64E-02	1.23±0.10	5.53E-04	0.80±0.18	8.21E-06	0.43±0.11
$\Sigma11\{113\}$					3.52E-06	0.63±0.03
$\Sigma9\{114\}$					6.19E-05	0.98±0.07

A set of interatomic potentials used in the present study was developed in [12]. We shall only notice that the Fe-Cr interaction is described by the two band model potential [13], which was extensively used over the last decade to model properties of lattice defects, dislocations, collision cascades and other atomic featured phenomena in the Fe-Cr system.

3   Results and Discussions

3.1   Stability of He-Vac Clusters

At first, the stability of He-Vac clusters was investigated in bulk and compared with available ab initio data [4]. As shown in Fig. 1(a), there is overall good agreement between our results and ab initio data, except for the discrepancy of about 1 eV for He_4V complex. Alternative calculations have also shown good agreement with ab initio results [4].

The binding energies for He-Vac clusters obtained in Fe-10%Cr alloy bulk (see Fig. 1(b)) show the same trend as obtained in pure Fe, which means that addition of Cr has no effect on the stability of He-Vac clusters.

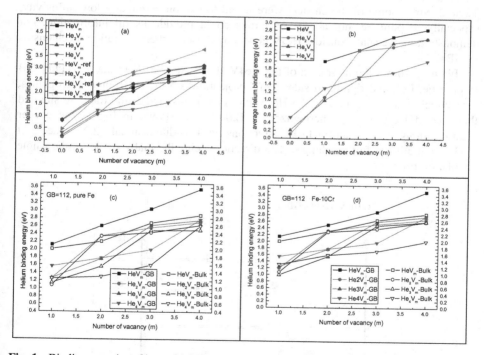

Fig. 1. Binding energies of interstitial He to the He-Vac clusters in bulk and GBs in pure Fe and Fe-10%Cr alloy. (a) Binding energies of interstitial He to the He-Vac clusters in bulk of pure Fe and compared with ab initio data; (b) average binding energies of interstitial He to the He-Vac clusters in bulk of Fe-10%Cr alloy; (c) Binding energies of interstitial He to the He-Vac clusters in 112 GB in pure Fe; (d) average binding energies of interstitial He to the He-Vac clusters in 112 GB in Fe-10%Cr alloy

Then, we computed the binding energies of an interstitial He and a vacancy in the He-Vac clusters placed at GB interfaces. Prior to that, the most efficient trapping sites for the He-Vac clusters were determined by two-dimensional mapping. As we expected, trapping of He by He-Vac clusters in GBs is stronger than in bulk. This statement is valid for both Fe and Fe-10Cr random alloy. Figure 1(c and d) provides an example of the results obtained for the $\sum 3\{112\}$ in pure Fe and Fe-10%Cr alloy. It shows that the binding energy of He to the He-Vac clusters strongly increases as function of vacancy content in the cluster, which means He can be deeply trapped by small vacancy clusters.

3.2   Diffusion of He-Vac Clusters in GBs

After determination of the lowest energy configurations of the He-Vac clusters at the GBs, we used them as initial configurations to study their migration at the GB interfaces. The position of the He-Vac clusters was traced in time to select the frames corresponding to the migration in the GB zone only, since for some clusters the dissociation from the GB interface was also observed. The migration mechanisms have been analyzed by reconstruction of the computer-generated trajectories.

A series of MD runs to assess the diffusivity of the He-Vac clusters are listed in Table 2. Since some of the clusters were found to exhibit essentially low diffusivity, especially in pure Fe, not all the MD runs could provide useful information. For demonstration, we shall consider He_4V cluster and discuss their migration mechanisms in GBs.

Figure 2 shows the migration of the He4V cluster at 1200 K in the $\sum 3\{111\}$ GB in pure Fe. Left and righthand sides show projections on the (110) and (112) planes, respectively. At the beginning, the He4V cluster was inserted at the trapping site and then the MD crystal was thermalized at 1200 K. As shown in Fig. 2, the cluster diffuses along <112> and <110> directions in two-dimensional (2D) space. At 32.35 ns, it diffuses further along <112> direction, being thermally stable for the whole simulation time span.

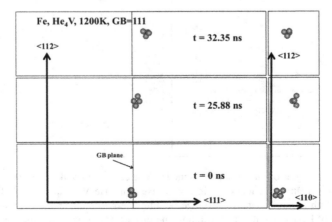

Fig. 2. Snapshot of He4V migrated at $\sum 3\{111\}$ GB in pure Fe at 1200 K. the left side is (110) plane and the right side is (111) plane.

In the case simulations at 1000 K in Fe-10Cr alloy, the same clusters did not experience migration within 30 ns. At 30.74 ns, see Fig. 3, one He interstitial is emitted from the cluster, and recombines back to it at 33.56 ns. After the dissociation, the remained He3V cluster was seen to diffuse along <112> and <110> directions, while He interstitial exhibit fast three dimensional diffusion.

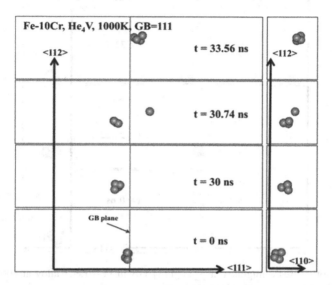

Fig. 3. Snapshot of He$_4$V migrated at $\sum$3{111} GB in Fe-10%Cr alloy at 1000 K. the left side is (110) plane and the right side is (111) plane

The migration of the He$_4$V placed at the $\sum$11{113} GB in Fe-10%Cr is found to be one-dimensional (1D) process, as shown in Fig. 4. The cluster migrates along <332> direction, which demonstrates clearly that the diffusion mode depends on the GB core structure.

Table 2 summarizes the diffusion coefficient pre-factor (fitted using Arrhenius relationship), and migration energy of all the studied clusters at different GBs in Fe-10%Cr alloy. According to the results summarized in Table 2, one can state that the clusters with He/V ratio exceed-ing unity (henceforth called He-rich clusters) diffuse faster than those with He/V < 1 (vacancy-rich). We attribute this difference to the fact that vacancy-rich clusters displace via vacancy diffusion, while He-rich clusters via interstitial He atoms. The latter are eventually faster than vacancies, providing a consistent explanation for the obtained results.

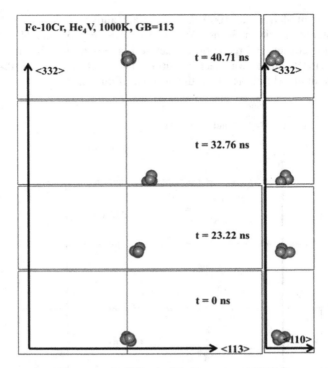

Fig. 4. Snapshot of He4V migrated at $\sum 11\{113\}$ GB in Fe-10%Cr alloy at 1000 K. the left side is (110) plane and the right side is (113) plane

Diffusion mechanisms of other studied He-Vac clusters will not be discussed in the present work in detail due to space limitations. The migration energies and diffusion coefficients are summarized in Table 2 and Fig. 5. It is important to mention, that frequent dissociation of He-rich clusters (by emission of He atoms) was observed in different GBs in Fe-10%Cr alloy, but not in pure Fe. We still have to clarify the reasons for this effect, but it is obvious that the frequent dissociation and reformation of the He-Vac clusters constituted an alternative migration of mechanism provoked by Cr random solution. To demonstrate this, we provide Fig. 6 showing the diffusion coefficient as a function of temperature for the He4V cluster at GBs in pure Fe and Fe-10Cr alloy. One can see a remarkable Cr effect on the cluster diffusivity.

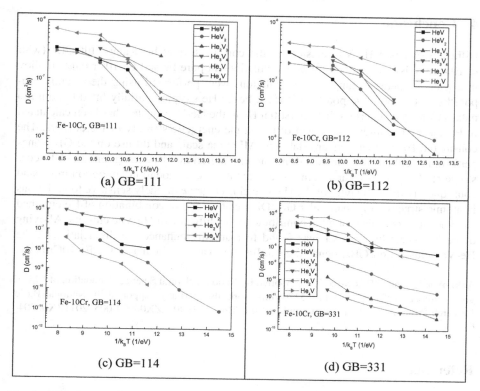

Fig. 5. Diffusion coefficients calculated for the He-Vac clusters migrating on the $\Sigma3\{111\}$, $\Sigma3\{112\}$, $\Sigma9\{114\}$, and $\Sigma19\{331\}$ GBs as a function of reciprocal temperature in Fe-10%Cr alloy

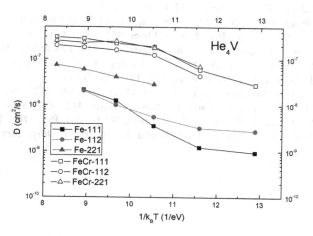

Fig. 6. Critical shear stress of Cu, Cu-Ni and Cu-Mn precipitates versus $(D^{-1} + L^{-1})^{-1}$.

4   Conclusion

Diffusion of small He-Vac clusters in the core of several high angle tilt GBs (with <110> tilt axis) was studied by MD simulations in pure Fe and Fe-10Cr random alloy in a wide temperature range. All calculations were performed using the recently proposed set of interatomic potentials for the Fe-Cr-He system, partially fitted to ab initio data. The binding energy of an interstitial He to the He-Vac clusters has been calculated in Fe and Fe-Cr, finding no effect of Cr on the energetic stability of the clusters. The considered He-Vac clusters are stable on MD time scale and diffuse on the GB planes performing either one- or two-dimensional migration, depending on the GB core structure. The results clearly demonstrate that the accommodation, migration mode and consequently the diffusivity of the He-Vac clusters are extremely sensitive to variations in atomic structure of a particular GB. Dissociation and re-combination of He enriched He-Vac clusters is also found to contribute to the diffusion of He-Vac clusters. Alloying of Fe bicrystals by 10% Cr was found to markedly enhance the dissociation of the He-Vac clusters on GBs, hence their diffusivity was also higher in the Fe-10Cr alloy.

Acknowledgment. This work was supported by National Natural Science Foundation of China, grant number 51201184 and 11375270; this work also partially supported by National Basic Research Program of China, grant number 2011CB610503, 2012ZX06004-005, 2011ZX06004-002.

References

1. Stoller, R.E.: J. Nucl. Mater. **174**, 289 (1990)
2. Zinkle, S.J.: Workshop on Decadal Challenges for Predicting and Controlling Materials Performance in Extremes, New Mexico, 6–10 December 2009
3. Samaras, M.: Mat. Today **12**, 46–53 (2009)
4. Fu, C.C., Willaime, F.: Phys. Rev. B **72**, 064117 (2005)
5. Zhang, L., Zhang, Y., Lu, G.: J. Phys. Condens. Matter **25**, 095001 (2013)
6. Gao, F., Heinisch, H., Kurtz, R.J.: J. Nucl. Mater. **351**, 133–140 (2006)
7. Gao, F., Heinisch, H., Kurtz, R.J.: J. Nucl. Mater. **367–370**, 446–450 (2007)
8. Terentyev, D., He, X., Terentyev, D., He, X.: Comput. Mater. Sci. **49**, 858–864 (2010)
9. Caturla, M.J., Ortiz, C.J.: J. Nucl. Mater. **362**, 141–145 (2007)
10. Ono, K., Miyamoto, M., Arakawa, K.: J. Nucl. Mater. **367–370**, 522–526 (2007)
11. He, X., Terentyev, D., Lin, Y., Yang, W.: J. Nucl. Mater. **442**, S660–S666 (2013)
12. Terentyev, D., Juslin, N., Nordlund, K., Sandberg, N.: J. Appl. Phys. **105**, 103509 (2009)
13. Olsson, P., Wallenius, J., Domain, C., Nordlund, K., Malerba, L.: Phys. Rev. B **72**, 214119 (2005)

Effect of Ni and Mn on the Interaction of an Edge Dislocation with Cu-rich Precipitates in Bcc Fe

Yankun Dou[1(✉)], Dongjie Wang[1], Xinfu He[1(✉)],
Muhammad Rizwan[2], Lixia Jia[1], Shi Wu[1], Han Cao[1], and Wen Yang[1]

[1] Reactor Engineering Technology Research Division, China Institute
of Atomic Energy, Beijing 102413, People's Republic of China
douyankun3@163.com, xinfuhe@gmail.com
[2] Department of Physics, University of Gujrat, HH Campus, Gujrat, Pakistan

Abstract. The interactions of a 1/2 <111> {110} edge dislocation with nano-sized Cu, Cu-Ni and Cu-Mn precipitates have been investigated by using of molecular dynamics method. It is found that the increase of precipitates size enhances their obstacle strength, while, the rise of temperature causes the reducing of obstacle strength. The results prove that Cu-Mn precipitates will have maximum resistance for dislocation gliding, followed by Cu-Ni and Cu precipitates. It is originated from Mn atoms in Cu-rich precipitate that exhibit attractive to dislocation segment. And Mn atoms can improve the fraction of transformed atoms from bcc structure to 9R structure for Cu-Mn precipitates with a diameter of 4 nm. These will lead to the increase of obstacle strength of Cu-Mn precipitates. For 4 nm Cu-Ni precipitate, the critical resolved shear stress is much bigger than that of 4 nm Cu precipitate, due to Ni atoms promoting the phase transition from bcc to 9R structure. Moreover, the fraction of transformed atoms is inversely proportional to temperature. Eventually, these features are confirmed that the appearance of Ni or Mn atoms enhances the obstacle strength of Cu precipitates for dislocation gliding in bcc Fe matrix, especially for Mn atoms.

Keywords: Cu-Ni precipitates · Cu-Mn precipitates · Hardening ·
Molecular dynamics method

1 Introduction

Cu-rich precipitates are the subject of extensive investigation for many years regarding operation and extending lifetime of nuclear reactor pressure vessels (RPV) with high or medium contents of copper [1–3]. Since Cu has limited solubility in Fe, Cu-rich precipitates with a high density can be produced in Fe matrix under neutron irradiation. The Cu-rich precipitate is the structural origin of irradiation-induced hardening and embrittlement of RPV. Experiment results reveal that nanometric (~ 2nm size) Cu-rich precipitates with fine dispersion ($\geq 10^{23} \text{m}^{-3}$) were formed under neutron irradiation at about 563K to the dose of technological relevance (~ 0.1 dpa), which were detected by the atom probe tomography and small angle neutron-scattering techniques [4–6].

© Springer Nature Singapore Pte Ltd. 2019
C. Hu et al. (Eds.): HPCMS 2018/HiDEC 2018, CCIS 913, pp. 135–151, 2019.
https://doi.org/10.1007/978-981-32-9987-0_12

Meanwhile, Cu precipitates have attracted reasonable consideration to develop low-carbon ultra-high-strength steels for structural and infrastructural applications [7, 8]. Using suitable compositional adjustment and heat treatment, the combination of Cu-rich precipitates and low carbon content can offer a substantial increase in strength, weldability and ductility [9]. In order to attain high strength, a great effort has been devoted to the characterization of nano-sized precipitates in the Fe-Cu system [10–12].

Previous investigations have revealed that irradiation hardening of RPV or strengthening of low-carbon steels induced by Cu-rich precipitates originates from the impeding dislocations gliding [13, 14]. It is important to understand the interaction between dislocations and Cu precipitates in Fe matrix. The principal mechanism of how dislocations interact with Cu precipitates has been considered in perspective of numerical simulations [13, 15, 16]. Osetsky et al. found that the mechanism of dislocation passing through a Cu precipitate depends on the size of precipitate using the molecular dynamics method (MD) [17]. The simulation results of dislocation stated that the dislocation pinning effect is influenced by the volume density, size and space distribution of Cu precipitates [18]. Bacon et al. proved that the critical resolved shear stress (τ_c) as a function of temperature for 2 nm Cu, Cu-Ni and Cu-Mn precipitates. It is see of Cu precipitates varies inversely with temperature [19]. Kohler et al. found that the shape of precipitates affects the τ_c in case of Cu precipitates [20]. It was shown that the obstacle strength of Cu precipitates is dependent on the interactive geometry of dislocations and precipitates [21]. A significant screw dislocation pinning effect is derived from the dislocation-induced precipitate transformation [22]. It is reasonable to believe that the mechanism of irradiation hardening or strengthening induced by Cu-rich precipitates is correction with the temperature, interaction geometry and microscopic features of precipitates. As the research proceeded, solute elements such as Ni and Mn were observed in Cu-rich precipitates revealed by atom probe tomography [23–25]. Zhang et al. evaluated the influence of Ni and Mn on Cu precipitates in body centred cubic structure (bcc) Fe matrix by using of non-classical nucleation theory [26]. The results showed that the exertion for the formation of a Cu critical nucleus is reduced by the addition of Ni and Mn. In addition, the nucleation rate and number of Cu particles is improved by the presence of alloy elements like Ni and Mn. The appearance of Ni could significantly affect the formation and stability of Cu-rich precipitates. Ni can effectively increase the amount of Cu-rich precipitates leading to an obvious improvement in yield strength [8]. As for dislocation glide, the small size Cu-Ni clusters prove to be little weak obstacle than pure Cu cluster [27]. However, there is a dissimilar view that the critical stress required to unpin the dislocation of the 2.38 nm Cu-Ni precipitates is larger than that of Cu precipitates [28]. Xie et al. [29] reported that Mn atoms can segregate to Cu precipitates in ferritic matrix both under the conditions of irradiation and thermal aging. Meanwhile, compared to Fe atoms, Mn atoms are more positively attracted to the self-interstitial atoms to form dumbbells. So far, the effect of Mn atoms on the interaction of a dislocation with Cu precipitates is rarely investigated and the influence of Ni remained a debating subject [27, 28]. Hence, it is worthwhile to make a detailed and systematic study on the contribution of Mn and Ni atoms to hardening induced by Cu-rich precipitates.

The purpose of this study is to model the effects of Mn and Ni on the interaction of a 1/2 <111> {110} edge dislocation and nano-sized coherent Cu precipitates with diameters of 0.5 nm–4 nm in bcc Fe by using of MD simulations. The impact of different temperatures (100K–600K) on the interactions of an edge dislocation and pure Cu, Cu-Mn or Cu-Ni precipitates are further explored. The results reveal that Cu-Mn precipitates show the maximum resistance for the dislocation gliding, followed by Cu-Ni and Cu precipitates. The mechanism of enhancement of obstacle strength by Mn and Ni of Cu precipitates is discussed.

2 Method

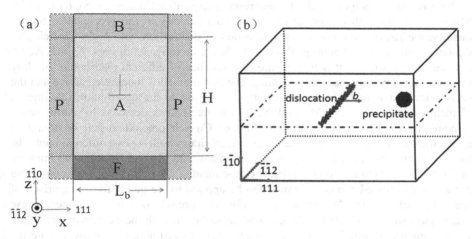

Fig. 1. (a) Schematic presentation of simulated crystallite; (b) Periodic cell of MD Simulation for the interaction of an edge dislocation and precipitate.

The models used for studying the interaction of an edge dislocation and precipitates were developed by Osetsky and Bacon [30]. As shown in Fig. 1a, the bcc crystal simulation box with the principal axes x, y and z of oriented along the [111], [$\bar{1}\bar{1}2$] and [$1\bar{1}0$] direction was built firstly. Regions P represent part of image crystallites whose atoms interact with those from the inner region A. The box was divided into three parts along z-direction. The inner region A has x, y, and z dimensions Lb, L and H. The atoms of the inner region A can move freely during the MD running. Periodic boundary conditions were applied in the x- and y-direction. The upper region B and lower region F are blocks of a "perfect" crystal, in which atoms are immobile. These rigid blocks were subject to periodic replication along the x and y directions. The block F was fixed and shear strain deformation was applied by the incremental displacement of the block B in the x-direction. As shown in Fig. 1b, an infinitely long and straight edge dislocation with {$1\bar{1}0$} slip plane x-y was created along the y direction, which had burgers vector $b = 1/2[111]$ parallel to the x axis. A glide force on the dislocation was introduced by the incremental displacement of the upper parts of the box in the x-direction. The corresponding resolved shear stress induced by the applied deformation was calculated as $\tau = F_x/A_{xy}$, where F_x is the total force in x-direction from all atoms of the middle block to the upper region, and A_{xy} is the xy cross-section area of the box. The size of the middle region of the MD box is 100×3, 29×6 and 25×2 atomic planes along x, y and z, respectively. The corresponding box volume is $25 \times 20 \times 10$ nm^3, and contained about 0.5×10^6 freely mobile atoms. Cu, Cu-Ni and Cu-Mn precipitates with their equator lying on the glide plane of dislocation were introduced into the middle region of the MD box. In previous researches the contribution of Cu-Ni precipitates with the proportion of Cu and Ni approximately 1.5:1 to the hardening of RPV was studied using the same interatomic potentials and calculation methods [27].The interaction of an edge dislocation and Cu-Ni precipitate with 50% Cu atoms replaced by Ni was also investigated [28]. In the present paper, 40% Cu atoms were replaced by Mn or Ni atoms with diverse size, distributed randomly in the precipitates. Subsequently, the stress-strain curves for interaction of dislocation with 4 nm Cu-rich precipitates built by two different methods at 100K are investigated in Figs. A1 and A2 (A denotes the Appendix). It is to compare the influence of different distribution of alloy elements in Cu precipitates on hardening. The first method is mentioned above and the second method is to build Cu precipitates according to the distribution of different elements such as Cu, Fe, Mn and Ni in Cu precipitates detected by Atom probe tomography [8]. The construction method of Cu-rich precipitate can be found in supplementary information. For the Cu-rich precipitates built by two different methods, the dependence of stress curves on strain is similar, and Mn and Ni atoms all improve the obstacle strength of Cu precipitates. Consequently, Cu-rich precipitates containing randomly distributed Mn or Ni atoms can be applied to the qualitative comparison of the effects of Mn and Ni atoms on the obstacle strength of Cu precipitates. These precipitates were all created with bcc structure coherent with the Fe matrix, according to experimental results [31]. The precipitates were placed about 7 nm away from the dislocation line to avoid a strong interaction with a dislocation before it glides. Diameter (D) of precipitates was in the range 0.5–4 nm and corresponding number of atoms was between 9 and 2862. After introducing the dislocation and precipitate in the box, the crystal was relaxed to minimize the potential energy. Strain was applied at a constant rate $\varepsilon = 10^8 s^{-1}$ to systems and the temperature was increased from 100K to 600K. The integration of Newton's equations in the MD code was performed using a constant time step equal to 2 fs at each temperature. The interaction of dislocation with precipitates at 0K was studied by the molecular static method. The stress is originated from straining the crystal by small increments, followed by relaxation using a combination of the conjugate gradient and quench algorithms at each loading step with an accuracy of 10^{-4} eV/atom [32]. The interatomic potentials in Fe-Cu, Fe-Cu-Ni and Fe-Cu-Mn systems were developed by Bonny et al. in [33]. The cross potentials for FeCu, FeNi, FeMn, CuNi and CuMn were fitted in [34, 35], respectively.

3   Results and Discussions

3.1   The Interactions of a Dislocation with Cu-Mn and Cu- Ni Precipitates at Different Temperature

Figure 2a presents the applied stress as functions of the applied strain, for Cu-Mn precipitates with diameter of 2 nm at the range of 100K–600K. The edge dislocation starts to move at 15 MPa under applied strain. The dislocation segment near the precipitates is absorbed into the Cu-Mn precipitates as soon as the dislocation contacts the Cu-Mn precipitates. The corresponding snapshots of interaction between the dis-location and Cu-Mn precipitate can be seen in the first and second inserts of Fig. 2b. As the dislocation starts to pass through the precipitate, the stress decreases and becomes negative. It is owing to the plastic strain of crystal due to dislocation movement is larger than the imposed strain [19]. While, the stress increases again with dislocation further gliding because of the dislocation segment inside the precipitates resisting the movement of dislocation. It is pinned at the precipitate and bows before detachment (as shown in the third inset of Fig. 2b). Eventually, the stress reaches the critical value. It is proved that the dislocation cuts through the precipitate rather than by-pass via the formation of the Orowan loop. After the dislocation breaking away from precipitate, it will continue to glide and the stress decreases rapidly. The process of the interaction of dislocation with Cu or Cu-Ni precipitates is similar with that of Cu-Mn precipitates. Figure 2b presents the critical resolved shear stress as a function of temperature for 2 nm Cu, Cu-Ni and Cu-Mn precipitates. It is seen that the τ_c is dependent on the temperature which decreases with the increasing of temperature. It is partly derived from atom thermal agitation deeply promoting the motion of dislocation under high temperature [36]. There is no obvious difference between τ_c of Cu and Cu-Ni pre-cipitates with a diameter of 2 nm. Compared with Cu and Cu-Ni precipitates, the τ_c of Cu-Mn precipitate is greatly improved at low temperature. The previous researches revealed that Mn atoms exhibit attractive interaction with <111> crowdion, vacancy and grain boundary in Fe matrix, and Mn atoms might potentially be dragged by the motion of a vacancy or grain boundary [37–39]. Solute atoms show the segregation of partial dislocations and binding energy between Mn atoms and a partial edge dislo-cation is about 3.5 times larger than other alloy atoms in Cu matrix [40]. Therefore, it is reasonable to believe that Mn atoms in Cu-rich precipitates might be attractive to dislocation segment and be dragged by mobile dislocation during dislocation gliding. This will enhance the obstacle strength of Cu-rich precipitates.

The critical line shapes in the $(1\bar{1}0)$ slip plane for edge dislocations detaching precipitates with a diameter of 2 nm are shown in the Fig. 3. The dislocation line shows the biggest bending under the critical stress. The corresponding critical angle, φ, formed by two opposite dislocation arms provides an indication of the obstacle strength in the framework of the constant line tension [32], using the following equation,

$$\tau_c = \frac{F_{MAX}}{bL} = \frac{Gb}{L}\cos(\frac{\varphi}{2}) \tag{1}$$

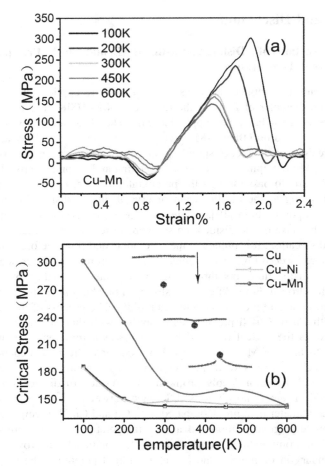

Fig. 2. Dependence of Stress-strain curves for 2 nm precipitates on temperature: (a) for Cu-Mn precipitates; (b) the critical shear stress of Cu, Cu-Ni and Cu-Mn precipitates, the insert pictures are MD snapshots of the interaction between an edge dislocation and 2 nm Cu-Mn precipitate.

Where F_{MAX} is the defect resisting force, G is the effective isotropic shear modulus. b is the Burgers vector and L is the defect spacing (defined as the length of the box along the y axis). The φ determined from the dislocation curvature is expected to predict values for the corresponding critical stress according to Eq. (1). Smaller the value of φ bigger the value of τ_c and it's vice versa.

As shown in the Fig. 3a, the values of φ, between the dislocation segments emerging from 2 nm Cu-Mn precipitate, increase with the increasing of temperature from 100K to 600K. It is revealed that the τ_c shows decline characteristic with the increasing of temperature, which agrees with the results directly obtained by MD. The Fig. 3b depicts φ for Cu-Mn precipitate at 100K is clearly smaller than Cu or Cu-Ni precipitates, which indicates that the Cu-Mn precipitate is strongest obstacle among these three different kinds of precipitates. For the Cu-Ni precipitates, the value of φ is

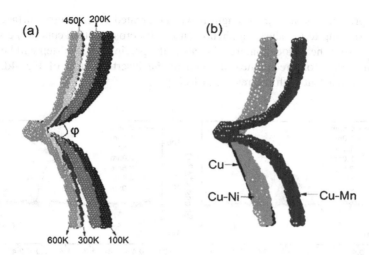

Fig. 3. Critical line shape for an edge dislocation passing through precipitates with a diameter of 2 nm: (a) Cu-Mn precipitates at different temperature. (b) Cu, Cu-Ni and Cu-Mn precipitates at 100 K.

almost similar to that of Cu precipitate. There is no parallel screw segments of dislocation formed when dislocation passes through Cu, Cu-Ni or Cu-Mn precipitate with diameter of 2 nm at range of 100K to 600K.

3.2 The Interactions of a Dislocation with Cu-Mn and Cu-Ni Precipitates with Different Sizes

Figure 4 presents the stress-strain curves for the interaction of different diameter precipitates with an edge dislocation in bcc Fe matrix at 600K. As shown in Fig. 4, it appears that the τ_c of Cu precipitates show the size-dependence. The τ_c are proved to increase with the increasing diameter of precipitates. This is in agreement with findings of Bacon and Osetsky [41]. The τ_c of 4 nm Cu precipitate increases 6.69 times compared to 0.5 nm Cu precipitate. Nevertheless, it is up to 6.89 and 9.77 times for Cu-Ni and Cu-Mn precipitates with the diameter increased from 0.5 nm to 4 nm. It is known that coherent bcc Cu precipitates will form in bcc Fe matrix at initial aging stage, which are metastable structure, and then subsequently transforms to 9R, 3R and finally to face center cubic (fcc) Cu [31, 42]. Coherent strain energy caused by lattice misfit between the bcc Cu precipitates and Fe matrix plays a key role in bcc-9R transformation [31]. Compressive stresses on the bcc Cu precipitates and interaction of a dislocation with Cu precipitates all can assist the transformation of a bcc Cu precipitate into a close-packed 9R structure, which is composed by fcc and close packed hexagonal (hcp) structure [43]. The fractions of transformed atoms in 4 nm diameter Cu, Cu-Ni and Cu-Mn precipitates at 600K in present paper are about 7.7%, 9.4% and 19.0%, respectively. The transformed precipitate is a stronger obstacle to the dislocation glide. The appearance of Mn or Ni atoms can promote the phase transition from the bcc to fcc structure in big size precipitates, resulting in the higher τ_c. To Cu, Cu-Ni or Cu-Mn precipitates, a step of length *b* will be created on the entry surface of the precipitate, owning to the shearing phenomenon with cross-section cuts of the sheared precipitates. After the dislocation breaking away the precipitates, the step will be leaved on the exit surface of precipitates, as seen in the insert pictures of Fig. 4d. These findings are consistent with the results in Ref. [17].

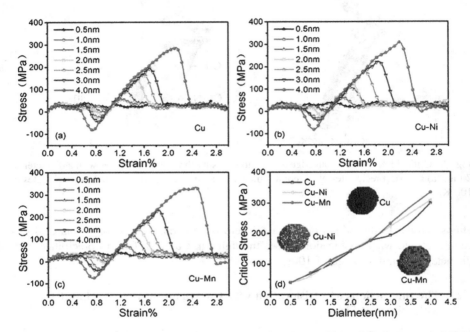

Fig. 4. Dependence of stress-strain curves on sizes at 600K: (a) Cu precipitates; (b) Cu-Ni precipitates; (c) Cu-Mn precipitates; (d) the corresponding critical shear stress, the insert pictures are the morphology of Cu, Cu-Ni and Cu-Mn precipitates after the dislocation breakaway.

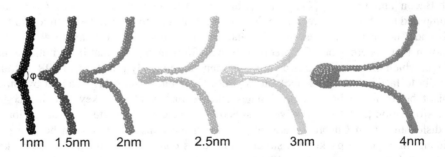

Fig. 5. Critical line shape for an edge dislocation passing through the center of Cu-Mn precipitates with different diameters at 100K.

The size-dependence of the τ_c partly attributes to the length dislocation segment entering the precipitates. That is to say the longer length of the dislocation segment entering the precipitates, for further motion, the dislocation needs to be subjected to the larger resistance. Meanwhile, the dislocation segment entering the precipitates will lead to an energy gain due to the decrease in length of the dislocation. Phase transition and longer length of the dislocation segment entering the precipitates all would lead to a strong obstacle and formation of parallel screw segments of dislocation (seen as in Fig. 5). For Cu-Mn precipitates, the φ decrease with increasing of precipitates diameter. It is equal to zero and screw segments are formed when dislocations pass through 2.5 nm, 3 nm and 4 nm Cu-Mn precipitates. And the corresponding length of screw segments of dislocation is 2.6 nm, 3.1 nm and 4.8 nm respectively. As to the dislocation passing through the Cu or Cu-Ni precipitates with diameter of 1 nm–4 nm, the change of φ or the variation length of screw segments of dislocation is similar with that of Cu-Mn precipitates. The specific parameters can be found in Table 1. Screw segments of dislocation are only found in 4 nm Cu precipitates, while it can be seen in 3, 4 nm Cu-Ni precipitates. According to the order of Cu, Cu-Ni and Cu-Mn precipitates with the same diameter, the length of screw segments of dislocation is gradually increased and the value of φ is decreased.

Table 1. The angle, φ, between dislocation segments as they emerge from a precipitate under the critical stress and the corresponding length of the screw segments of dislocation.

Precipitates	Diameter (nm)	φ (°)	Screw dislocation (nm)
Cu	1.0	156.6	0.0
	1.5	135.1	0.0
	2.0	121.5	0.0
	2.5	110.4	0.0
	3.0	11.6	0.0
	4.0	0.0	1.6
CuNi	1.0	154.9	0.0
	1.5	118.3	0.0
	2.0	107.3	0.0
	2.5	9.7	0.0
	3.0	0.0	1.2
	4.0	0.0	1.5
CuMn	1.0	119.7	0.0
	1.5	91.6	0.0
	2.0	30.7	0.0
	2.5	0.0	2.6
	3.0	0.0	3.1
	4.0	0.0	4.8

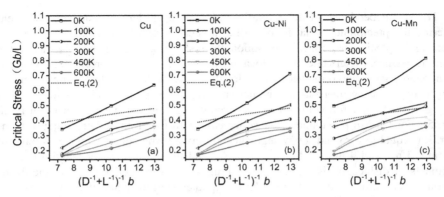

Fig. 6. Critical shear stress of Cu, Cu-Ni and Cu-Mn precipitates versus $(D^{-1} + L^{-1})^{-1}$.

A comparison of τ_c for Cu, Cu-Ni and Cu-Mn precipitates is plotted against the harmonic mean $(D^{-1} + L^{-1})^{-1}$ on a log scale for all the combinations of D and L, as shown in the Fig. 6. Gb/L and Burgers vector b are denoted as units of the ordinate and abscissa, respectively. The reason for plotting the data in this way is the following correlation between these quantities is found in the computer based elasticity treatment of dislocation self-stress during its interaction with a regular array of impenetrable obstacles (Orowan strengthening) or voids with dislocation self-stress included [44, 45].

$$\tau_c = \frac{Gb}{2\pi L}[\ln(D^{-1} + L^{-1})^{-1} + \Delta] \tag{2}$$

Where $G = 63000$ MPa and $\Delta = 0.77$. Δ depends on the obstacle type ranging from 0.77 to 1.52, which equals 0.77 for the precipitates and 1.52 for voids.

The τ_c calculated from the Eq. (2) are plotted in the dash line in the Fig. 6. It can be seen that the τ_c of 2 nm Cu precipitates fall below the calculated values no matter any temperature. It is worth mentioning that the τ_c are much closer to the values calculated from the Eq. (2) with the increasing of diameter or decreasing of temperature. It is expected that the τ_c for Cu precipitates with diameters of 3 nm and 4 nm at 0K are bigger than the values calculated from the Eq. (2). Compared to Cu precipitates, the τ_c of 4 nm Cu-Ni precipitate even exceeds the value calculated from the Eq. (2) at 100K. Meanwhile, the τ_c of Cu-Mn precipitates with diameters of 2 nm, 3 nm and 4 nm are all higher than the values calculated with Eq. (2) at 0K. And the τ_c of 3 nm Cu-Mn precipitate at 100K almost equals to the value calculated with Eq. (2), and that of 4 nm Cu-Mn precipitate at 100K or 200K are almost bigger than the values calculated with Eq. (2). It is again demonstrated that the Cu-Mn precipitate is the strong obstacle. When the dislocations break away from the strong obstacles, the dislocation segments that emerge from the obstacles are almost parallel to form the screw segments, which matches the conditions for the Orowan stress. As described in the previous sections, the screw segments will be formed when the dislocation passes through the big precipitates. Among these precipitates with same diameter, the length of screw segments is longest for Cu-Mn precipitates under the critical stress (seen in Table 1).

Experimental results showed that the transformation of Cu precipitate with a diameter of 4 nm from the bcc to 9R phase (be composed of ordered stacks of fcc and hcp atoms) in binary Fe-1.3 wt%Cu alloy [46]. Heo et al. has confirmed the transformation sequence of Cu precipitates during aging in a Fe-3Si-2Cu alloy using Cs-corrected high-angle annular dark-field microscopy, and found that bcc Cu precipitates transformed to twinned and untwinned 9R Cu particles, turning to fcc Cu particles eventually [47]. The mechanism of transformation of Cu precipitates has also been investigated by using of MD simulations. The calculated results reported the strong size-temperature of Cu precipitates at which the bcc-9R transition occurs [48]. The screw dislocation interaction with a bcc Cu precipitate in bcc Fe matrix has been performed using MD simulations. It has found that a screw dislocation assists the transformation of a bcc Cu precipitate into a close-packed structure (mainly hcp structure), and the transformed precipitate is a stronger obstacle to the dislocation glide [49]. Hence, it is believed that formation of a fraction of new phase inside the Cu precipitates can result in high τ_c, accompanied by the decrease of φ and increase of screw dislocation length in the critical condition. This should be ascribed to the fact that dislocation segment inside the precipitate needs to change local structure to cross the interface between two different phases and, inside the new phase, glide locally on a different plane. Our study found that the introduction of Mn in 4 nm Cu precipitates will improve fraction of transformed atoms in precipitates, similar to influence of Ni atoms on phase transition of Cu precipitates [28]. The appearance of Mn or Ni in Cu precipitates may improve the lattice misfit of the Cu precipitates and Fe matrix. It induces the coherent strain energy, which plays a key role in bcc-9R transformation. Figure 7 presents the projection of atoms positions in $(\bar{1}\bar{1}2)$ and $(1\bar{1}0)$ planes near the equator of a 4 nm Cu-Mn precipitate after dislocation breakaway at 100K. It can be seen that the bcc structure has turned into close-packed structure. The specific fraction of transformed atoms in 4 nm Cu, Cu-Mn and Cu-Ni precipitates can be seen in Table 2. The hcp fraction of the 4 nm Cu precipitate reaches about 30.5% and the fcc fraction is about 4.8% at 100K. Importantly, it confirms that introduction of Mn and Ni can improve the total fraction of transformed atoms in 4 nm Cu precipitates to 52.7% and 44.3% at 100K, respectively. It reveals that 4 nm Cu-Mn and Cu-Ni precipitates are stronger obstacles for the glide of dislocation compared to Cu precipitate, especially for Cu-Mn precipitates. The fraction of transformed atoms is inversely proportional to temperature. According to ref. [47], the strong temperature dependence of transformation atoms is because of the entropic stabilization of bcc Cu structure which is mechanically unstable as a bulk phase. While at high temperatures the transition exhibits first-order characteristics, the hysteresis, and thus the nucleation barrier. In contrast, both hysteresis and nucleation barrier vanish at temperatures below approximately 300K. The MD simulations results found that the hcp and fcc fraction atoms in the presence of a screw dislocation for bcc Cu precipitates with a diameter of 4 nm are more than 30% and 10%, respectively [50]. Bacon and Osetsky carried out a similar analysis as a function of temperature for 6 nm Cu precipitates. They found that more than 50% of Cu atoms underwent a transformation at about 100K while this fraction dropped to about 10% at 600K [19]. These are consistent with the results reported in the present paper.

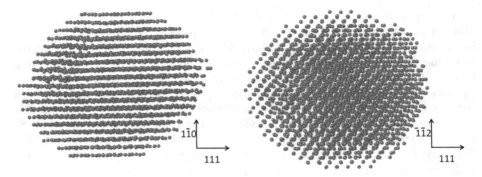

Fig. 7. Schematic presentation of position of atoms in 4 nm Cu-Mn precipitates in different planes at the centre of Cu-Mn precipitate after dislocation breakaway at 100K.

Table 2. the fractions of transformed atoms in Cu, Cu-Mn and Cu-Ni precipitates at different temperature

T	Type					
	Cu		Cu-Mn		Cu-Ni	
	fcc (%)	hcp (%)	fcc (%)	hcp (%)	fcc (%)	hcp (%)
100 K	4.7	30.5	5.8	46.9	5.8	38.5
200 K	4.5	23.5	4.6	46.1	5.3	34.5
300 K	3.9	18.7	3.8	35.9	4.3	29.5
450 K	3.1	16.9	4.1	28.1	3.4	17.3
600 K	2.4	5.3	2.8	16.2	2.7	6.7

4   Conclusion

The interactions of a 1/2 <111> {110} edge dislocations with coherent Cu, Cu-Ni and Cu-Mn precipitates in bcc Fe matrix have been studied with the method of molecular dynamics method, respectively. The results reveal that obstacle strength of precipitates depends on the temperature and precipitate size, which decreases with the increasing of temperature and increases with the increasing of precipitates size. It is found that Cu-Mn precipitates make a much more significant contribution to hardening in bcc Fe matrix, compared to Cu-Ni and Cu precipitates. It is originated from Mn atoms in Cu-rich precipitate exhibiting attractive to dislocation segments and being dragged by mobile dislocation probably. And Mn atoms can improve the fraction of transformed atoms from bcc to 9R structure in big size precipitates. Dislocation segment inside the precipitate needs to change local structure to cross the interface between two different phases and, inside the new phase, glide locally on a different plane. These will lead to the increase of the τ_c. The value of the τ_c of 2 nm Cu-Ni precipitate is similar to that of Cu precipitate. But for 4 nm Cu-Ni precipitate, the obstacle strength is obviously stronger than that of 4 nm Cu precipitate, due to Ni atoms also promote the bcc structure transform to 9R structure. In summary, the introduction of Ni or Mn atoms in

Cu precipitates enhances the irradiation hardening of RPV or strengthening of low carbon steels, particularly Mn atoms.

Acknowledgment. The authors gratefully acknowledge the financial support of the National Key Research and Development Program of China (Grant Number. 2017YFB0202300), The China National Nuclear Corporation Centralized Research and Development Project (Grant Number. FA16100820) and the National Natural Science Foundation of China (Grants Number. 11375270).

Appendix

Two methods of creating Cu-rich precipitates are carried out in the present paper. The first one is developed by Osetsky and Bacon [30]. It introduces the Cu precipitate directly in modes. Cu-Mn and Cu-Ni precipitates are built by randomly replacing 40% Cu atoms in Cu precipitate by Mn or Ni atoms. The second method is to create precipitates according to experiment results. The Cu precipitates detected by Atom probe tomography in ref.8, contains some amount of Fe and Cu, as well as a little of Mn and Ni atoms. We first attain the contents of Fe, Cu, Mn and Ni elements in Cu-rich precipitates at different distances from the precipitate core to the interface. The precipitates are divided into as many isometric layers as possible, and with each layer filled using corresponding contents according to the distribution of different elements in Cu precipitates from the core to the interface. The precipitates will be introduced into the calculation models to relax adequately. The precipitates after relaxation are stable enough and interface effect between different layers in precipitates can be ignored. The corresponding pure Cu precipitate is created by substitution of the Mn and Ni atoms for Cu atoms in order to study the influence of Mn and Ni atoms on the obstacle strength of Cu-rich precipitates.

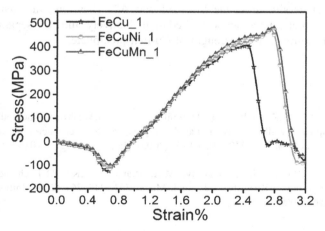

Fig. A1. Stress–strain curves for 4 nm precipitates created by the first method at 100K

Figure A1 presents the stress-strain curves for interaction of dislocation with 4 nm Cu, Cu-Mn and Cu-Ni precipitates created by the first method. It can be seen that the Mn or Ni atoms enhance the critical resolved shear stresses of Cu-rich precipitates.

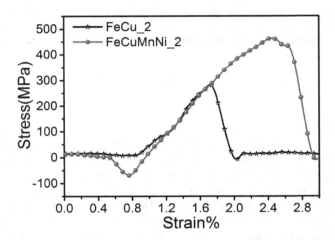

Fig. A2. Stress–strain curves for 4 nm precipitates created by the second methods at 100K

Figure A2 shows the stress-strain curves for interaction of dislocation with 4 nm pure Cu precipitate and Cu-rich precipitate containing Fe, Mn and Ni atoms built by the second method. The critical resolved shear stress for Cu-rich precipitate built by experimental results is more than 450 MPa, which is much bigger than that of pure Cu precipitate ($\sim$260 MPa). More strain (about 3%) should be applied before the dislocation departure from the Cu-rich precipitate. It reveals that the Mn and Ni atoms can improve the obstacle strength of the Cu-rich precipitate built by experimental results. It agrees with the conclusion obtained in the Fig. A1 and the dependence of stress-strain curves on strain is similar in the Figs. A1 and A2. Therefore, the first method of creating Cu-rich precipitates can be applied to qualitatively study the separate influence of Mn and Ni on the obstacle strength of Cu-rich precipitate.

References

1. Fukuya, K., Ohno, K., Nakata, H., Dumbill, S., Hyde, J.M.: Microstructural evolution in medium copper low alloy steels irradiated in a pressurized water reactor and a material test reactor. J. Nucl. Mater. **312**, 163–173 (2003). https://doi.org/10.1016/S0022-3115(02)01675-6
2. Miller, M.K., Russell, K.F., Sokolov, M.A., Nanstad, R.K.: APT characterization of irradiated high nickel RPV steels. J. Nucl. Mater. **361**, 248–261 (2007). https://doi.org/10.1016/j.jnucmat.2006.12.015

3. Glade, S.C., Wirth, B.D., Odette, G.R., Asoka-Kumar, P.: Positron annihilation spectroscopy and small angle neutron scattering characterization of nanostructural features in high-nickel model reactor pressure vessel steels. J. Nucl. Mater. **351**, 197–208 (2006). https://doi.org/10.1016/j.jnucmat.2006.02.012

4. Meslin, E., Radiguet, B., Pareige, P., Barbu, A.: Kinetic of solute clustering in neutron irradiated ferritic model alloys and a French pressure vessel steel investigated by atom probe tomography. J. Nucl. Mater. **399**(2-3), 137–145 (2010). https://doi.org/10.1016/j.jnucmat.2009.11.012

5. Miller, M.K., Sokolov, M.A., Nanstad, R.K., Russell, K.F.: APT characterization of high nickel RPV steels. J. Nucl. Mater. **351**(1–3), 187–196 (2006). https://doi.org/10.1016/j.jnucmat.2006.02.013

6. Vaynman, S., Isheim, D., Kolli, R.P., Bhat, S.P., Seidman, D.N., Fine, M.E.: Temperature dependence of irradiation hardening due to dislocation loops and precipitates in RPV steels and model alloys. J. Nucl. Mater. **464**(2), 6–15 (2015). https://doi.org/10.1016/j.jnucmat.2015.04.014

7. Vaynman, S., Isheim, D., Kolli, R.P., Bhat, S.P., Seidman, D.N., Fine, M.E.: High-strength low-carbon ferritic steel containing Cu-Fe-Ni-Al-Mn precipitates. Metall. Mater. Trans. A **39**(2), 363–373 (2008). https://doi.org/10.1007/s11661-007-9417-x

8. Jiao, Z.B., Luan, J.H., Zhang, Z.W., Miller, M.K., Ma, W.B., Liu, C.T.: Synergistic effects of cu and ni on nanoscale precipitation and mechanical properties of high-strength steels. Acta Mater. **61**(16), 5996–6005 (2013). https://doi.org/10.1016/j.actamat.2013.06.040

9. Yu, X., Caron, J.L., Babu, S.S., Lippold, J.C., Isheim, D., Seidman, D.N.: Characterization of microstructural strengthening in the heat-affected-zone of a blast-resistant naval steel. Acta Mater. **58**(17), 5596–5609 (2010). https://doi.org/10.1016/j.actamat.2010.06.031

10. Nakamichi, H., Yamada, K., Sato, K.: Sub-nanometre elemental analysis of cu cluster in fe–cu–ni alloy using aberration corrected stem-eds. J. Microsc. **242**(1), 55 (2011). https://doi.org/10.1111/j.1365-2818.2010.03438.x

11. He, S.M., et al.: In situ determination of aging precipitation in deformed Fe-Cu and Fe-Cu-B-N alloys by time-resolved small-angle neutron scattering. Phys Rev B **82**(17), 174111 (2010). https://doi.org/10.1103/PhysRevB.82.174111

12. Kar'kina, L.E., Kar'kin, I.N., Gornostyrev, Y.N.: Computer simulation of the interaction between an edge dislocation and Cu precipitates in bcc iron. Bull. Russ. Acad. Sci. Phys. **74**(5), 650–652 (2010). https://doi.org/10.3103/S1062873810050187

13. Shim, J.H., Kim, D.I., Jung, W.S., Cho, Y.W., Hong, K.T., Wirth, B.D.: Atomistic study of temperature dependence of interaction between screw dislocation and nanosized bcc Cu precipitate in bcc Fe. J. Appl. Phys. **104**(8), 083523–083523-4 (2008). https://doi.org/10.1063/1.3003083

14. Harry, T., Bacon, D.J.: Computer simulation of the core structure of the <111> screw dislocation in α-iron containing copper precipitates: II. dislocation–precipitate interaction and the strengthening effect. Acta Mater. **50**(1), 209–222 (2002). https://doi.org/10.1016/S1359-6454(01)00332-9

15. Lehtinen, A., Granberg, F., Laurson, L., Nordlund, K., Alava, M.J.: Multiscale modeling of dislocation-precipitate interactions in Fe: from molecular dynamics to discrete dislocations. Phys. Rev. E **93**(1), 013309 (2016). https://doi.org/10.1103/PhysRevE.93.013309

16. Chen, Z., Kioussis, N., Ghoniem, N.: Influence of nanoscale Cu precipitates in α-Fe on dislocation core structure and strengthening. Phys. Rev. B **80**(18), 184104 (2009). https://doi.org/10.1103/PhysRevB.80.184104

17. Osetsky, Yu.N., Bacon, D.J., Mohles, V.: Atomic modelling of strengthening mechanisms due to voids and copper precipitates in α-iron. Philos. Mag. **83**(31-34), 3623–3641 (2003). https://doi.org/10.1080/14786430310001603364

18. Liao, Y., Ye, C., Gao, H., Kim, B.J.: Dislocation pinning effects induced by nano-precipitates during warm laser shock peening: dislocation dynamic simulation and experiments. J. Appl. Phys. **110**(2), 291 (2011). https://doi.org/10.1063/1.3609072

19. Bacon, D.J., Osetsky, Y.N.: Mechanisms of hardening due to copper precipitates in α-iron. Philos. Mag. **89**(34–36), 3333–3349 (2009). https://doi.org/10.1080/14786430903271377

20. Kohler, C., Kizler, P., Schmauder, S.: Atomistic simulation of precipitation hardening in α-iron: influence of precipitate shape and chemical composition. Model. Simul. Mater. Sci. **13** (1), 35 (2004). https://doi.org/10.1088/0965-0393/13/1/003

21. Grammatikopoulos, P., Bacon, D.J., Osetsky, Y.N.: The influence of interaction geometry on the obstacle strength of voids and copper precipitates in iron. Model. Simul. Mater. Sci. **19** (19), 015004 (2011). https://doi.org/10.1088/0965-0393/19/1/015004

22. Harry, T., Bacon, D.J.: Computer simulation of the core structure of the, screw dislocation in α-iron containing copper precipitates: I structure in the matrix and a precipitate. Acta Mater. **50**(1), 195–208 (2002). https://doi.org/10.1016/S1359-6454(01)00331-7

23. Isheim, D., Gagliano, M.S., Fine, M.E., Seidman, D.N.: Interfacial segregation at Cu-rich precipitates in a high-strength low-carbon steel studied on a sub-nanometer scale. Acta Mater. **54**(3), 841–849 (2006). https://doi.org/10.1016/j.actamat.2005.10.023

24. Edmondson, P.D., Miller, M.K., Powers, K.A., Nanstad, R.K.: Atom probe tomography characterization of neutron irradiated surveillance samples from the RE Ginna reactor pressure vessel. J. Nucl. Mater. **470**, 147–154 (2016). https://doi.org/10.1016/j.jnucmat.2015.12.038

25. Wen, Y.R., Hirata, A., Zhang, Z.W., Fujita, T., Liu, C.T., Jiang, J.H.: Microstructure characterization of Cu-rich nanoprecipitates in a Fe-2.5 Cu-1.5 Mn-4.0 Ni-1.0 Al multicomponent ferritic alloy. Acta Mater. **61**(6), 2133–2147 (2013). https://doi.org/10.1016/j.actamat.2012.12.034

26. Zhang, C., Enomoto, M.: Study of the influence of alloying elements on Cu precipitation in steel by non-classical nucleation theory. Acta Mater. **54**(16), 4183–4191 (2006). https://doi.org/10.1016/j.actamat.2006.05.006

27. Terentyev, D., Malerba, L., Bonny, G., Al-Motasem, A.T., Posselt, M.: Interaction of an edge dislocation with Cu–Ni-vacancy clusters in bcc iron. J. Nucl. Mater. **419**(1–3), 134–139 (2011). https://doi.org/10.1016/j.jnucmat.2011.08.021

28. Lv, G., Zhang, H., He, X., Yang, W., Su, Y.: Atomistic simulation of Cu–Ni precipitates hardening in α-iron. J. Phys. D Appl. Phys. **48**(11), 115302 (2015). https://doi.org/10.1088/0022-3727/48/11/115302

29. Xie, Y.P., Zhao, S.J.: The segregation behavior of manganese and silicon at the coherent interfaces of copper precipitates in ferritic steels. J. Nucl. Mater. **445**(1–3), 43–49 (2014). https://doi.org/10.1016/j.jnucmat.2013.10.054

30. Osetsky, Y.N., Bacon, D.J.: An atomic-level model for studying the dynamics of edge dislocations in metals. Model. Simul. Mater. Sci. **11**(4), 427–446 (2003). https://doi.org/10.1088/0965-0393/11/4/302

31. Jenkins, M.L.: High-resolution electron microscopy studies of the structure of Cu precipitates in α-Fe. Philos. Mag. A **70**(1), 1–24 (1994). https://doi.org/10.1080/01418619408242533

32. Terentyev, D., Haghighat, S.M.H., Schäublin, R.: Strengthening due to Cr-rich precipitates in Fe–Cr alloys: effect of temperature and precipitate composition. J. Appl. Phys. **107**(6), 061806 (2010). https://doi.org/10.1063/1.3340522

33. Bonny, G., Terentyev, D., Bakaev, A., Zhurkin, E.E., Hou, M., Neck, D.V.: On the thermal stability of late blooming phases in reactor pressure vessel steels: an atomistic study. J. Nucl. Mater. **442**(1–3), 282–291 (2013). https://doi.org/10.1016/j.jnucmat.2013.08.018

34. Pasianot, R.C., Malerba, L.: Interatomic potentials consistent with thermodynamics: the Fe–Cu system. J. Nucl. Mater. **360**(2), 118–127 (2007). https://doi.org/10.1016/j.jnucmat.2006.09.008

35. Bonny, G., Pasianot, R.C., Malerba, L.: Fe-Ni many-body potential for metallurgical applications. Model. Simul. Mater. Sci. **17**(2), 025010 (2009). https://doi.org/10.1088/0965-0393/17/2/025010

36. Terentyev, D., Malerba, L., Bacon, D.J., Osetsky, Y.N.: The effect of temperature and strain rate on the interaction between an edge dislocation and an interstitial dislocation loop in α-iron. J. Phys. Condens. Matter **19**(45), 456211 (2007). https://doi.org/10.1088/0953-8984/19/45/456211

37. Olsson, P., Klaver, T.P.C., Domain, C.: Ab initio study of solute transition-metal interactions with point defects in bcc Fe. Phys. Lett. B **81**(5), 054102 (2010). https://doi.org/10.1103/PhysRevB.81.054102

38. Barashev, A.V., Arokiam, A.C.: Monte Carlo modelling of Cu atom diffusion in α-Fe via the vacancy mechanism. Phil. Mag. Lett. **86**(5), 321–332 (2006). https://doi.org/10.1080/09500830600788927

39. Bakaev, A., Terentyev, D., Bonny, G., Klaver, T.P.C., Olsson, P., Van Neck, D.: Interaction of minor alloying elements of high-Cr ferritic steels with lattice defects: an ab initio study. J. Nucl. Mater. **444**(1–3), 237–246 (2014). https://doi.org/10.1016/j.jnucmat.2013.09.053

40. Varschasky, A.: Ordering and solute segregation to dislocations in Cu-20at.%Mn. Mater. Sci. Eng. **89**, 119–128 (1987). https://doi.org/10.1016/0025-5416(87)90255-2

41. Bacon, D.J., Osetsky, Y.N.: Hardening due to copper precipitates in α-iron studied by atomic-scale modeling. J. Nucl. Mater. **329**, 1233–1237 (2004). https://doi.org/10.1016/j.jnucmat.2004.04.256

42. Lee, T.H., Kim, Y.O., Kim, S.J.: Crystallographic model for bcc-to-9R martensitic transformation of Cu precipitates in ferritic steel. Phil. Mag. **87**(2), 209–224 (2007). https://doi.org/10.1080/14786430600909014

43. Hu, S.Y., Li, Y.L., Watanabe, K.: Calculation of internal stresses around Cu precipitates in the bcc Fe matrix by atomic simulation. Model. Simul. Mater. Sci. **7**(4), 641 (1999). https://doi.org/10.1088/0965-0393/7/4/312

44. Scattergood, R.O., Bacon, D.J.: The strengthening effect of voids. Acta Metall. **30**(8), 1665–1677 (1982). https://doi.org/10.1016/0001-6160(82)90188-2

45. Bacon, D.J., Kocks, U.F., Scattergood, R.O.: The effect of dislocation self-interaction on the Orowan stress. Philos. Mag. **28**(6), 1241–1263 (1973). https://doi.org/10.1080/14786437308227997

46. Lozano-Perez, S., Jenkins, M.L., Titchmarsh, J.M.: Titchmarsh, Evidence for deformation-induced transformations of Cu-rich precipitates in an aged FeCu alloy. Philos. Mag. Lett. **86**(6), 367–374 (2006). https://doi.org/10.1080/09500830600815365

47. Heo, Y.U., Kim, Y.K., Kim, J.S., Kim, J.K.: Phase transformation of Cu precipitates from bcc to fcc in Fe–3Si–2Cu alloy. Acta Mater. **61**(2), 519–528 (2013). https://doi.org/10.1016/j.actamat.2012.09.068

48. Erhart, P., Marian, J., Sadigh, B.: Thermodynamic and mechanical properties of copper precipitates in α-iron from atomistic simulations. Phys. Rev. B **88**(2), 024116 (2013). https://doi.org/10.1103/PhysRevB.88.024116

49. Shim, J.H., Kim, D.I., Jung, W.S., Cho, Y.W., Wirth, B.D.: Strengthening of nanosized bcc Cu precipitate in bcc Fe: a molecular dynamics study. Mater. Trans. **50**(9), 2229–2234 (2009). https://doi.org/10.2320/matertrans.M2009040

50. Shim, J.H., Cho, Y.W., Kwon, S.C., Kim, W.W., Wirth, B.D.: Screw dislocation assisted martensitic transformation of a bcc cu precipitate in bcc Fe. Appl. Phys. Lett., **90**(2), 021906–021906-3 (2007). https://doi.org/10.1063/1.2429902

The Performance Test and Optimization of Crystal-MD Program on Tianhe-2

Jianjiang Li, Kai Zhang, Peng Wei[✉], Jie Wang, and Changjun Hu

Department of Computer Science and Technology, University of Science and Technology Beijing, Beijing 100083, China
weissnh@163.com

Abstract. In the research field of virtual reactor, the study of materials is one of the most significant issues, and in the research of materials irradiation effect, Molecular Dynamics (MD) is the widely used method. In this paper, the existing Crystal-MD simulation program has been tested in a homogeneous way on the platform of Tianhe-2 supercomputer, and the program has also been rewritten according to the heterogeneous multi-core architecture of Tianhe-2, and finally tested on the Tianhe-2 platform. Our experimentation results show that homogeneous Crystal-MD simulation program has a good expansion on Tianhe-2 and with the same number of nodes, the heterogeneous program is more efficient than the homogeneous one.

Keywords: Molecular dynamics · Homogeneous · Heterogeneous · Tianhe-2 supercomputer

1 Introduction

1.1 Tianhe-2

Tianhe-2 is a supercomputer developed by the National University of Defense Technology. In 2012, it ranked top on the list with a peak computing speed of 549 billion times per second and a continuous calculation speed of 3.39 billion double-precision float operations per second. On October 16, 2015, a new list of the world's top 500 supercomputers was announced, and the Tianhe-2 supercomputer took the sixth consecutive victory [1,2].

Before 2018, the Tianhe-2 consisted of 16,000 compute nodes, each of which had 2 Intel Xeon E5-2692 v2 processors and 3 Intel Xeon Phi coprocessors, so it was 32,000 Intel Xeon processors and 48,000 Intel Xeon Phi coprocessors in total [14]. And it has been upgraded to 2 processors and 8 coprocessors per node, 16 cores per processor and 64 cores per coprocessor respectively now. And the Tianhe-2 supercomputer uses a cluster system structure to connect multiple computing nodes that can operate independently, and can communicate with each other through a high-speed interconnection network which is called TH express-2.

© Springer Nature Singapore Pte Ltd. 2019
C. Hu et al. (Eds.): HPCMS 2018/HiDEC 2018, CCIS 913, pp. 152–163, 2019.
https://doi.org/10.1007/978-981-32-9987-0_13

1.2 Molecular Dynamics

The MD simulation method originated in the 1950s and gradually received wide attention. It is a method of simulating motion under Newton's laws of motion in a system of molecules or atoms.

The combination of high-performance computing and Molecular Dynamics simulation expands the number of molecules that the program can simulate. Even so, due to the limitations of memory bandwidth, molecular dynamics can reach the maximum atomic number level at the spatial scale of 10^{12}. Therefore, the key to the development of molecular dynamics simulation is the expansion of the spatial and time scale. Only when the number of atoms is big enough and the calculation time is long enough, can we truly reflect the macroscopic behavior of material properties.

The mainstream Molecular Dynamics simulation software such as LAMMPS and IMD both have some defects. One of the them is that the required memory is too much so the simulation scale are not able to reach a higher level. [5] propose a new MD simulation software called Crystal-MD, and it solves the above problem and shows a good performance.

However, the Crystal-MD program can not take advantage of the heterogeneous resources on Tianhe-2, and as stated above, heterogeneous resources is a very important part of Tianhe-2, the simulation scale of program can reach a higher level if the heterogeneous resources are made full use of.

2 Related Work

Molecular Dynamics simulates the trajectory of atom by solving the equations of motion of all particles in the system. The interaction of microscopic particles in the system are computed, and obtain temperature, volume, pressure, stress, and other macroscopic and microscopic process quantities of the system according to the calculation. Since the development in the 1950s [8,9], it has been widely used in many fields including physics, computational chemistry, computational biology, materials science and drug design. MD simulation, as a very effective material calculation technique, has become an equally important scientific research method.

Currently, the widely used MD simulation softwares are as below:

LAMMPS software [10] is a general-purpose large-scale Molecular Dynamics parallel computing software developed by the United States Sandia National Laboratory, is one of the most widely used Molecular Dynamics software in the world.

Based on the development of IMD [11], a classical Molecular Dynamics simulation of open source software packages, the MD code "Ls1-MarDyn" jointly developed by the University of Stuttgart, University of Kaiserslautern, Technische and the University of Paderborn, aiming to challenge the Molecular Simulation of the trillion level [12,13]. Ls1-MarDyn keeps record of the largest MD simulations at the moment, using a 140,000-core molecular simulation of $4*10^{12}$ particles on the supercomputer at the Leibniz Supercomputing Center in Germany.

COMD [6] is an MD code developed and designed by the Exascale Co-Design Center for Materials in Extreme Environment Center funded by the US Department of Energy. It is developed and maintained on the basis of the Molecular Dynamics of SPaSM.

Currently, there are two most commonly used data structures in MD programs: Cell List and Neighbor List [3]. However, both of these data structures use a large amount of memory space in order to effectively find neighbor atoms, which limits the simulation scale.

Parallel MD programs are designed according to the critical material characteristics of the reactor to achieve the desired large-scale Molecular Dynamics simulation. Aiming at the structure characteristics of Body Centered Cube (BCC) metal, a data structure Lattice Neighbor List which can greatly reduce the occupation of memory is proposed [4]. This kind of data structure does not need to maintain the neighbor list or the required memory of the cell list structure, which decreases the need of storage capacity greatly. And for this kind of data structure, the communication model in parallel MD simulation is designed. Based on this data structure and communication model, a massively parallel MD simulation software, Crystal-MD, is developed [5].

3   Original Crystal-MD Program

The MD program calculates the atom force between each pair of atom with the Newton's third law, and there may have some write conflicts during the program running time. To solve the problem, the simplest way is to abandon the use of Newton's third law, but the flaw of the method is also obvious: the calculation of the force between atoms will be doubled [6]. The second way is to use critical sections [7], but the method will cost more extra time because of the synchronization. The Crystal-MD proposed in [4] uses the Partition-and-Separate-Calculation (PSC) method to solve the write conflicts problem. The method can mainly be divided into two aspects, one aspect is region splitting and the other is calculation of the nonadjacent region. And the PSC method can ensure that there is no write conflict between the regions:

(1) If the total number of threads used in the simulation is N, the simulation area will be divided into $2N$ blocks. And the $2N$ blocks will be divided into two groups, the adjacent blocks will not be included in the same group.

(2) The calculation process is performed in two steps. The N non-adjacent blocks will be calculated with N threads concurrently in each step.

The flow chart of the existing Crystal-MD program is illustrated as Fig. 1.

The program can be divided into 5 phases.

(1) Prepare the data

The configuration file and the initial atomic data will be read, and the atomic space will be constructed based on the input data. And then the potential function file will also be read.

(2) Exchange the atom data

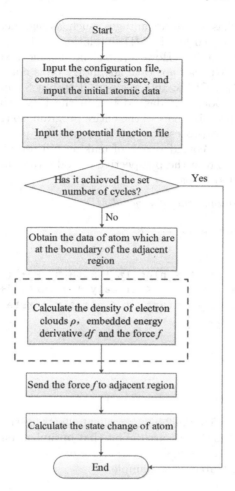

Fig. 1. The flow chart of original Crystal-MD program

The data such as the initial location and speed of the atoms in the lattice boundary will be sent to the adjacent region with MPI.

(3) Calculate the results

The program uses the data in phase (1) and (2) to calculate the results such as the density of electron clouds ρ, embedded energy derivative df and the force f.

(4) Exchange the force data

The force data f will be sent to the adjacent block in order to update the atomic location and motion state.

(5) Calculate the state change of atom

According to Newton's mechanical equations, the location and motion state of atom in all the blocks will be calculated.

The Crystal-MD has many advantages, such as significantly reducing the amount of memory required for the MD simulation, and using the PSC to solve the problem of write conflict. However, on the Tianhe-2 supercomputer, the homogeneous Crystal-MD can not take advantage of as many cores as possible, because there are only 2 CPUs, 16 cores per CPU, but 8 coprocessors, 64 cores per coprocessor in a node. The dashed box in the Fig. 1 shows the compute-intensive and time-consuming part of the entire program, so this part of program should be calculated in coprocessors, and the remaining part of program still be run on the CPUs for the consideration of making full use of the heterogeneous resources of Tianhe-2. From the perspective of code, the most time-consuming part is a series of nested loops.

The most time-consuming code of Crystal-MD

```
void computeEam(eam* pot,.....)
{
    ......
    for(int k = zstart; k < nlocalz + zstart; k++){
        for(int j = ystart; j < nlocaly + ystart; j++){
            for(int i = xstart; i < nlocalx + xstart; i++){
                ......
            }
        }
    }
    ......
}
```

The coprocessors of the Tianhe-2 have excellent effects for the compute-intensive part of program. So it is the research point that optimization work should focus on. There are many nested loops like the above one in *computeEam()*, and this nested loop is demonstrated as a example.

4   Optimized Crystal-MD Program

To solve the situation we have mentioned above, a optimal strategy has been used as Fig. 2.

The main idea of the optimal strategy is to transmit the computationally intensive code and the data to coprocessors and transmit the computation result back to CPUs. And the PSC which proposed in [4] is used to divide the whole loop area into blocks, and each core in coprocessor computes a block.

The Pseudo code of computeEam function in Crystal-MD

```
Input: The atom location array x and the potential function
       array spline and so on
Output: The density of electron clouds rho, embedded energy
```

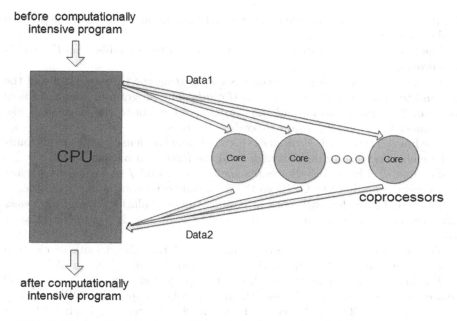

Fig. 2. The optimal strategy which takes advantage of the coprocessor cores

```
         derivative df and the force f
1   createEnvironment();
2   for each va in Input
3        move va from CPUs to coprocessors;
4   for each core in a coprocessor
5        myid <- getId();
6        num_threads <- getThreadNumber();
7        index1 <- myid * 2 % (num_threads * 2);
8        simu_areas1 <- setArea(index1);
9        calculate rho in each simu_areas1 in parallel;
10       calculate df in each simu_areas1 in parallel;
11       calculate f in each simu_areas1 in parallel;
12       for each rho, df and f
13            move rho, df and f from coprocessors to CPUs;

14       index2 <- (myid * 2 + 1) % (num_threads * 2);
15       simu_areas2 <- setArea(index2);
16       calculate rho in each simu_areas2 in parallel;
17       calculate df in each simu_areas2 in parallel;
18       calculate f in each simu_areas2 in parallel;
19       for each rho, df and f
20            move rho, df and f from coprocessors to CPUs;
```

The line 1: creating the variable mapping environment on coprocessors to prepare for data movement.

The line 2–3: for each variable in Input, moving the variable from the CPUs to coprocessors.

The line 4–8: for each core in coprocessor, getting the thread id $myid$ of the core and total number of threads $num\_threads$. The program divides the whole area into 2 * $num\_threads$, and the $simu\_areas1$ refers to the even areas like the number 0, 2, ..., 2 * ($num\_threads - 1$) areas.

The line 9–11: for each $simu\_areas1$, calculating the density of electron clouds ρ, the embedded energy derivative df, and the force f in parallel.

The line 12–13: moving the results such as ρ, df and f in each $simu\_areas1$ from coprocessors back to CPUs so the data can be computed in CPUs side.

The line 14–15: for each core in coprocessor, calculating the $simu\_areas2$ which refers to the even areas like the number 1, 3, ..., 2 * $num\_threads - 1$ areas.

The line 16–18: for each $simu\_areas2$, calculating the density of electron clouds ρ, the embedded energy derivative df, and the force f in parallel.

The line 19–20: moving the results such as ρ, df and f in each $simu\_areas2$ from coprocessors back to CPUs so the data can be computed in CPUs.

Each node of Tianhe-2 has 2 CPUs and 8 coprocessors. Each CPU can run up to 24 threads, and each coprocessor can run up to 64 threads. On the Tianhe-2, the OpenMP guidance statement can be used for heterogeneous transplantation of the program. In OpenMP guidance statement, the $omp\ target\ data\ map$ is used to create a map envirorment in coprocessor, and the $map\ to\ /from$ is used to transmit the data from CPUs to coprocessors or from coprocessors to CPUs respectively.

In the code, the required data (potential function file, atomic location information data x, etc.) is transmitted from main memory to coprocessor, and the calculated result (electronic cloud potential energy ρ and force f, etc.) is transmitted from coprocessor to memory. The nested loop has been put in a parallel environment so that it can be executed in parallel by multiple threads.

And the OpenMP statements support not only homogeneous multi-thread parallelism but also heterogeneous programming. The $map(alloc :)$ is used to create the variable mapping environment in coprocessors, and the $update\ to/from$ statement is used to transmit the data between CPUs and coprocessors. And as the homogeneous programming, the $parallel\ for$ can be employ for calculation in parallel in a heterogeneous way.

The optimized code of Crystal-MD

```
void computeEam(eam* pot,.....)
{
    ......
    #pragma omp target data map(alloc:spline[0:7*(nr_d+1)],
      x[0:numberoflattice*3],rho[0:numberoflattice],......)
    {
```

```
#pragma omp target update to(spline[0:7*(nr_d+1)],
        x[0:numberoflattice*3],......)
#pragma omp target
{
    cal_rho1(x,neighbour_array,spline,rho);
    cal_rho2(x,neighbour_array,spline,rho);
}
#pragma omp target update from(rho[0:numberoflattice],......)
......
}
......
}
```

The variables has been mapped into coprocessor space with the *map()* statement in the above function, and transmitted between CPUs and coprocessors with *updateto/from()* statement. The calculation function has been put into the *target* environment, so the threads of coprocessors can be made full use of.

The implementation of the PSC on Tianhe-2

```
void cal_rho1(double *x,......)
{
    #pragma omp parallel num_threads(set_numth)
    {
        my_id = omp_get_thread_num();
        num_threads = omp_get_num_threads()*2;
        subindex_z = (my_id * 2) % num_threads;
        z_start = begin_of_area(nlocalz, zstart,subindex_z);
        z_end = end_of_area(nlocalz, zstart,subindex_z);

        #pragma omp for private(k,j,i,......)
        for(k = z_start; k < z_end; k++){
            for( j = ystart; j < nlocaly + ystart; j++){
                for( i = xstart; i < nlocalx + xstart; i++){
                    ......
                }
            }
        }
        ......
    }
}
```

The nested loop can be executed in parallel in the omp parallel environment, and the number of threads used in each coprocessor can be set with the variable *set_numth*. The function implements the Partition-and-Separate-Calculation method with the thread id which can be get by the interface *omp_get_num_threads()*. And the *cal_rho2()* function is similar to *cal_rho1()* function, the difference is that when calculating the variable $subindex\_z$, $(my_i d * 2 + 1)\%\ num\_threads$ will be used.

5   Experiment and Analysis

The section states the experiment results and the correlative analysis. The experimental environment of the original Crystal-MD program is shown as Table 1.

The homogeneous and heterogeneous Crystal-MD simulation tests have been run on Tianhe-2. The running time of original Crystal-MD on different simulation scales and core numbers is illustrates as Table 2, and the unit of running time is seconds, the data we have not tested are shown as the symbol '/'.

Table 1. The experimental environment

Item	Specifications
Operation System	Kylin Linux
MPI Version	MPI 3.0
CPU	32000 Intel Xeon CPU, 24 cores per CPU
Coprocessor	128000 Matrix 2000, 64 cores per coprocessor
Node	16000 compute nodes in total
Interconnect	TH Express-2
Memory	1.4PB in total
Storage	12.4PB in total
Cabinets	162 Cabinets in total

Table 2. The running time of original Crystal-MD on different simulation scales and core numbers

Core numbers	Simulation scales			
	100^3	200^3	400^3	800^3
1	153.85	/	/	/
2	79.76	/	/	/
4	42.61	/	/	/
8	22.15	178.38	/	/
16	11.12	89.11	/	/
32	4.84	44.71	/	/
64	2.78	22.32	178.80	/
128	/	11.16	89.20	/
256	/	5.54	44.78	/
512	/	2.78	22.25	178.52
1024	/	/	11.12	89.17
2048	/	/	5.54	44.79
4096	/	/	2.78	22.33
8192	/	/	/	11.13
16384	/	/	/	5.54
32768	/	/	/	2.77

The homogeneous test results are demonstrated with scales of 100*100*100, 200*200*200, 400*400*400 and 800*800*800 respectively in Fig. 3 according to the Table 2.

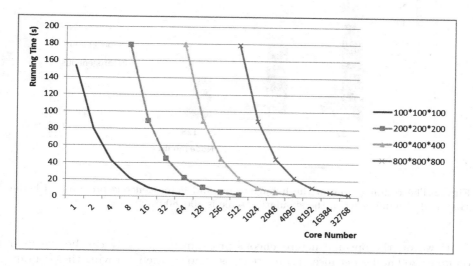

Fig. 3. The homogeneous program test results with different scales

As can be seen from the Fig. 3, for each molecular scale, when the number of cores used increases, the running time nonlinearly decreases, and the rate of decline is faster in the beginning, indicating that the Crystal-MD simulation program is suitable for running with multiple processes. However, when the number of cores comes to be big enough, the running time decline much slower. The main reason is that less data are allocated to each core, so some computing power has been wasted.

Comparing the scale of each molecule laterally, the descending trajectories of the four kinds of curves are very similar. For the adjacent curves, the ratio of the simulated atom numbers is exactly equal to the ratio of the core numbers when the running time is settled. This demonstrates that the homogeneous Crystal-MD simulation program has a good expansion on the Tianhe-2 supercomputer.

The Fig. 4 shows the running time of the homogeneous and heterogeneous program respectively. The program has been tested on different number of nodes, the homogeneous program is just executed in CPUs of each node, and the heterogeneous program is executed both in CPUs and coprocessors.

From the Fig. 4, it is obvious that with the same number of nodes, the heterogeneous program is less time-consuming than the homogeneous one, because the heterogeneous program can utilize more resource of each node, and the coprocessor is suitable for compute-intensive part of the program.

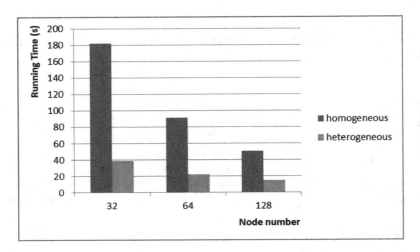

Fig. 4. The running time of the homogeneous and heterogeneous program with the same nodes' number when the simulation scale is 800*800*800

However, the optimal heterogeneous program temporarily can be executed on up to 200 nodes because of some reasons. And we are improving the program continuously.

6   Conclusion

With the development of supercomputer such as Tianhe-2, many programs can be transplanted to the supercomputer. The Crystal-MD can be run in a scalable way on Tianhe-2, and the program can be rewritten to a heterogeneous way, then executed on both CPUs and coprocessors. And the test results show that the heterogeneous Crystal-MD is less time-consuming and can take advantage of the resource in Tianhe-2. The future work is to improve the heterogeneous program, making it can be executed on a larger number of nodes.

Acknowledgments. This work was supported by the National Key R&D Program of China (2017YFB0202003, 2017YFB0202104).

References

1. TOP500 supercomputer sites. https://www.top500.org
2. Li, D., Xu, C., Wang, Y., et al.: Parallelizing and optimizing large-scale 3D multiphase flow simulations on the Tianhe-2 supercomputer. Concurrency Comput. Pract. Experience **28**(5), 1678–1692 (2016)
3. Sandia National Laboratories. LAMMPS user manual, p. 996 (2014)
4. Hu, C., Wang, X., Li, J., et al.: Kernel optimization for short-range molecular dynamics. Comput. Phys. Commun. **211**, 31–40 (2016)

5. Bai, H., Hu, C., He, X., Zhang, B., Wang, J.: Crystal MD: molecular dynamic simulation software for metal with BCC structure. In: Chen, W., et al. (eds.) BDTA 2015. CCIS, vol. 590, pp. 247–258. Springer, Singapore (2016). https://doi.org/10.1007/978-981-10-0457-5_23

6. CoMD. http://www.exmatex.org/comd.html

7. Lawson G, Sosonkina M, Shen Y.: Performance and energy evaluation of CoMD on Intel Xeon Phi co-processors. In: Proceedings of the 1st International Workshop on Hardware-Software Co-design for High Performance Computing, pp. 49–54. IEEE Press, New York (2014)

8. Alder, B.J., Wainwright, T.E.: Phase transition for a hard sphere system. J. Chem. Phys. **27**(5), 1208 (1957)

9. Alder, B.J., Wainwright, T.E.: Studies in molecular dynamics. I. General method. J. Chem. Phys. **31**(2), 459–466 (1959)

10. Lammps manual. http://lammps.sandia.gov

11. Stadler, J., Mikulla, R., Trebin, H.R.: IMD: a software package for molecular dynamics studies on parallel computers. Int. J. Mod. Phys. C **8**(5), 1131–1140 (1997)

12. Large systems 1: molecular dynamics. http://www.ls1-mardyn.de

13. Niethammer, C., Becker, S., Bernreuther, M., et al.: ls1 mardyn: the massively parallel molecular dynamics code for large systems. J. Chem. Theor. Comput. **10**(10), 4455–4464 (2014)

14. Peng, S., Zhang, X., Lu, Y., et al.: High-scalable collaborated parallel framework for large-scale molecular dynamic simulation on Tianhe-2 supercomputer. IEEE/ACM Trans. Comput. Biol. Bioinform. **PP**, 99 (2018)

Research on Large Scale Parallel Hydrological Simulation

Genshen Chu[1,2], Changjun Hu[1(✉)], Xiaoning Qin[3], Jiahao Wu[1], and Yanfei Wu[1]

[1] University of Science and Technology Beijing, Beijing, China
genshenchu@gmail.com, huchangjun@ies.ustb.edu.cn
[2] Beijing Key Laboratory of Knowledge Engineering for Material Science, Beijing, China
[3] Shuguang Information Industry (Beijing) Limited Company, Beijing, China

Abstract. In recent years, hydrological simulation has become an effective and significant method for achieving accurate and effective flood forecasting to decreasing losses of human's belongings caused by floods disaster. In this paper, we will analyse challenging problems in large scale parallel hydrological simulation. As an important data structure for effective channel routing, river network codification methods will be introduced in Sect. 2. And some issues about parallel tasks decomposition methods and parallel simulation strategies will also be discussed in this paper. As an significant part of parallel issues, the comparison of static parallel tasks decomposition method and dynamic parallel tasks decomposition methods will be presented. At last, we discussed the pipline parallel strategy of hydrological simulation.

Keywords: Parallel hydrological simulation ·
River network codification · Tasks decomposition

1   Introduction

Floods disaster causes great losses of human's belongings and even lives every year. Hydrological simulation is an effective and significant method for achieving accurate and effective flood forecasting to decreasing those losses. The water cycle is the most active energy exchange and material transfer process on the earth, which presents complex spatial and temporal variability, nonlinearity, and uncertainty. Sundry physics based hydrologic models for representing this kind of process are necessary parts of effective hydrological simulation, which normally couple multiple geographic processes such as interception, infiltration, surface depression, overland-flow routing and channel-flow routing process [3,6].

With the growth of computing power, especially high performance clusters and supercomputers, larger area and longer term simulation with more complex hydrologic models can get involved. Meanwhile, simulation using distributed hydrologicalmodels [5] over large area and long-term periods also requires a large mount of computation, which makes the parallel hydrological simulation based on distributed hydrological models an inevitable choice. The basic idea for parallel hydrological simulation is dividing the whole simulation area into several parts spatially [2] which are called simulation units [6]. We denote those simulation units as set U. Each processor i undertake a subset of U, denoted as U_i, where $\bigcup_{i=1}^{n} U_i = U$ with n processors. This has been implemented by several studies [1, 3, 4].

We also concern following things while carrying out the parallel hydrological simulation:

1. The partition results of simulation area are normally irregular. That is, dividing a drainage basin into some sub areas with regular shape like square or cube shape may be not a good approach due to the guideline of following the organization of nature rivers [1], which will lead a complex dividing process [7].
2. As an important data structure for effective channel routing, river network codification methods plays an important role in hydrological simulation. A general purpose of river network codification is to find where the downstream simulation units and upstream simulation units of a simulation unit is, which is critical for efficient river routing. River network codification methods will be disscussed in Sect. 2.
3. Bad algorithm for dispatching computing tasks from different simulation units to different processors may cause load unbanlance and large communication among processors. Therefore, load banlance strategies and communication optimization among processors are the points worthy of study [1], which will be disscussed in Sect. 3.
4. The process of river routing from upstream to downstream must follow timing relationship, In the same time steps, each downstream simulation unit have to wait for the simulation results passed from its upstream simulation units, which will result in a poor parallel efficiency due to the sequential river routing process. We will introduce a assembly line river routing algorithm for improving parallel efficiency in Sect. 3.

2   River Network Codification Methods

Usually, the topological structure of river network is a sparse graph. A sparse graph is a graph $G = (V, E)$ in which $|E| = O(|V|)$, indicating nodes in graph are sparsely connected. We should also notice that the river network topological structure have high and coarse resolution, normally the coarse resolution river network is used in simulation process [4].

2.1 Binary Tree Based Codification Method

Based on following assumption, [8] proposed a binary treebased and dyadic indi-
cated codification method:

1. One simulation unit only has physical interactions with its adjacent upstream
   and downstream river reach, and there is only one river channel between two
   adjacent river reach.
2. There are no circles in river network. We may ignore the circles in graph or
   convert those circles to other format due to few circles in river network graph,
   the topological structure of river network can be a forest containing of several
   trees.
3. One simulation unit only receive two upstream units.

In binary tree based codification method, the binary tree is the topological
structure of river network, nodes represent river reaches of simulation units,
edges represent river channel in simulation units. Each node was denoted by
pair (L, V), in where L denotes the level of node in tree, V denotes sequential
integer starting with zero from left to right at the same level of tree. Given a
node (L, V), its parent node will be $(L - 1, \left\lfloor \dfrac{V}{2} \right\rfloor)$ if it exists, and its direct
children will be $(L + 1, 2V)$ and $(L + 1, 2V + 1)$ if it exists. Figure 1 show an
example of the result of binary tree based codification of value V.

In practical application, [9] found V can be extremely large, even overflow,
when L grows, because V increases exponentially with L. But in fact, in the same
level l, due to the incomplete binary trees characteristic, many integer from 0
to $2^l - 1$ do not appear in codification. Therefore, [9,10] developed a modified
binary tree codification based on the application of binary-tree structures and
hierarchical zones. [11] proposed the Multi-tree Code Method (MCM).

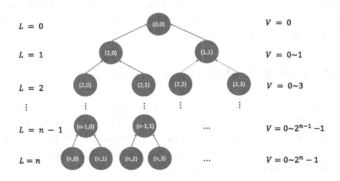

Fig. 1. An example of binary tree based codification

2.2   Modified Binary Tree Codification Method

In modified binary tree codification method, it use a triple (Z, L, V) to represent a river confluence point, namely node in topology binary tree, in river network, in which, Z denotes global unique zone index, L denotes level of node in tree as the same as in binary tree based codification method, and V denotes sequential integer number starting from 0 in this zone. The generate idea of this method is divide the whole binary tree into several subtree. Then codify each subtree with different zone index by using binary tree based codification method mentioned in Sect. 2.1.

The basic process of modified binary tree codification method is shown in Algorithm 1. First, it codify the binary tree using binary tree based codification method, with setting all values of Z to 0. And check and append all nodes i with $V_i > V_{max}$ into a list. Second, for each node in list, select a ancestor node of node i whose value V is less than or equal to V_{max} but greater than zero, denoted as node p, and recodify this subtree starting from node p with a new global unique zone index recursively. Here, V_i denote the value V of node i, and V_{max} denote a predefined constant less than or equal to the overflow upper limit.

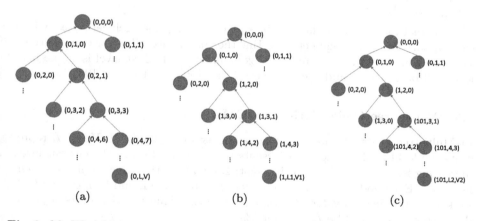

(a)   (b)   (c)

Fig. 2. Modified binary tree codification method. (a) Codify the binary tree using binary tree based codification method first, but some nodes's values of V may be larger than V_{max}, such as node $(0, L, V)$. (b) Make a zones for the subtree containing node $(0, L, V)$ whose corresponding ancestor node is node $(0, 2, 1)$. Then recodify the subtree rooted at node $(0, 2, 1)$ with zone index 1. (c) The value V of node $(1, L1, V1)$ is still larger than V_{max}. Recodify the subtree rooted at node $(1, 2, 1)$ with zone index 101.

In [10]'s study, ancestor node p of denoted as node i is selected according to following condition: node p has a left brother node q whose value V is 0. As shown in Fig. 2a, node $(0, 2, 1)$ is the ancestor node of node $(0, L, V)$ mentioned above. And the zone index is calculated by formula $Z_{new} = 100 \times Z_{old} + i; 0 < i < 100$, which can represent at most 99 sub zones in the same zone. Meanwhile, the

---

Algorithm 1. codify$(T, Z, List)$

1: **for** *node* in T **do**
2:    codify_node$(node, Z)$
3:    **if** $node.V > V_{max}$ **and** (**not** *node* in $List$) **then**
4:       $List \leftarrow$ append$(List, node)$
5:    **end if**
6: **end for**
7: **for** *node_i* in $List$ **do**
8:    $List \leftarrow$ remove$(List, node\_i)$
9:    **if** $node\_i.V > V_{max}$ **then**
10:       $node\_p \leftarrow$ find_ancestor$(node\_i)$
11:       $new\_zone\_index \leftarrow$ generate_new_zone_index$()$
12:       codify $(node\_p, new\_zone\_index, List)$
13:    **end if**
14: **end for**

---

adjacent downstream of node (Z, L, V) will be $(Z, L - 1, \left\lfloor \dfrac{V}{2} \right\rfloor)$ if $V \neq 0$, or

$(\left\lfloor \dfrac{Z}{100} \right\rfloor, L - 1, 0)$ if $V = 0$.

This method can avoid large values of V by using hierarchical zones, which can support large drainage network. But the zone index will grow exponentially with the zone level. For example, the zone index in the first level is 1, the next level will be $100 + i_1$, and the lth level will be $100^l + i_l, 1 < i_l < 100^l$.

2.3   Multi-tree Code Method (MCM)

In Multi-tree Code Method, each node consists of a triple (L, V, Z). L represents the level of the node; V represents the node location at the current level, increasing from the left zero to the right; Z equals to the V value of the parent node [11]. Each node can be uniquely identified by value L and V of this node. If we known a node with value (L_0, V_0, Z_0), then the value L and V of its adjacent downstream node will be $L_0 - 1$ and Z_0.

This codification method can deal with multitree effectively, while it can be a challenge for both binary tree based codification and modified binary tree codification method. But given a node, both modified binary tree codification method and MCM will have difficulty searching its upstream nodes.

3   Parallel Tasks Decomposition

In order to perform parallel simulation, we must partition temporal domain or spatial domain into sub domains. However, due to the dependency of temporal dimension, which means the results of current timestep depend on the results from last timestep, almost parallel hydrological simulation method is based on spatial decomposition [4,15] (e.g. [1,3,4,12,13]).

In parallel hydrological simulation, we define a *static* tasks decomposition that a subbasin would be located on this processor permanently in the entire simulation cycle when a simulation unit is dispatched to a processor. In other words, any simulation unit would not migrate to other processors in the entire simulation cycle. While a *dynamic* tasks decomposition refers to that a simulation unit is located on this processor, but it would migrate to other processor in next simulation timestep.

Static tasks decomposition and related parallel program can be implemented more easily compared to dynamic tasks decomposition. By using static tasks decomposition, we can take task decomposition before executing parallel program. After finishing decomposition, each processor of parallel program can just read decomposition results of itself. And the later execution of parallel program can also use this decomposition result, because the topological structure of river network is almost unchanged. For efficient program performance, we must design a decomposition algorithm to implement load-balance and minimize communication among processors. [1] developed a parallel hydrological module, tRIBS, which use graph partitioning software METIS [16,17] to decomposite simulation units to different processors. In tRIBS, load-balance and two kind of communication minimization strategies were considered, which obtained approximately 70 speedup at 512 processors. METIS tools was also used in [3] for a two-level parallelization method, which obtained more then 25 speedup at 48 parallel units (processors and threads).

In dynamic tasks decomposition, tasks schedule is determined by schedule algorithm, and tasks may migrate to other processors at runtime. [4] developed a parallel hydrological simulation algorithm with dynamic tasks decomposition. It use a master processor to maintain a binary tree coded using modified binary-tree codification method, several slave processors to conducting all hydrological simulation, a data transfer process to temporarily stores intermediate simulation results and a database server to manage input and output data. Every slave processor request tasks, namely simulation unit, from master processor, followed by requesting upstream inflow data from data transfer process if necessary and reading simulation data from database. Then it will start simulation for this simulation unit. After finishing simulation, it will store inflow data to data transfer process, and request next simulation unit. And the maximum speedup ratio curve (MSC) was discussed in detail for this parallel method based on the binary-tree theory [14]. [15] developed a parallel hydrological computing framework using analogous strategy above. Through theoretical analysis, the restriction of maximum speedup ratio of M/L has found, where M is the number of sub-basins in the entire river basin, and L is the number of binary-tree layers. Besides, in their tests, they found I/O occupied most of the simulation time by using dynamic tasks decomposition strategy. An advantage of dynamic tasks decomposition strategy is that it can adjust load balance at runtime by migrating tasks to different processors using task scheduling algorithm. But tasks migration make simulation program reading hydrological related data again and again, which can cause a large I/O overhead, and it may cause an increase of communication.

4   Parallel Strategies

To expand our program to a large scale, static tasks decomposition can be a better choice, because static tasks decomposition has less additional performance overhead such as I/O and communication. In this section, we will discuss parallel strategies based on static tasks decomposition. Wang Hao [18,19] proposed a river routing parallel method called "temporal-spatial discretization method (TSDM)". In this method, one sub-basin is treated as a river channel plus two or three hillslopes. Hillslopes simulation can be calculated independently, which is not restricted by the river routing dependency. And pipeline strategy can be used for the river routing process of river channels (the following will discuss in detail). In pipeline strategy when finished calculation of one simulation unit at time step t_1, then it will pass simulation to its downstream, and start simulation at time step t_2. [3,20] proposed layered approach at the sub-basin level and the basic simulation-unit level such as grid cell. [21] also implemented a grid based algorithm, which is based on single-flow D8 algorithm of grid flow, in distributed hydrological model simulations by using OpenMP technology. The speed-up ratio of this parallel algorithm 2.42 under 4 cores.

4.1   Pipeline Parallel River Routing Strategy

In non-pipeline strategy, after one simulation unit finished simulation in time step t_1, it must wait the whole simulation units to finish their simulation in this time step, then start simulation of next time step t_2. But in pipeline strategy, one simulation unit can carry out next time step(t_2) simulation after it has finished its simulation of this time step(t_1) and passed simulation results of t_1 to its downstream, if all its upstream dependencies of t_2 has been satisfied. Figure 3a shows the result of non-pipeline strategy when running with n processors. When river routing goes to the near root of river network tree, there are only a few nodes can be counted in, which will result in a large amount of idleness of computing resources. Extremely in the root node, there is only one processor in calculating state, while other processors are in idle state. And it is also easy to conclude, in this strategy, the more processors get involved, the worse performance the program may have. Figure 3b and c show the comparison of non-pipeline strategy and pipeline strategy. In which, A_i represents simulation process of sub-basin A in time step t_i, and so forth.

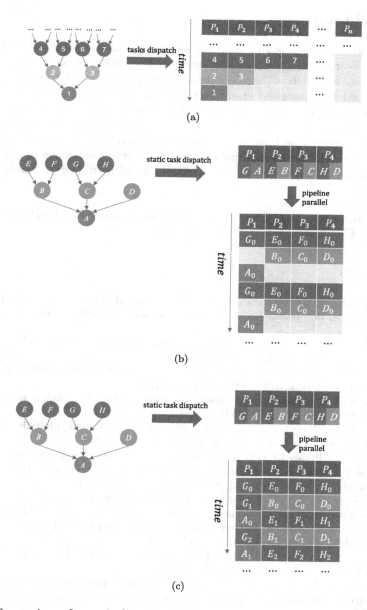

(a)

(b)

(c)

Fig. 3. Comparison of non-pipeline parallel strategy and pipeline parallel strategy. We assume that each simulation unit has the same amount of calculations for convenient analysis. (a) Non-pipeline parallel strategy with n processors, which can cause a large amount of idleness of computing resources (grey blocks). (b) Non-pipeline parallel strategy with 4 processors (P_1, P_2, P_3, P_4) and 8 simulation units ($A, B, \cdots, G$). (c) Pipeline parallel strategy with 4 processors and 8 simulation units. This strategy can improve program efficiency compared to non-pipeline parallel strategy.

5   Conclusion

Hydrological simulation is an important technology for flood forecast and water resources research. In this paper, we analyzed river network codification methods, which are almost tree based codification methods in published works. Then we introduced and discussed static and dynamic tasks decomposition method. Static decomposition method can be more efficient compared to dynamic tasks decomposition method, especially with a low I/O overhead relatively, but we must design a good load balance and communication minimizing algorithm. By using pipeline river routing parallel strategy, the parallel efficiency of river routing process can be improved, which can lead parallel hydrological simulation to large scale.

Acknowledgments. The research is supported by National Key R&D Program of China No.2017YFB0203100 and 2017YFB0203103.

References

1. Vivoni, E.R., et al.: Real-world hydrologic assessment of a fully-distributed hydrological model in a parallel computing environment. J. Hydrol. **409**(1–2), 483–496 (2011)
2. Junzhi, L.I.U., et al.: Review on parallel computing of distributed hydrological models. Prog. Geogr. **32**(4), 538–547 (2013)
3. Liu, J., et al.: A two-level parallelization method for distributed hydrological models. Environ. Modell. Softw. **80**, 175–184 (2016)
4. Li, T., et al.: Dynamic parallelization of hydrological model simulations. Environ. Modell. Softw. **26**(12), 1736–1746 (2011)
5. Freeze, R.A., Harlan, R.L.: Blueprint for a physically-based, digitally-simulated hydrologic response model. J. Hydrol. **9**(3), 237–258 (1969)
6. Dehotin, J., Braud, I.: Which spatial discretization for distributed hydrological models? Proposition of a methodology and illustration for medium to large-scale catchments. Hydrol. Earth Syst. Sci. **12**(3), 769–796 (2008)
7. Apostolopoulos, T.K., Georgakakos, K.P.: Parallel computation for streamflow prediction with distributed hydrologic models. J. Hydrol. **197**(1–4), 1–24 (1997)
8. Li, T., Wang, G., Liu, J.: Drainage network codification method for digital watershed model. Adv. Water Sci. **17**(5), 664 (2006)
9. Hao, W., et al.: Binary-tree coding for drainage network of large-scale basins. J. Hohai Univ. Nat. Sci. **37**(5), 499–504 (2009)
10. Li, T., Wang, G., Chen, J.: A modified binary tree codification of drainage networks to support complex hydrological models. Comput. Geosci. **36**(11), 1427–1435 (2010)
11. Wang, H., Xudong, F., Wang, G.: Multi-tree coding method (MCM) for drainage networks supporting high-efficient search. Comput. Geosci. **52**, 300–306 (2013)
12. Vivoni, E.R., et al.: Parallelization of a fully-distributed hydrologic model using sub-basin partitioning. EOS Trans. AGU **86**, 52 (2005)
13. Cui, Z., et al.: Parallelisation of a distributed hydrologic model. Int. J. Comput. Appl. Technol. **22**(1), 42–52 (2005)

14. Wang, H., et al.: Maximum speedup ratio curve (MSC) in parallel computing of the binary-tree-based drainage network. Comput. Geosci. **38**(1), 127–135 (2012)

15. Wang, H., et al.: A common parallel computing framework for modeling hydrological processes of river basins. Parallel Comput. **37**(67), 302–315 (2011)

16. METIS - serial graph partitioning and fill-reducing matrix ordering. http://glaros.dtc.umn.edu/gkhome/metis/metis/overview

17. Karypis, G., Kumar, V.: A fast and high quality multilevel scheme for partitioning irregular graphs. SIAM J. Sci. Comput. **20**(1), 359–392 (1998)

18. Hao, W., et al.: Parallel characteristics of river basin based on temporal-spatial-discrete approach. Sciencepaper Online **7**, 005 (2010)

19. Wang, H., et al.: A high-performance temporal-spatial discretization method for the parallel computing of river basins. Comput. Geosci. **58**, 62–68 (2013)

20. Liu, J., et al.: A layered approach to parallel computing for spatially distributed hydrological modeling. Environ. Modell. Softw. **51**, 221–227 (2014)

21. Xu, R., et al.: A new grid-associated algorithm in the distributed hydrological model simulations. Sci. China Ser. E: Technol. Sci. **53**(1), 235–241 (2010)

The Study of Parallelization of SWAT Hydrology Cycle

Qiang Li[1(✉)], Ningming Nie[2(✉)], Zhonghua Lu[2],
and Yangang Wang[2]

[1] Qingdao University, Qingdao 266000, SD, China
lq.sxt@163.com
[2] Computer Network Information Center, Chinese Academy of Sciences,
Beijing 100190, China
nienm@sccas.cn

Abstract. The accurate simulation of large scale hydrology cycles is a hot topic in the field of hydrology and parallel computing. Due to the huge computation amount, the process of the hydrology cycle should be parallelized and the high-performance computing is required. In this study, a parallel scheme of hydrology cycle is proposed by the parallelization of SWAT-the most popular hydrology simulation software. The potential parallelizable sections have been analyzed and exploited. Then a parallel framework based on MPI and OpenMP is proposed according to the structure of SWAT. Finally, the performance of this parallelism has been tested in the Shule River and the rivers in the northern slope of Tianshan Mountains. And the results show that this parallelism is suitable for the large scale hydrology simulations.

Keywords: SWAT · Hydrologic model · Parallel computing · MPI · Omptl

1 Introduction

As the key process in the hydrologic simulations, hydrologic cycle simulates the rainfall, flow production and converge by some physical and chemistry models. In the large scale hydrologic simulations, the computation of cycle process is very time-consuming, especially in the parameter calibration part. Thousands of cycle process simulations during parameter calibration process cost a long time to obtain the optimal solution. While as the constitution of the calibration, the parallelization of the hydrology cycle plays a significant role.

With the development of supercomputer and parallel computing in the scientific and industry fields [1–8], parallel hydrologic simulation attracts more and more scholars' attention. Apostolopoulus and Georgakakos [9] analysed the hydrologic forecast by means of parallel computing for the first time. Singh and Woolhiser [10] studied the order of magnitude of hydrologic simulation. Rodell [11] analysed the possibility of applying the large hydrologic models in Europe. Cui [12] proposed a parallel flood forecast model based on finite element analysis. Vivoni [13] proposed a parallel distributed hydrologic model based on the sub-basin decomposition (tRIBS). Kollet and Maxwell [14] implemented large area hydrologic simulation in almost

© Springer Nature Singapore Pte Ltd. 2019
C. Hu et al. (Eds.): HPCMS 2018/HiDEC 2018, CCIS 913, pp. 174–185, 2019.
https://doi.org/10.1007/978-981-32-9987-0_15

100 cores and got relatively high efficiency. Yalew and van Griensven [15] studied the parallelization of SWAT hydrologic cycle for the first time. Vivoni [16] built a distributed hydrologic assessment model for the real world. Li and Wang [17] proposed a dynamic parallel model for the hydrologic simulation. Based on these scholars' work, the computation performance of hydrologic simulation has been increased a lot, but it still cannot meet the demand of large scale hydrology cycle simulation. Meanwhile, most of the current parallel hydrologic model are based on some certain river, not for general use. This study will propose a new parallel scheme to parallelize and accelerate the hydrologic cycle for the SWAT model based on MPI+OpenMP.

The structure of this paper is as follows. In Sect. 2, we describe and analyze the structure of SWAT model. In Sect. 3, we proceed some performance analysis for SWAT hydrologic cycle computing, in order to get the parallelizability and break-through point of hydrologic cycle. Then, we propose our parallel strategy for SWAT hydrologic cycle simulation in Sect. 4 and Sect. 5. In Sect. 6, we present a numerical experiment to verify the effectiveness of our parallel scheme. Finally, we summarize our results in Sect. 7.

2 Structure of SWAT Model

SWAT (Soil and Water Assessment Tools) is a distributed environmental hydrologic model, developed by Dr. Jeff Arnold in USDA-ARS. SWAT is a dynamic simulation model for continuous time step based on natural physical process. It is used for different land use and multiple agricultural management measures' influence on the river's water, sediment and chemistry. It is widely used to manage and control non-point source pollution.

After about 15 years' development, with more function modules added, the size of SWAT's source code is larger and larger. Then the total running time increased a lot, especially in the case of large scale simulation, in which the time elapsed is quite considerable. But on the whole, although the SWAT developer integrated more and more features and optimize the algorithms continually, the essential structure of the hydrologic model hasn't been changed.

From the model point of view, the hydrologic cycle includes 3 sections: input, simulation and output.

(1) Input

There are a large number of input files and different formats. The most popular measure to deal with the input files is using the existing tools (for example, ArcSWAT), although some research teams get the formatted input files with databases. The main characteristics of SWAT input file are large number of quantity and formats, which produces a negative impact on the efficiency. In SWAT codes, the files named fig.fig and file.cio play an important part in the input files. Fig.fig controls the input and output of the whole model, and file.cio controls the input parameters in the runtime.

(2) Simulation

As is shown in Fig. 1, the hydrologic cycle of SWAT is divided into two levels: time level and space level. In the time level, the basic computation unit is the runoff every day. The month runoff is calculated by gathering the runoff each day. The outermost layer is the iteration loop based on each year. While in the space level, there are two layers in the computation unit: sub-basin and HRU (Hydrologic Response Unit). Sub-basin is the river channel, divided by the whole basin. While HRU is some area composed by the same hydrologic characteristic like forest, farmland, lake and many other undivided homogeneous units.

SWAT model obtains the HRU division of the whole river by reading the input files. With the physical and chemistry models integrated, the runoff of each HRU is calculated according to the current precipitation, then the runoff of the sub-basin will be obtained by the confluence. At last the runoff of the whole basin is calculated by the confluence of each sub-basin in it.

(3) Output

SWAT model has a large number of output files and formats. The output files are generated in each day, month and year, which bring many difficulties to the parallelization and make the efficiency hard to raise.

The whole structure of SWAT is shown in Fig. 1. The outer two layers are the year and day loops, while the inner layers are the sub-basin and HRU loops. If both of the HRU and time step are divided densely enough, the computation of SWAT hydrologic cycle simulation will be quite time-consuming.

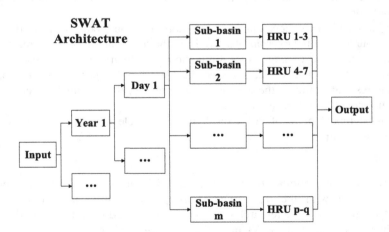

Fig. 1. The whole structure of SWAT program

3   The Performance Analysis of SWAT Hydrologic Cycle

An efficient way to improve the computational efficiency of a software is to speed up the hot spot section in it. It is unrealistic to analyze the code line by line for the distributed hydrologic model, which has a large amount of code, like SWAT. We can obtain the actual performance results with the help of some performance analysis tools from different angles.

From an efficient point of view, it is better to keep the main structure of SWAT complete and change less no matter how the algorithms update. In the reading input phase, there are thousands of input files. Although we can use parallel I/O schemes to accelerate reading files, it isn't applicable to the scattered files of SWAT data, while parallel I/O is applicable to the continuous large files. If we reconstitute the scattered files to a continuous one, the whole structure of SWAT should be modified either, that isn't what we want to see. We hope to accelerate the SWAT hydrologic cycle with as little change as possible. Then the reading input files section is not applicable to modify. While from the point of parallel computing, the loops are the most applicable to parallelize.

The best way to parallelize a multiple loop is to start from the outer layer. Because dividing from the outer makes the most coarse-grained parallelization, then each process or thread has enough work to do. For SWAT model, there are two time-layers in the outer and two space layers in the inner. If the parallelization is started from the outer layers, the hydrologic cycles of different years will proceed concurrently, which violates the natural principle of SWAT model. Actually, the input data of the current year in this loop has to be obtained from the output data of the last year in the last loop. On the other hand, the final purpose of SWAT is to forecast, while simulations of different years proceed separately will be meaningless. Then the outer two layers of loop will be not applicable to be parallelized.

In the inner two layers of sub-basin and HRU, a medium scale river is generally divided into hundreds of sub-basins and thousands of HRUs. In such case, the total running time is more than ten seconds, including input and output. Although it may be more efficient if HRU is selected as the dividing unit, it will mostly alter the whole structure of SWAT. However, if we start parallelizing from the sub-basin layer, a relatively coarse-grained parallelization would be implemented. Due to the sub-basins are composed of HRU, starting parallelization from sub-basins layer will not change the whole structure of SWAT too much. Then in this study, the parallelization will be based on this layer.

On the other hand, we apply VTune, produced by Intel, to test and analyze the application performance of SWAT. By adding the compile option -g, the application will be started by VTune, then the functions requested, I/O and the memory status will be snapshot and shown in a graphical interface.

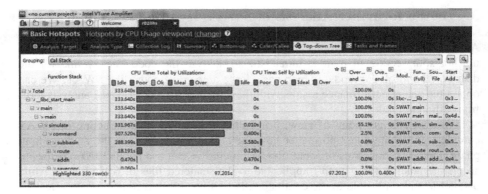

Fig. 2. The performance analysis by VTune

The performance analysis of SWAT is shown in Fig. 2 by VTune. The whole test, in which the input data includes 246 sub-basins and 5334 HRUs for 5 years, costs about 333 s, and the sub-basin part costs 288 s, which accounts for about 86%. This result is supported our analysis, that parallelization should be started from the sub-basin layer.

4   The Parallelization Study of SWAT Hydrologic Cycle with MPI

In this section, we will propose the details of parallel scheme for SWAT hydrologic cycle with MPI.

(1) Task allocation

Based on the analysis above, the tasks should be parallelized in the sub-basin level. While the sequence of every hydrology process should also be considered. In the input files of SWAT, the sequence of the whole hydrology processes was recorded in the file fig.fig. The runoff of sub-basin is separated from the confluence, which is an accumulated section. So only the sub-basin section can be parallelized. The number of processes can be obtained from the MPI functions, and SWAT can read the number of sub-basins from the input files. Then in order to allocate the tasks to the processes, a map of the processes and the sub-basins can be drawn by the principle of load balancing, which is shown in Fig. 3. Then the runoff and confluence of sub-basins can be running on different processes averagely.

(2) Result reduction

After the parallelization of sub-basins, the total model can be running concurrently on different processes. But the output may be not the same as the original SWAT, the reason is that these tasks are finished by different processes. To the hydrologists, they have used to the outputs of the original SWAT model. Then, after parallelization, the outputs should insure to be identical to the original SWAT. There are 3 circumstances:

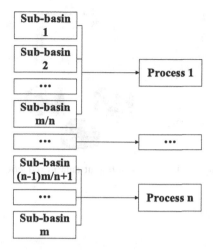

Fig. 3. The Scheme of Task Allocation

(a) Some results ordered by the time sequence, such as the output of precipitation, surface flow, ground water and many other outputs. After the SWAT is parallelized, these results are actually the sum of the variables in each process, which is shown in Fig. 4.

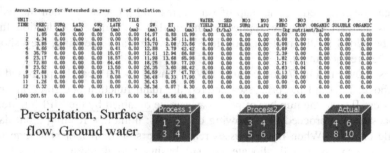

Fig. 4. The sum of output data in reduction

(b) Many crops data ordered by the sequence of sub-basin or HRU. These results are actually the union of the variables in each process after the model is parallelized, which is shown in Fig. 5.

(c) The runoff result in output.rch file, which is shown in Fig. 6, cannot be reduced before output, because there are much more operations before that. Then this kind of data should be reduced in the processing stage.

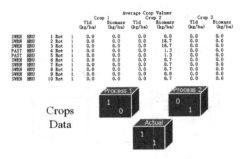

Fig. 5. The union of output data in reduction

```
  SWAT  Sept '05 VERSION2005                                         0/ 0/ 0      0: 0: 0

  General Input/Output section (file.cio): ArcSWAT 2.3.4
  2013/5/29 0:00:00ARCGIS-SWAT interface AV

         NCH    GIS  NON   AREAkm2   FLOW_INcms FLOW_OUTcms   EVAPcms   TLOSScms  SED_INtons SED_OUTtonsSEDCONCmg/kg   ORGN_INkg  ORGN_OUTkg   ORGP_INkg
  REACH    1     0    1  0.1105E+05 0.1064E-05 0.0000E+00 0.0000E+00 0.1064E-05 0.9284E-07 0.0000E+00 0.0000E+00 0.2859E+00 0.0000E+00 0.5719E+00
  REACH    2     0    1  0.2330E+03 0.2692E-05 0.0000E+00 0.0000E+00 0.2692E-05 0.2479E-06 0.0000E+00 0.0000E+00 0.7219E+00 0.0000E+00 0.1444E+01
  REACH    3     0    1  0.1073E+05 0.4402E-05 0.0000E+00 0.0000E+00 0.4402E-05 0.2790E-06 0.0000E+00 0.0000E+00 0.1179E+01 0.0000E+00 0.2358E+01
  REACH    4     0    1  0.9239E+04 0.1760E-06 0.0000E+00 0.0000E+00 0.1760E-06 0.9300E-07 0.0000E+00 0.0000E+00 0.4715E-01 0.0000E+00 0.9430E-01
  REACH    5     0    1  0.2104E+03 0.2434E-05 0.0000E+00 0.0000E+00 0.2434E-05 0.9294E-07 0.0000E+00 0.0000E+00 0.6524E+00 0.0000E+00 0.1305E+01
  REACH    6     0    1  0.1106E+04 0.7584E-06 0.0000E+00 0.0000E+00 0.7584E-06 0.1550E-06 0.0000E+00 0.0000E+00 0.2031E+00 0.0000E+00 0.4063E+00
  REACH    7     0    1  0.4338E+03 0.5005E-05 0.0000E+00 0.0000E+00 0.5005E-05 0.9273E-07 0.0000E+00 0.0000E+00 0.1345E+01 0.0000E+00 0.2690E+01
  REACH    8     0    1  0.6069E+03 0.4762E-06 0.0000E+00 0.0000E+00 0.4762E-06 0.1240E-06 0.0000E+00 0.0000E+00 0.1276E+00 0.0000E+00 0.2551E+00
  REACH    9     0    1  0.1884E+03 0.2175E-05 0.0000E+00 0.0000E+00 0.2175E-05 0.6187E-07 0.0000E+00 0.0000E+00 0.5842E+00 0.0000E+00 0.1168E+01
  REACH   10     0    1  0.9013E+04 0.5109E-05 0.0000E+00 0.0000E+00 0.5109E-05 0.1860E-06 0.0000E+00 0.0000E+00 0.1369E+01 0.0000E+00 0.2737E+01
```

Fig. 6. The data reduction in processing stage

The task allocation is the core of the parallelization. Because of the particularity of SWAT structure, there are two layers of loops outside the sub-basins. The task allocation can be achieved by the map of sub-basins and processors. Then the reduction functions above can also be applied in the model, and different reduction function should be added in different location in SWAT. Generally speaking, they should be located before the output.

As is shown in Fig. 7, the parallel SWAT based on MPI can be proposed by the study above. First, all the processes entered the main function and run concurrently. The process ID and the number of processes can be obtained by the MPI functions. All the processes will proceed the following operations: initialing, reading input data and temp file creation. When the processes reached the sub-basin loop, the map of sub-basins and processed will allocate the sub-basins into different processes, which implement the parallelization. But the sub-basins in each process run sequentially. After all the computation, every process runs the same code for the confluence. Then in the reduction phase, before each output, different result would be reduced according to different reduction functions to make the final results be the same.

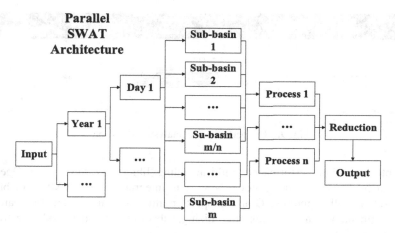

Fig. 7. Parallel SWAT architecture

5 The Parallelization of SWAT Hydrology Cycle with OpenMP

Now the sub-basins are allocated into different processes and the parallelization is implemented. But from hotspot of the Intel VTune, there are still several functions, which are very time-consuming.

From the Figs. 8 and 9, amax1, amin1 and many other functions consume much more time than others and repeated many times in the whole program. Then it is necessary to accelerate these functions to achieve more parallel efficiency.

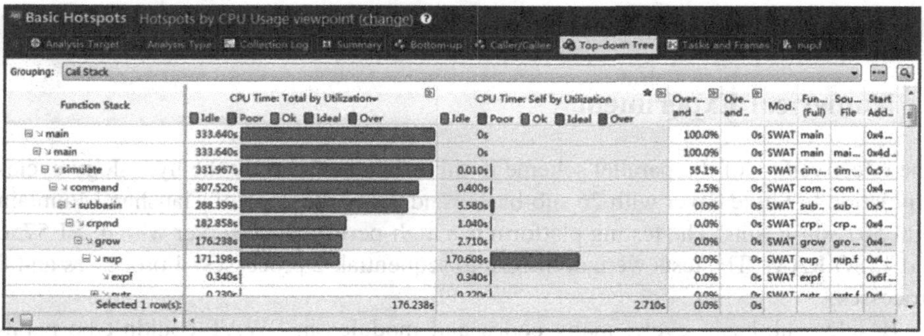

Fig. 8. The performance analysis by VTune

Amax1 and amin1 are the library functions in Fortran, whose function was sorting the array and stored. Sorting is always the most time-consuming algorithm, and there are many fast-sorting algorithms now. Omptl is an efficient multi-threading software pack, which could achieve fast-sorting.

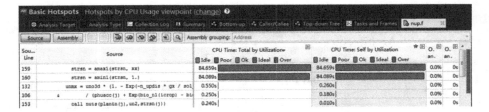

Fig. 9. The performance analysis by VTune

Omptl is a high performance multi-threading library by the use of OpenMP, developed by Université de Genève. Now it is integrated into CVMLCPP, but the omptl itself is still supported. Omptl supports multi-threading version for searching, sorting, segmentation, maximizing, minimizing, substitution and many other operations based on OpenMP.

Because the omptl only supported C++, the SWAT was written in fortran, then the hybrid programming of C++ and fortran is needed to apply omptl in SWAT. By omptl, the time cost in amax1 and amin1 function was shown in Fig. 10, from which we can see the time consumed by these two functions declined 40% in two threads.

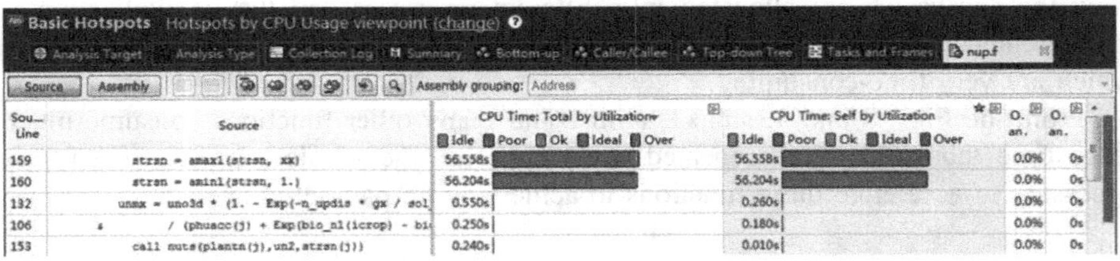

Fig. 10. The optimized performance analysis by Vtune

6   Numerical Experiment

The effectiveness of the parallel scheme in this study is tested by the hydrology cycles simulation in Shule River with 26 sub-basins and the north slope of Tianshan Mountain with 507 sub-basins. The testing platform is a high-performance server with 4 * E5750 and 128G RAM. The tests were divided into sequential, 2 processes, 4 processes and 8 processes.

Besides sub-basin cycle, many codes and modules in SWAT couldn't be parallelized. So the only proportion of the sub-basin cycle would determine the parallel efficiency. The calculation time of sub-basin section in the two rivers is shown in Fig. 11, which shows that computing efficiency of these two hydrology cycles simulations are accelerated by parallel computing. The speedup of Shule River and the north slope of Tianshan Mountain was about 4 and 5 with 8 processes. Because of the larger computation amount, the calculation on the north slope of Tianshan Mountain is more efficient than the Shule River.

From the Fig. 12, because the total running time includes the reading of input data, writing output data to the disk, confluence and the reduction of output data, many of which are sequential. Then the parallel efficiency is not as high as ideal. In Shule River, 8 processes even slower than 4 processes. For the reason that less sub-basins computing in Shule river, the computation proportion of parallelizable in this river is relatively low. While in the case of the north slope of Tianshan Mountain, although the input, output and the reduction time are more than Shule River, the number of sub-basin is much more than the Shule River. So the speedup is 3 in 8 processes. This shows the computation proportion of the sub-basin cycle determines the parallel efficiency and the parallelization scheme is more suitable for large scale simulations.

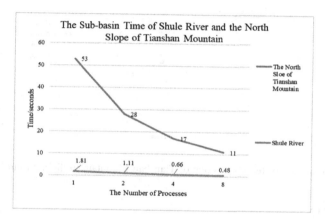

Fig. 11. The sub-basin time of Shule River and the north slope of Tianshan Mountain

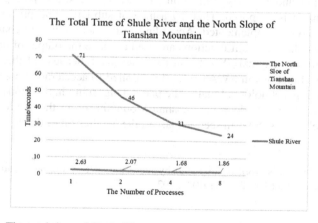

Fig. 12. The total time of Shule River and the north slope of Tianshan Mountain

From Fig. 13, in the MPI+OpenMP hybrid parallelization model, with the increasing of processes and threads, the total computation time is declining continuously. Although the declining range is not large, because of the applying of multithreading is only on the sorting functions, and the proportion of these functions in SWAT is a constant. Then with the increasing of computation amount, the total performance of MPI+OpenMP will be better than the MPI only version.

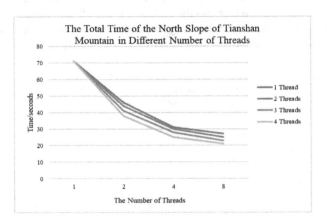

Fig. 13. The total time of the north slope of Tianshan Mountain in different number of threads

7 Summary

In this study, the SWAT model is analyzed from the structure of model and program. From the hotspot and memory utilization by VTune, the strategy of parallelization based on sub-basin is proposed. Then by a map of sub-basin and process, the parallelization of SWAT is implemented. According to the definition and characteristic of different outputs, the reduction functions are used to make the output of parallelization be identical with the original SWAT. On the other hand, because of there are several time-consuming functions in SWAT, omptl is applied to accelerate these functions by the multi-threading technology. Finally, the parallel algorithm in this study is applied in Shule River and the north slope of Tianshan Mountain. From the results we can see, with the parallelizable sub-basin sections larger, the parallelism of this algorithm can be better.

Acknowledgement. This work is supported by the National Key Research and Development Program of China (Grant No. 2017YFB0203102).

References

1. Wang, J., Gao, F., Vazquez-Poletti, J.L., Li, J.: Preface of high performance computing or advanced modeling and simulation of materials. Comput. Phys. Commun. **211** (2017)

2. Wang, J., Liu, C., Huang, Y.: Auto tuning for new energy dispatch problem: a case study. Future Gener. Comput. Syst. **54**, 501–506 (2016)
3. Li, S., Zhang, Y., Xiang, C., Shi, L.: Fast convolution operations on many-core architectures. In: Proceedings of the 17th International Conference on High Performance Computing and Communications (HPCC 2015), pp. 316–323. IEEE (2015)
4. Li, S., Hoefler, T., Snir, M.: NUMA-aware shared-memory collective communication for MPI. In: Proceedings of the 22nd International Symposium on High-Performance Parallel and Distributed Computing (HPDC 2013), pp. 85–96. ACM (2013)
5. Li, S., Hu, C., Zhang, J., Zhang, Y.: Automatic tuning of sparse matrix-vector multiplication on multicore clusters. Sci. China Inf. Sci. **58**(9), 1–14 (2015)
6. Li, S., Hoefler, T., Chungjin, H., Snir, M.: Improved MPI collectives for MPI processes in shared address spaces. Cluster Comput. **17**(4), 1139–1155 (2014)
7. Li, S., Hu, J., Cheng, X., Zhao, C.: Asynchronous work stealing on distributed memory systems. In: Proceedings of the 21st Euromicro International Conference on Parallel, Distributed and Network-Based Processing (PDP 2013), pp. 198–202. IEEE (2013)
8. Zhang, Y., et al.: Parallel processing systems for big data: a survey. Proc. IEEE **104**(11), 2114–2136 (2016)
9. Apostolopoulos, T.K., Georgakakos, K.P.: Parallel computation for streamflow prediction with distributed hydrologic models. J. Hydrol. **197**(1–4), 1–24 (1997)
10. Singh, V.P., Woolhiser, D.A.: Mathematical modeling of watershed hydrology. J. Hydrol. Eng. **7**(4), 270–292 (2002)
11. Rodell, M., Houser, P.R., Jambor, U., et al.: The global land data assimilation system. Bull. Am. Meteorol. Soc. **85**(3), 381–394 (2004)
12. Cui, J., Li, C., Sun, G., et al.: Linkage of MIKE SHE to Wetland-DNDC for carbon budgeting and anaerobic biogeochemistry simulation. Biogeochemistry **72**(2), 147–167 (2005)
13. Vivoni, E.R., Ivanov, V.Y., Bras, R.L., et al.: On the effects of triangulated terrain resolution on distributed hydrologic model response. Hydrol. Process. **19**(11), 2101–2122 (2005)
14. Kollet, S.J., Maxwell, R.M.: Integrated surface–groundwater flow modeling: A free-surface overland flow boundary condition in a parallel groundwater flow model. Adv. Water Resour. **29**(7), 945–958 (2006)
15. Yalew, S.G., Griensven, A.V.: Parallel computing of a large scale spatially distributed model using the Soil and Water Assessment Tool (SWAT). In: International Environmental Modelling and Software Society (iEMSs), 2010 International Congress on Environmental Modelling and Software, Modelling for Environment's Sake, Fifth Biennial Meeting, Ottawa, Canada, July 2010
16. Vivoni, E.R., Mascaro, G.: Real-world hydrologic assessment of a fully-distributed hydrological model in a parallel computing environment. J. Hydrol. **409**, 483–496 (2011)
17. Li, T., Wang, G., Chen, J., et al.: Dynamic parallelization of hydrological model simulations. Environ. Model Softw. **26**(12), 1736–1746 (2011)

Research on Shared Resource Contention of Cloud Data Center

Jingyuan Hu[1(✉)] and Jianjiang Li[2]

[1] Virtualization Laboratory, School of Information Science and Technology,
Peking University, Beijing 100871, China
hujingyuan0303@gmail.com
[2] Department of Computer Science and Technology, School of Computer
and Communication Engineering, University of Science and Technology of Beijing,
Beijing 100083, China

Abstract. In the process of cloud computing development and popularization, virtualization provides a viable solution to solve the problem of energy consumption and resource utilization. Meanwhile, Virtualization leads to multiple virtual machines competing for shared resources. This paper summarizes the shared resources contention caused by multiple co-tenant virtual machines in cloud data centers. We expound and analyze the main aspects of resource contention, and describe the key technologies to solve this problem. We focus on two main resources: memory and cache. At the end of this paper, the development trend of virtualization is also discussed.

Keywords: Cloud computing · Data center applications ·
Virtualization · Resource contention

1 Introduction

Compared with conventional data centers, cloud data centers have effectively improved information and resource sharing capability, as well as computation and storage capacity. Data security has also been highly improved. Meanwhile, cloud data centers face challenges such as huge power source consumption and low utilization of computational resources.

Virtualization is a viable solution for cloud data centers to solve these problems. System virtualization provides an abstract layer between hardware and the operation system, which is called a virtual machine monitor (VMM) or hypervisor. It allows multiple guest operation systems to run on a single physical machine. These guest systems are encapsulated in different virtual machines (VM), managed by the VMM. Virtualization can improve hardware resources utilization of a single machine and save energy for a data center. Besides, it has good resource and performance isolation. Using VM migration technology, we can transport VMs between different servers without suspension. Virtualization has become the core technology of resource management in cloud data centers.

© Springer Nature Singapore Pte Ltd. 2019
C. Hu et al. (Eds.): HPCMS 2018/HiDEC 2018, CCIS 913, pp. 186–197, 2019.
https://doi.org/10.1007/978-981-32-9987-0_16

Virtualization also faces great challenges. In the shared resource environment in a cloud data center, VMs often interfere with each other when the number of VMs in a server exceeds a certain limit. This interference is mostly caused by shared resource contention on a single server, which leads to performance degradation of each VM. The main resources of contention include CPU, memory, cache, Network I/O, and Disk I/O.

In this paper, we firstly describe the problem of VM interference. We then analyze and survey existing work of resource contention, focusing on two main shared resources: memory and cache. Finally we give our brief perspective for cloud data centers. The rest of paper is organized as follows. In Sect. 2, we outline several hardware resources that cause VM interference. We present current solutions for shared memory and cache in Sect. 3. The final section concludes the study and presents further research work.

2   Interference in Cloud Data Center

2.1   Characteristic of Application in Cloud Data Center

After analyzing several realistic cloud data center workloads, we find that data center applications show the following characteristics:

- Most users' operations are: search, add, delete, index
- Require for short respond time while having large amount of data interaction
- Require high data reliability
- Multiple clients can demand services simultaneously
- Many applications with short execution time and uncertain running frequency

According to these characteristics, applications in cloud data centers can be classified into two main categories: data-intensive applications and compute-intensive applications.

- Data-intensive applications: A data-intensive application contains a large number of data analysis tasks and can be distributed in different servers in a cluster. Most data intensive applications also have a data flow. Its bottleneck usually appears in data I/O.
- Compute-intensive applications: A compute-intensive application demonstrates high utilization of CPU and memory for scientific computation and logic decision. Compute-intensive applications span across high performance computing, scientific grid computing, and super computing.

2.2   Analysis of Shared Resource Contention

When multiple VMs run on the same server, they share hardware resources such as CPU and memory. Shared resource contention happens when the total demand of certain resource used by all VMs goes beyond the amount that the server can provide. The VMM then uses its default resource allocation policy to re-allocate this resource, and tries to satisfy all VMs. This can lead to VM performance degradation for each of them. After analyzing applications in cloud data centers, we find that memory and cache are the most important resources susceptible to resource contention. We also list other shared resources and analyze the reason of contention.

Memory. Traditional servers used by cloud data centers are chip multiprocessors (CMPs). Memory is one of the most important shared resource which affects all system performance. Three parameters that affect memory performance are: size, latency and bandwidth. If a VM does not receive enough memory from the host, it will lose performance due to the swap process. When multiple processors access memory, memory requests are delivered to the memory controller and put into an FIFO queue. Requests waiting in queue bring additional delay and cause memory latency. In a multi-VM environment, memory bandwidth has become an important performance factor for applications [1]. A cloud data center creates a large number of VMs and is very sensitive to latency, so memory contention occurs frequently and needs to be mitigated.

Cache. Cache is an important resource between CPU and memory. The last level cache (LLC) is often shared by multiple CPU. Although the size of the LLC can be only a dozen of mega-bytes, its load and store speed matches the CPU better than the DRAM. Using cache can efficiently decrease memory latency and improve CPU performance when dealing with computation of big data. Because of the limitation of size, cache can suffer a high cache miss rate when multiple processes or VMs running on the same server.

Other Shared Resources. Big data applications generate a lot of disk accesses within a short period of time. They continuously read/write data from disk. Due to the large speed gap between CPU and disk, disk I/O becomes a bottleneck in such cases. Applications in different VMs share disk I/O bandwidth and their I/O requests are managed by the VMM using a default FIFO queue.

More and more network I/O intensive applications are deployed in cloud data centers, such as online learning, video/audio web-site and online games. In cloud service, computation node or resources can be settled in different physical locations. They need good Internet service to communicate with each other and guarantee QoS. In a physical server, VMs share the network interface card (NIC) and contend for network bandwidth. A single VM cannot hold alone the NIC and co-run VMs have to share. Adding new VMs to a physical server makes the partitioning of NIC bandwidth even more difficult.

Both disk I/O and network I/O are managed by the VMM. A possible solution for reducing the shared source contention is to develop new mechanism and policy in the VMM for dealing with network/disk requests.

In a virtual execution environment, the way of pining CPU cores affects VM performance. When running multiple VMs on the same server, the CPU core used by a VM, which is called the VCPU, has to be mapped from the physical CPU core (called PCPU). When we activate Hyper-Threading technology in

BIOS, one core can be pinned by two VCPUs. Tang et al. find that in the multi-VM environment, the best CPU pinning method is different than the solo-VM environment [2].

For conclusion, in this section we present the main shared resources that cause VM interference. Sometimes more than one resource will be in contention. When we detect VM performance degradation, firstly we need to indicate the bottleneck resources, and then we use better resource management mechanism to improve performance.

3   Main Contention Causes and Solutions

Virtualization has been used to solve large energy consumption and low resource utilization problem, but it also causes performance problem. After analyze in Sect. 2, the main problem is to solve shared memory and cache contention.

3.1   Memory Performance

3.1.1   Memory Management in Virtualization Environments

Operation system uses a page table to manage physical memory. In virtualization environments, the VMM manages memory allocation and address translation of all VMs. Memory virtualization allows multiple VMs to share physical (machine) memory, which needs dynamic memory allocation and periodically memory reclamation. When memory using by guest VM exceeds the amount that host has offered, guest OS will trigger the swap mechanism which causes a great performance overhead.

The two main technologies to realize dynamic memory allocation are: the balloon driver technology and the memory hot-plug. Balloon driver is a VM process which adjusts VM memory by inflating and deflating the balloon module in the VM. For better understanding, we use Fig. 1 to present a inflate scenario of ballooning. Memory hot-plug changes the memory state into available/unavailable to increase/decrease amount of memory. In a memory hot-add case, the firmware notifies the OS when a physical DIMM is plugged. The OS kernel initializes all memory in the DIMM as free pages and makes it available for users.

We compare these two techniques in Table 1.

3.1.2   Solutions to Determine Memory Size

In the previous section, we discuss technologies using in memory management in virtualization environments. If we can predict the memory demand by applications and guarantee all VMs to have enough memory, we can easily reduce shared memory contention. The common method to determine the size of memory demand is to use a sampling method to calculate the working set size (WSS) of an application in a time interval. The most efficient way to estimate WSS is constructing Miss Ratio Curve (MRC), which indicates the relationship between

Table 1. Comparison of solutions of virtual memory management.

Solutions	Advantages	Disadvantages
Memory Hot-plug	1. Dynamic allocation	1. Performance overhead in section-level memory control
	2. Contiguous and large memory space added/removed; do not cause memory fragmentation	2. Difficult to implement
Balloon driver	1. Dynamic allocation	1. The time and size of allocation is unknown
	2. Allocation size can be set	2. Memory fragmentation

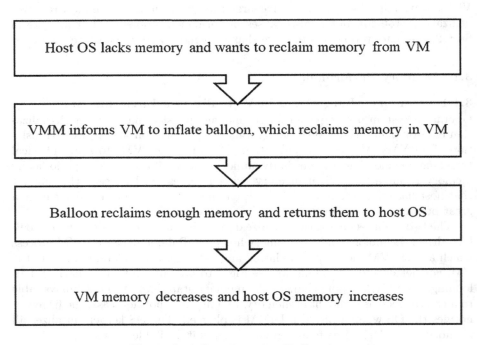

Fig. 1. An inflate scenario of ballooning.

VM performance and memory allocation. Zhao et al. [3] propose a method of chasing WSS using dynamic hot set and intermittent memory tracking in order to reduce the sampling overhead. Based on this work, Wang et al. [4] propose a memory balancer system to realize dynamic memory management (MEB). It contains a predictor and a balancer. Figure 2 presents a sketch of the whole system. The functions of the system are as follows:

1. Use hardware tools to monitor an applications phase change and determine whether to sample
2. Use hot set to filter frequently accessed pages and monitor the rest
3. Based on LRU list and reuse distance, construct the miss ratio curve
4. Calculate the WSS of each VM and store them in the predictor
5. Allocate memory based on the result of the predictor

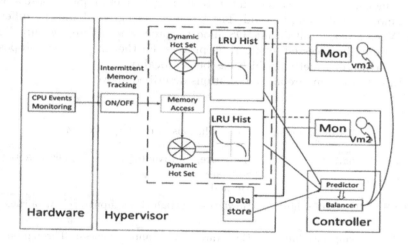

Fig. 2. The structure of MEB system.

3.1.3 Solutions to Memory Latency

In a CMP system, multiple processors share memory that can lead to memory contention. When different processors access memory, their memory requests are sent to the memory controller (MC). Most of them are waiting to be handled in order and cause memory latency. Memory latency often depends on whether a memory request can hit rapidly on the row-buffers of DRAM. It also depends on the scheduling policy. In a memory request scheduling policy, we consider throughput and fairness as two parameters of evaluation.

There are many researches in reducing memory latency. In early period, people focused on hardware methods which modify the scheduling algorithm in the MC. Traditional MC in DRAM uses a First Ready First Come First Serve (FR-FCSD) algorithm. It prioritizes row buffer hit requests and then the old (first come) requests waiting in queue. The advantage is high throughput, but it lacks of fairness. In [5], Mutlu et al. give a fair policy: Stall-Time Fair Memory Access Scheduling (STFM). They propose a factor S equal to the latency of solo run divided by the latency of multi-process. The MC will follow FR-FCSD if the fairness is no greater than a threshold α. Otherwise, the MC will prioritize the requests from the thread with the highest slowdown. Further in [6], Multu et al. design a policy which gives attention to both throughput and fairness:

Parallelism-Aware Batch Scheduling (PAR-BS). They use different policies for different class of processes. These are all static scheduling policies. Kim et al. in [7] propose a dynamic policy: they divide processes into bandwidth sensitive and latency sensitive. At each time interval, the system checks the number of processes of the two types in the MC, and handles latency sensitive processes with priority. For bandwidth-sensitive processes, they design a special policy.

Besides hardware solutions, page coloring technology is a software method to optimize memory system. Based on this technology, Liu et al. [8] propose a bank level memory partitioning method. The key idea is to group banks by different colors. When a page fault occurs, OS allocates process to different group. These banks can only be accessed by a certain process. Further in [9] , they propose a channel partitioning method which has better locality.

In Table 2, we compare all the solutions described above.

Table 2. Comparison of solutions of memory latency.

Solutions	Characteristics	Hardware/ Software Method	Advantages	Disadvantages
FR-FCFS	Row buffer hit priority	Hardware	High throughput	Low fairness
STFM	Using speedup to ensure fairness	Hardware	Guarantee fairness; low latency	Throughput loss
PAR-BS	Using sampling to classify process; package process to execute together	Hardware	Guarantee both throughput and fairness	
Page coloring	Tagging bits in physical address as color bits; process access fix part of memory	Software	First software method; low overhead	
BMP	Tagging BANK	Software	Little bank visit conflict; using bank parallelism	Bank using limitation
Channel level partitioning	Tagging channel	Software	Good locality	

3.1.4   Solutions to Memory Bandwidth Contention

In multi-process/VM environments, each process/application occupies certain memory bandwidth. To reduce the bandwidth contention, a common method is to predict bandwidth usage for each application, and match the high-consuming applications with the low ones in order to meet the peak bandwidth of a server. A study in [10] uses bus transactions rate (BTR) as a key factor of evaluating bandwidth consuming. They first calculate available BTR for each CPU. Then they choose a process with BTR adapted from the waiting queue to match with CPU. This strategy keeps bandwidth utilization always in peak level and reduces bandwidth competition. Because of different phases of an application, using only BTR to predict bandwidth utilization is not precise. Eklov [11] design a bandit application and co-run it with the target application to detect its phases and corresponding bandwidth. Xu et al. [12] find that a system cannot always reach peak bandwidth because of the contention. They focus on maintaining applications performance rather than high utilization of system bandwidth.

3.2   Analysis of Cache Performance

3.2.1   Solutions Based on Replacement Policy

To improve cache performance, solutions in early days are mostly based on hardware and focused on cache replacement policy. Traditional cache replacement algorithm considers data access frequency or time stamp for replacement. Least Recently Used (LRU) policy is the basic replacement policy for cache. In [13], Qureshi et al. propose a dynamic insertion policy (DIP), which uses different cache miss rate to guide the replacement. In [14], Jaleel et al. propose a method in a multi-core system which searches for recent cache activities, predicts future cache activities and gives a better replacement policy. They classify cache lines into re-reference intervals for replacement decision.

Table 3 presents a comparison of these replacement policies.

3.2.2   Solutions Based on Cache Prediction

Cache prediction can help cache partitioning. Miss ratio curve (MRC) is used to present a relationship between miss ratio and cache size. It presents precise cache demand of an application and widely used in cache prediction. There are two basic methods in cache miss ratio curve prediction: reuse distance (RD) based and reuse time (RT) based.

The original MRC is calculated based on the reuse distance distribution tracked with an LRU queue. This method needs to monitor every memory access and update the LRU list for these accesses. LRU list maintenance and LRU position tracking lead to significant performance overhead. Improvement methods such as Scale Tree algorithm [15], Footprint algorithm [16], and Counter Stacks [17], etc., have a limitation which requires the full memory access trace of an application to calculate its MRC. This brings great overhead in tracing the memory accesses. In order to reduce the overhead, some studies propose to sample memory access. SHARDS [18] is a typical model using sampling to calculate MRC. It considers a sampling rate, using a threshold divided by the cache size. The threshold is a variable depending on the number of accesses sampled and sampling rate change simultaneously.

Table 3. Comparison of cache replacement policy.

Solutions	Key ideas	Advantages	Disadvantages
Traditional LRU replacement	Replace the least recently used data out of cache	Easy to realize, with low overhead; high performance for good locality applications	Bad performance in cache contention: performance degradation without fairness guarantee
DIP	Analyze dynamically cache miss variation and propose replacement policy with smallest miss ratio	Cache miss ratio; guarantee fairness	Applications with different cache: phases and high cache miss: ratio
Jaleel's replacement	Use recent cache activities to predict further activity; replacement based on prediction	Propose better replacement policy related to cache activity	

For RT-based method, Hu et al. [19] propose an average eviction time (AET) method to calculate MRC. They sample reuse time distribution and infer miss ratio curve based on the average eviction time of any given cache size. Compared with other methods, this method use less space to keep track of different data structures. It only saves the number of accesses to track a data's reuse. We note the RT distribution **rtd**, **rtd[i]** presents the number of occurrences of a reuse time equal to **i**. For a given memory size **c**, AET calculates the average time **AET(c)** of an element moving from the top of LRU list to the position **c**. When the next access of this element arrives and if its reuse time is greater than **AET(c)**, it will incur a miss. Otherwise it will be a hit. The equation of calculating miss ratio for a cache size **c** is presented below:

$$MissRatio(c) = \frac{\sum_{k=AET(c)+1}^{+\infty} rtd[k]}{\sum_{k=0}^{+\infty} rtd[k]}$$

3.2.3 Solutions Based on Cache Partitioning

Page coloring technology used in memory can also be used in cache. In [20], Sherwood et al. use page coloring to reduce the cache contention and cache misses. This is a static partitioning approach. In further research, Lin et al. [21] propose page re-coloring method, dynamically dividing cache. They choose several factors to evaluate cache, and use speedup after partitioning to evaluate fairness. In [22], Suh et al. use hardware counters to guide cache partitioning and increase total cache hits. In [23], Moreto et al. propose a dynamic cache partitioning policy to allocate more cache to the slowest running process.

In [24], Lee et al. propose a cloud-cache model, which can divide both shared and non-shared cache to ensure QoS.

3.3 Solutions on Considering Two or More Shared Resources

Memory and cache have a strong relationship. When the number of cache misses increase, these missed requests are transported to main memory, which will cause memory contention. So many researchers orchestrate both resources to develop a more accurate and efficient prediction or management model.

In [1], Zhao et al. analyze the usage of memory and cache and build a quantity model to predict the usage of both resources. They takes a machine learning approach to study thousands of application groups and learn a staged function between memory and cache size. It can accurately predict the performance of memory and cache in multi-application environments. In the Paragon [25] model, Delimitrou et al. use a movie recommendation algorithm to estimate the performance of an application when running on different servers. Each application has a point on each type of server. Then it uses a greedy algorithm to distribute applications to the most adapted server. The authors then propose in Quasar model which can not only guarantee performance, but also keep a high utilization of shared resources on servers [26]. Normal resource management is based on high level parameters such as CPU utilization, memory utilization, etc. In [27], Wang et al. propose a system using hardware counters to guide resource allocation. They use the last level cache miss rate, memory bandwidth usage and memory latency to evaluate performance. The key idea is to avoid resource contention. They also use VM mitigation to avoid resource contention. Table 4 presents a comparison of these solutions.

Table 4. Comparison of multi-resources models.

Solutions	Key ideas	Target
Paragon	Using file recommendation algo. to get performance rapidly; using greed algo. to match application with server	Fast distribution of a large number of applications to different servers
Quasar	Based on paragon plus high resource utilization of servers	Guarantee both VM performance and server resource utilization
A-DRM	Avoid resource contention using hardware counters; using VM mitigation	Solve problem of resource management with traditional high level parameters

4   Conclusion and Perspective

In this paper, we have surveyed related research in shared resource contention in cloud data centers. We analyze the reason of shared resource contention in virtualization environments and focus on the resources that can be interfered. For the most important two resources: memory and cache, we analyze the key factors and compare existing solutions to mitigate interferencd and guarantee the quality of service. The further research in this field can be developed as follows:

1. Searching for appropriate metrics to represent applications performance. Researchers usually use IPC to evaluate performance. Alamldeen et al. [28] point out that in multi-application environment or for parallel programs, IPC is not accurate. Execution time or throughput is suggested as a performance metric in cloud data centers.
2. If multi-resources are concurrent in contention, how to build a prediction model in cloud data centers to determine the performance degradation is a problem to solve. Most current researches are most focused on a single resource and a few studies extend to two resources (ex, memory and cache [1]).
3. One biggest concern of cloud data center is the energy consumption and resource utilization. It is still worthy to develop better resource management mechanism to achieve these goals.

To conclude, virtualization brings chances and challenges for cloud data centers. Shared resource contention is important to data center and need continuous attention.

References

1. Zhao, J., Cui, H., Feng, X., et al.: An empirical model for prediction cross-core performance interference on multicore processors. ACM (2013)
2. Linjia, T., Mars, J., Vachharajani, N., et al.: The impact of memory subsystem resource sharing on datacenter applications. ACM (2011)
3. Zhao, W., Jin, X., Wang, Z., et al.: Low cost working set size tracking. USENIX (2011)
4. Wang, Z., Wang, X., Hou, F., et al.: Dynamic memory balancing for virtualization. ACM Trans. Architect. Code Optim. **13**(1), 2 (2016)
5. Mutlu, O., Moscibroda, T.: Stall-time fair memory access scheduling for chip multiprocessors. IEEE (2007)
6. Mutlu, O., Moscibroda, T.: Parallelism-aware batch scheduling: enhancing both performance and fairness of shared dram systems. ACM (2008)
7. Kim, Y., Papamichael, M., Mutlu, O., Harchol-Balter, M.: Thread cluster memory scheduling: exploiting differences in memory access behavior. IEEE (2010)
8. Liu, L., Cui, Z., Xing, M., et al.: A software memory partition approach for eliminating bank-level interference in multicore systems. ACM (2012)

9. Liu, L., Cui, Z., Li, Y., et al.: BPM/BPM+: software-based dynamic memory partitioning mechanisms for migrating DRAM bank-channel level interferences in multi core system, vol. 11. ACM (2014)
10. Antonopoulos, C.D., Nikolopoulos, D.S., Papatheodorou, T.S.: Scheduling algorithms with bus bandwidth considerations for SMPs. (2003)
11. Eklov, D., Nkioleris, N., Black-Schaffer, D., Hagersten, E.: Bandwidth Bandit: quantitative characterization of memory contention. IEEE (2013)
12. Xu, D., Wu, C., Yew, P.C.: On mitigation memory bandwidth contention through bandwidth-aware scheduling. ACM (2010)
13. Qureshi, M.K., Jaleel, A., Patt, Y.N., et al.: Adaptive insertion policies for high performance caching. ACM (2007)
14. Jaleel, A., Theobald, K.B., Steely Jr., S.C., et al.: High performance cache replacement using re-reference interval prediction (RRIP). ACM (2010)
15. Ding, C., Zhong, Y.: Predicting whole-program locality through reuse distance analysis, pp. 245–257. ACM (2003)
16. Xiang, X., Bao, B., Chen, D., et al.: Linear-time modeling of program working set in shared cache. ACM (2011)
17. Wires, J., Ingram, S., Drudi, Z., et al.: Characterizing storage workloads with counter stacks. USENIX (2014)
18. Waldspurger, C.A., Park, N., Garthwaite, A., et al.: Efficient MRC construction with SHARDS. USENIX (2015)
19. Hu, X., Wang, X., Zhou, L., et al.: Kinetic modeling of data eviction in cache. USENIX (2016)
20. Sherwood, T., Calder, B., Emer, J.: Reducing cache miss using hardware and software page placement. ACM (1999)
21. Lin, J., Lu, Q., Ding, X., et al.: Gaining insights into multicore cache partitioning: bridging the gap between simulation and real systems. IEEE (2008)
22. Suh, G.E., Devadas, S., Rudolph, L.: A new memory monitoring scheme for memory-aware scheduling and partitioning. IEEE (2002)
23. Moreto, M., J. Cazorla, F., Sakellariou, R., Valero, M.: Load balancing using dynamic cache allocation. ACM (2010)
24. Lee, H., Cho, S., R.Childers, B.: Cloudcache: expanding and shrinking private caches. IEEE (2011)
25. Delimitrou, C., Kozyrakis, C.: Paragon: QoS-aware scheduling for hetergeneous datacenters. ACM (2013)
26. Delimitrou, C., Kozyrakis, C.: Quasar: resource-efficient and QoS-aware cluster management. ACM (2014)
27. Wang, H., Isci, C., Subramanian, L., et al.: A-DRM: architecture-aware distributed resource management of virtualized clusters. ACM (2015)
28. Alameledeen, A.R., Wood, D.A.: IPC considered harmful for multiprocessor workloads. IEEE Micro 26(1), 8–17 (2006)

A Sequence Anomaly Detection Approach Based on Isolation Forest Algorithm for Time-Series

Yu Weng and Lei Liu[✉]

College of Information Engineering, Minzu University of China,
Beijing 100081, China
aishangzoulu@gmail.com

Abstract. Anomalous behavior detection in many applications is becoming more and more important, especially for computer security and sensor networks domains, in which data are typical time-series. However, the sequence anomaly detection for time-series data exists lots of problems, for example, there is no anomalous point in time series sequence but the whole sequence may be anomalous. In this paper, we use the sliding window framework to split time-series into sequences and taking into account the time-series statistical features of the sequence, proposing a novel sequence anomaly detection algorithm based on iForest, namely iForestFS. The experimental results are performed on three real-world data sets derived from UCI repository demonstrate that the proposed algorithm can effectively detect anomalous sequence of time-series data.

Keywords: Sequence anomaly detection · Time-Series · Isolation forest · Sliding window

1 Introduction

Time series data is an important high-dimensional data type, which was a sequence composed of sampling values of a certain physical quantity of objective objects at different time points arranged in chronological order and was widely used in economic management and engineering fields. Time-series data itself has the features of high-dimension, complexity, dynamic, high-noise and the feature of easy to achieve large-scale. As a result, time series data mining is one of the ten challenging problems in data mining research area [1].

According to the type of anomaly, it can be divided into point anomalies, the contextual sequence anomalies and collection of anomalies. According to the application domains, it can be divided into intrusion detection, fraud detection, medical anomaly detection and sensor network detection. According to the methods of detection [2], it can be classified into classification based, neural network based, Bayesian network based, support vector machine based, rule based, distance of nearest neighbors based, clustering based and probability statistics based.

© Springer Nature Singapore Pte Ltd. 2019
C. Hu et al. (Eds.): HPCMS 2018/HiDEC 2018, CCIS 913, pp. 198–207, 2019.
https://doi.org/10.1007/978-981-32-9987-0_17

In the analysis of time series data, it is of great expectation to find out how these time series data are related at different time periods. This relationship is generally manifested as frequent patterns of change in time series and patterns of infinitesimal changes. This rare pattern of change is called anomalous pattern. It is easy to find some problems when detecting this kind of abnormal pattern.

Problem 1: There is no anomalous point in time series sequence, but the whole sequence is anomalous. For example, in the behavior sequence of a user's access to a website, and user is constantly trying to log in with different password, the operations of the user sequence are normal at each time point, but in a certain period, the user consistently tried to log in and failed [2]. This may be a malicious user trying to crack the password, which means that the sequence is anomalous.

Problem 2: Time series data have the features of fast speed, high real-time performance, and large scale and so on. The running speed of traditional anomaly detection algorithm can't reach the near real time standard in the model training, it is easy to have the outlier "flow past" and not be detected.

Other problems: Time series data is in large-scale and data labeling work is costly.

The main contributions of this paper are as follows: Firstly, we propose a sequence anomaly detection algorithm for time-series data. Secondly, the experiment demonstrates that the proposed algorithm is available and effective.

The next part of this article is organized as follows: Sect. 2 describes related work. In Sect. 3, the method proposed in this paper is gradually demonstrated. First, comparing the differences between statistical and machine learning methods on anomaly detection. Secondly, the sequence anomaly detection algorithm iForestFS is introduced and analyzed. In Sect. 4, we first demonstrate the experimental data sets and then analyze the experimental results to validate our proposed method. Finally, the conclusions and future research directions are provided.

2 Related Works

In 2009, Chandola et al. published "anomaly detection: A survey" [3] on ACM CSUR. In the paper, an overview of structured and comprehensive anomaly detection research is sought. Based on the basic approach taken by each technology, they classify the existing technology into different categories. For each category, a fundamental anomaly detection method is provided, and then they show the differences between other methods in this category and the fundamental method. In 2012, Chandola et al. further analyzed the detection of discrete sequence data anomalies and published a survey about the anomaly detection of discrete sequence data in the IEEE Transactions on Knowledge and Data Engineering named "Anomaly detection for discrete sequences: A survey" [2]. They classify the existing research into three different categories based on the statement of the problem that it is trying to solve. These questions are structured as follows: (1) to identify abnormal sequences in normal sequence databases; (2) to identify subsequences within an unusually long sequence; and (3) to identify patterns in frequently abnormal sequences. And showed how the concepts of these issues differ from one another, discussing their relevance in different application areas.

Some researchers use time series classification technology for time series anomaly detection. Unlike algorithms commonly used in time series analysis, time series classification takes the entire time series as input, the purpose of which is to assign a discrete label to the sequence. It is more difficult than the general classification problem, mainly because of the unequal length of the time series data to be classified, which makes the general classification algorithm cannot be directly applied. Even for the same time series, the general classification algorithm is still not suitable for direct application because the values of different sequences in the same location cannot generally be directly compared. In order to solve these difficulties, there are usually two ways: first, to define the appropriate distance measure (the most commonly used distance measure is the DTW distance) so that similar sequences in this measure have the same classification label, and such methods are domain-independent. Second, we first model the time series (using the dependency of the data in the sequence to establish the model), then use the model parameters to construct the equidistant vectors to represent each sequence, and finally train and classify them by the general classification algorithm, and such methods belong to domain-related methods. In [4], methods above are analyzed, and two kinds of methods which are domain-independent and domain-related are compared on different synthetic data sets and actual data sets respectively. The results show that when the training data is less, the domain-related algorithms are more appropriate; on the other hand, domain-independent algorithms are relatively less affected by noise. Some researchers also use other machine learning algorithms. In 2003, Zhang Xiaoqiang used a hierarchical hidden Markov model for anomaly detection [5].

Time-series data are large scale and it is very difficult to label the data manually. Some researchers have proposed some unsupervised anomaly detection algorithms. In 2008, Liu et al. proposed an unsupervised outlier-based isolated forest algorithm "Isolation forest" [6]. Isolated forest is an Ensemble-based fast anomaly detection method with linear time complexity and high precision. It is a state-of-the-art algorithm that meets the requirements of big data processing. It belongs to Non-parametric and unsupervised methods. It is suitable for the anomaly detection of continuous-valued data, and the anomaly is defined as "easily isolated outlier" - a point that can be understood as a remote point from a sparsely populated and densified population. Statistically, the sparsely populated areas in the data space indicate that the probability of the data occurring in this area is low, so that the data falling within these areas can be considered abnormal. In 2012, they optimized the iForest algorithm for isolated forests [7], which takes advantage of subsampling to achieve lower linear time complexity and smaller memory requirements, and to effectively handle swamping and masking effects. Empirical assessment shows that iForest has better processing time on AUC than ORCA, SVR, LOF and random forest, and has good robustness. iForest also works well in high-dimensional problems with many irrelevant attributes and in the absence of anomalies in training samples.

Time series data have typical contextual features. Some researchers use statistical features and machine learning methods for anomaly detection. In 2014, Vallis proposed a novel sequence anomaly detection technique [8], which mainly used statistical learning to detect anomalies. The data used included the measurement of application and system operation log. In addition, the algorithm uses robust statistical measures, that is, median, median absolute deviation (MAD), and underlying segment approximation long-term trends to accurately detect anomalies. In 2015, Yahoo's Laptev used a variety of statistical features (trend, seasonal, spectral entropy, etc.) of time-series data and then clustered them into clusters C based on these features. After clustering, they use the deviation between the centroids to detect the inter-cluster anomalies, and the deviation of the centroid in the cluster and the time series i to detect intra-frame anomalies [9]. In the meantime, Yahoo has implemented an anomaly detection framework EGADS. Compared with other anomaly detection systems for different time series features of real-time and composite data, the EGADS framework improves accuracy and recall by 50%–60%.

In addition, the timing data has the features of large flow velocity, high dynamic, high dimensionality and complexity. Some researchers have studied how to improve the streaming data algorithm for anomaly detection of time series data and further improve the detection efficiency.

Time series data can be converted to symbolic representations, and such representations will potentially allow researchers to utilize algorithms from text processing. In 2003, Lin and Jessica proposed a time-series notation [10] that is suitable for the streaming data algorithm. This notation is unique. It allows dimensionality/numerosity reduction. It also allows to define the distance measure method of the representation, reducing the limits of distance measure method on the original sequence. The latter feature allows running some symbolic data mining algorithms while producing the same result as the algorithm that manipulates the original data. Finally, their notation representation method could transform real and valuable data into streams with minimal time and space overhead.

3   Design Overview

3.1   Statistics and Machine Learning Based Anomaly Detection

In the probability statistics based anomaly detection algorithms, the algorithm often takes into account the time sequence statistical features of the data (e.g. distribution, deviation, etc.). In some specific application domain, the anomaly is just judged based on the experience threshold (e.g. 3sigma threshold in Gauss distribution model) and the local fluctuation points are easily identified as abnormal points. However, in machine learning based clustering and other anomaly detection algorithms, the contextual statistical features (such as trend and period) of the time series data are not taken into consideration. It is easy to miss the contextual information and ignore the anomalous case where the sequence is abnormal but each point in it is normal. At the same time, the sequential data has the features of high dimensionality, complexity and high noise. Thus, it is very difficult to label the training data, it is more suitable to use unsupervised algorithm [2].

Liu et al. proposed a unique anomaly detection algorithm in 2008 - the Isolated Forest Algorithm [6] and improved this algorithm in 2012. Commonly, anomalous instances are those objects that their attributes values are very different from the normal instances and are easier to being divided than normal instances [7]. Later, Ding et al.

implemented an algorithm for anomaly detection of streaming data based on the isolated forest algorithm and the sliding window technique [12]. Sun et al. proposed an algorithm based on isolated forest user anomaly detection [13] and applied it in the enterprise environment with good performance.

iForest's detailed algorithms and assessments can be seen in [Liu et al. 2008], we only describe the subject here part of the iForest algorithm.

```
Algorithm 1: iForest(X, T, N)
Inputs: X - input dataset, T - number of trees, N -
subsampling size
Output: a set of iTrees
Step 1: Initialize Forest={ };
Step 2: set iTree  height h = ceiling(log2N);
Step 3: for i = 1 to T do
            X' ← sample(X,N);
            Forest←Forest∪ iTree(X', 0, h);
Step 4: return Forest;
```

An iForest consists of multiple isolation trees, namely iTree, which are created by choosing attributes and the values of attributes randomly. At each node in the isolation trees, the samples are divided into two parts based on the selected attributes and its values. Here, the attributes are selected randomly and the split value for this selected attribute is chosen randomly as well between the minimum value and maximum value of this selected attribute. Commonly, anomalous instances are those objects that their attributes values are very different from the normal instances and are easier to being divided than normal instances. In the process of isolation, they are also closer to the root and more easily divided than the normal instances. In order to alleviate the effects imported by the random characteristic in the process of building the isolation forest, we calculate the average depth of the instance in the forest which is composed multiple isolation trees and use the average depth as the anomalous score (calculate by formula (1)) of the instance. The lower score the instance has, the higher probability it an anomaly. In the above algorithm, the procedure of creating the iTree is a key step. The detail creating procedure of iTree algorithm can be seen in [6].

$$S(x, N) = 2^{-\frac{E(h(x))}{c(N)}}$$
$$E(h(x)) = \frac{1}{L}\sum_{i=1}^{L} h_i(x)$$

(1)

3.2 Sequence Anomaly Detection for Time-Series Data

This shows that the isolated forest algorithm has a very good performance in the field of anomaly detection. Based on isolation forest, we proposed a sequence anomaly detection algorithm named iForestFS (iForest For Sequence).

```
Algorithm 2: iForestFS (S, T, N, K)
Inputs: S - input sequence data, T- number of trees, N -
subsampling size, K- in sliding window size;
Output: a set of iTrees;
   Step 1: Split S into sub-sequences {S1, S2…Si…} with
sliding window size K, initialize X={};
   Step 2: Select a continuous feature from Si, calculate
statistical features (Table 1) for it, named Xi;
   Step 3: add Xi to X;
   Step 4: invoke iForest(X, T, N);
   Step 5: return Forest;
```

(1) At first, we divide time-series data S into subsequence Si according to the sliding window size K.

(2) For each Si, we extract time-series statistical features (see Table 1, including autocorrelation, nonlinearity, skewness, kurtosis, Hurst Index, etc.) as the Si's feature vector Xi, we only use four statistical features (mean, Variance, Skewness, Kurtosis) in this paper.

Table 1. Time-series features used by iForestFS

Feature name	Feature description
Periodicity (frequency)	Periodicity is very important for determining seasonality
Trend	If there is a long-term change in the average level, it exists
Seasonality	When the time series is affected by seasonal factors, such as one day a month in a year or in a week
Mean	The average value
Variance	Sequence volatility metric
Auto-correlation	Express long-range dependency
Skewness	Measurement of symmetry
Kurtosis	Measures if the data has reached a peak relative to the normal distribution
Hurst exponent	Long-term memory of time series
Lyapunov exponent	Measuring the divergence speed of the nearby trajectories

(3) Then we use {Xi} namely X as training samples, with two parameters-number of trees T, and subsampling size N, invoking iForest (X, T, N) algorithm and getting forest returned by iForest method.

(4) Finally, in the anomaly evaluation phase, we calculate the average depth of the instance in the forest which is composed multiple isolation trees and use the average depth as the anomalous score of the instance. The lower score the sequence instance has, the higher probability it an anomaly.

4   Experiment and Evaluation

We have conducted extensive experiments using the three real data sets of the UCI University Machine Learning Library to evaluate sequence anomaly detection algorithms based on iForest and statistical features. Because the iForest algorithm is an unsupervised method, the category attribute is not needed in the exception process. The label of the abnormal data is only used to evaluate the final anomaly detection performance.

Our experiment was run on a server equipped with Intel Xeon E5-2620 @2.40 GHz (2 processors), 64 GB RAM, and centos7 operating system. The algorithm described in Sect. 3 is programmed using the Java language on the INTELLIJ IDEA integrated development environment and uses the machine learning library WEKA to process and analyze the results of the experiments.

4.1   Datasets

Table 2 shows the details of the three datasets selected because they contain known data using the anomaly class as a basic fact and these datasets were used multiple times in the anomaly detection algorithm literature to evaluate algorithm performance [13, 14].

Table 2. Information of four datasets

Dataset name	M (#instances)	N (#attributes)	Anomaly threshold
Http	567498	22	0.4%
Smtp	95156	22	0.03%
Shuttle	49097	9	7.15%

The Http dataset and the Smtp dataset are two subsets of the KDD-CUP99 network intrusion data. The KDD-CUP99 data set contains 4,898,431 instances, each of which has 41 attributes (duration, service, srcBytes, dstBytes etc.) and a class label. In our experiment, we only selected the numerical attributes (22 in total). The Shuttle dataset contains 9 attributes. Approximately 80% of the data belongs to class 1 and we regard labeled 2, 3, 5, 6, 7 as the anomaly class. In each data set, the class label attribute is used only to evaluate the algorithm.

Because the iForest algorithm only processes numerical attributes, all nouns and boolean attributes are removed. The attributes selected in our experiments are continuous values.

4.2   Experiment Settings and Result Evaluation

After the data set is built, the primary task is to train the iForest-based anomaly detector algorithm iForestFS to perform the sequence anomaly detection in the sliding window frame. The iForestFS sequence anomaly detection method has several important parameters, namely the size of the sliding window and the scale of ensemble learning.

For the former, because the size of the sliding window is time-sensitive, there is no parameter setting method for the theoretical direction. In our experiment, as shown in Fig. 1, the sliding window value ranges from 4 to 256.

For the latter, the number of iTree in iForestFS and the number of samples_size used to build iTree are included. For the itree_num value, there is actually no theoretical direction for ensemble learning. Zhou et al. found that the path length generally converges well when itree_num = 100. So, in our experiment, we use itree_num = 100 and sample_size = 256 as defaults.

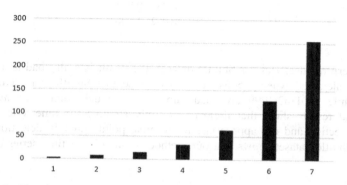

Fig. 1. The size of sliding window (y-axis) versus the i-th experiments (x-axis)

In anomaly detection domain, AUC (Area Under ROC) [6, 14] is commonly used to measure the overall performance of an anomaly detector, regardless of the threshold between true positive and true negative. Abnormal points are always considered positive during the abnormal process, and normal points are always detected as negative. The calculation formula is described as formula (2). n_a denotes the number of true outliers, n_n denotes the number of true normal points, and r_i denotes the rank of the i-th abnormality according to the anomaly score.

$$S = \sum_{i=1}^{n_a} r_i$$
$$AUC = \frac{S - \left(n_a^2 + n_a\right)/2}{n_a * n_n} \tag{2}$$

To evaluate the performance of our proposed iForestFS anomaly detection algorithm, we used AUC on four datasets. The test results can be seen in Table 3 and Fig. 2.

From the experimental results shown in Fig. 2 (the value of x axis is in log scale), we can easily find out when the size of sliding window increases, the value of AUC increases correspondingly. When the size of the sliding window increases to the desired value, for example 128 for the Http data set, iForestFS detection performance is stable and reliable, that is, there is no need to further increase the sliding window size. Because it increases processing time and memory size while there is no gain in

Table 3. AUC of different datasets for different sliding windows size

Sliding window size	Dataset		
	Http	Smtp	Shuttle
4	0.935	0.978	0.975
8	0.930	0.985	0.837
16	0.945	0.987	0.728
32	0.960	0.990	0.087
64	0.979	0.991	0.029
128	0.987	0.996	–
256	0.992	1.000	–

detection performance. But for Shuttle dataset, the result is really bad and the AUC cannot be calculated when $k > 64$. This is because that Shuttle consist of discrete samples while KDD-CUP99 are made up of contextual points. Meanwhile, the experimental results show that iForestFS is only suitable for time-series sequence anomaly detection and not appropriate for discrete point anomaly detection. Experiments on Shuttle dataset shows that our method is suitable for time-series data.

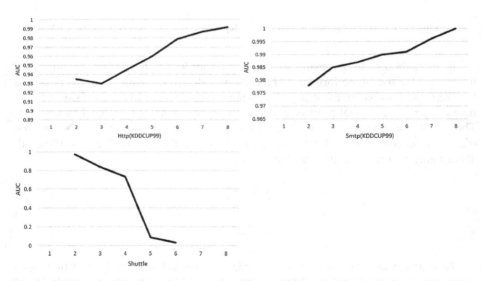

Fig. 2. AUC performance (y-axis) versus the different sliding window size in log scale (x-axis)

5   Conclusion and Future Work

This paper considers the statistical features of time series data, based on iForest's anomaly detection framework, and uses sliding window technology to implement a sequence anomaly detection algorithm, namely iForestFS. Experiments were conducted on three real data sets and the results demonstrated that the proposed method was effective and efficient. However, in our study, we only verified that our proposed method was suitable for sequence anomaly detection but did not compare with existing methods. More importantly, there are still some problems that need further discussion.

Our future work will focus on the following three directions: First, the size of the sliding window is fixed in this article, which may not be suitable for real applications. Second, we did not evaluate the influence of a single statistical feature on our anomaly detection effect. In actual applications, different data may have better detection effects using different statistical features. Third, in our research, when comparing abnormal datasets or streaming data for anomaly detection, our algorithm cannot detect anomalies quickly and efficiently. In many practical applications, it is often required to detect abnormalities in nearly real-time.

References

1. Yang, Q., Wu, X.: 10 challenging problems in data mining research. Int. J. Inf. Technol. Decis. Making **5**(4), 597–604 (2006)
2. Chandola, V., Banerjee, A., Kumar, V.: Anomaly detection for discrete sequences: a survey. IEEE Trans. Knowl. Data Eng. **24**(5), 823–839 (2012)
3. Chandola, V., Banerjee, A., Kumar, V.: Anomaly detection: a survey. ACM Comput. Surv. (CSUR) **41**(3), 15 (2009)
4. Xi, X., et al.: Fast time series classification using numerosity reduction. In: Proceedings of the 23rd International Conference on Machine Learning. ACM (2006)
5. Zhang, X., Fan, P., Zhu, Z.: A new anomaly detection method based on hierarchical HMM. In: Proceedings of the Fourth International Conference on Parallel and Distributed Computing, Applications and Technologies, PDCAT 2003. IEEE (2003)
6. Liu, F.T., Ting, K.M., Zhou, Z.-H.: Isolation forest. In: Eighth IEEE International Conference on Data Mining, ICDM 2008. IEEE (2008)
7. Liu, F.T., Ting, K.M., Zhou, Z.-H.: Isolation-based anomaly detection. ACM Trans. Knowl. Disc. Data (TKDD) **6**(1), 3 (2012)
8. Vallis, O., Hochenbaum, J., Kejariwal, A.: A novel technique for long-term anomaly detection in the cloud. In: HotCloud (2014)
9. Laptev, N., Amizadeh, S., Flint, I.: Generic and scalable framework for automated time-series anomaly detection. In: Proceedings of the 21st ACM SIGKDD International Conference on Knowledge Discovery and Data Mining. ACM (2015)
10. Lin, J., et al.: A symbolic representation of time series, with implications for streaming algorithms. In: Proceedings of the 8th ACM SIGMOD Workshop on Research Issues in Data Mining and Knowledge Discovery. ACM (2003)
11. Ding, Z., Fei, M.: An anomaly detection approach based on isolation forest algorithm for streaming data using sliding window. IFAC Proc. Vol. **46**(20), 12–17 (2013)
12. Sun, L., et al.: Detecting anomalous user behavior using an extended isolation forest algorithm: an enterprise case study. arXiv preprint arXiv:1609.06676 (2016)
13. Cao, F., Ester, M., Qian, W., Zhou, A.: Density-based clustering over an evolving data stream with noise. In: Proceedings of the 2006 SIAM conference on data mining (SDM), Bethesda, MD, pp. 328–339 (2006)
14. Yamanishi, K., Takeuchi, J.: A unifying framework for detecting outliers and change points from non-stationary time series data. Knowl. Data Eng. **18**(4), 482–492 (2006)

Hourly Day-Ahead Power Forecasting for PV Plant Based on Bidirectional LSTM

Hui He[(⊠)], Ran Hu, Ying Zhang, Runhai Jiao, and Honglu Zhu

School of Control and Computer Engineering,
North China Electric Power University,
Beijing 102206, People's Republic of China
huihe@ncepu.edu.cn

Abstract. A novel hourly day-ahead power forecasting approach for PV plant based on bidirectional LSTM is proposed in this paper. Firstly, after analyzing the periodic characteristics of PV plant daily power curves, we employ K-means to cluster days into different types of weather according to the irradiance index. Then, a bidirectional Long Short-Term Memory (LSTM) is presented to build forecasting models for each type of weather in four seasons. An empirical study on a real dataset shows that the proposed method can effectively use multivariate time series information to predict the power for PV plants and obtain better performance than Autoregressive Integrated Moving Average model (ARIMA), Extreme Learning Machine (ELM) and Multilayer Perceptron (MLP).

Keywords: Irradiance index ·
Bidirectional Long Short-Term Memory (LSTM) · PV power forecasting ·
PV plant

1 Introduction

With the global energy crisis, renewable energy such as wind power and solar energy has been vigorously developed, and renewable energy generation has gradually shifted from supplementary energy to alternative energy. However, due to the intermittency and the non-controllable characteristics of the solar production, when large-scale PV power generation is connected to the power grid, it will bring a number of other problems such as voltage fluctuations, local power quality, and stability issues. Reasonable allocation and dispatch of PV system power generation are of great importance to the power balance of the entire power grid. Precise PV power forecasting is the premise to guarantee the safe and stable operation of PV grid-connected power generation, and it is also an important basis for rational distribution and dispatching of PV system power generation.

PV power forecasting [1] is to construct a prediction model based on the Numerical Weather Prediction (NWP) data or/and measured data combining with the geographical information of PV power plants and to estimate the output power of PV power plants in a certain period of time in the future. According to different time scales, the forecasting task can be divided into ultra-short term (0–6 h), short-term (6 h–1 day) and long-term (1 month–1 year). Short-term PV power forecasting can be used for scheduling

C. Hu et al. (Eds.): HPCMS 2018/HiDEC 2018, CCIS 913, pp. 208–222, 2019.
https://doi.org/10.1007/978-981-32-9987-0_18

planning and demand response in the electricity market, etc. Besides, short-term power forecasting requires relatively low spatial and temporal resolution of meteorological data, which can utilize the NWP data rather than sky image data. Therefore, short-term PV power forecasting draws a lot of attention from the scholars and researchers in energy and environment areas.

The most used short-term forecasting algorithms include neural network [2–4], non-linear regression algorithms [5, 6], time series algorithms [7, 8], wavelet analysis [9], and random forest [10] and so on. Among them, because neural networks and non-linear regression algorithm have good generalization ability and fault tolerance, they are the most frequently used models in PV power prediction. However, these methods only use single sample information in model training, which means that they ignore the strong correlation between multiple samples in the same time series, and lose the sequence information. The time series algorithms are suitable for the cases that the weather does not change obviously. When the weather changes quickly, the prediction accuracy will drop sharply. The wavelet analysis is employed to mine the multi-resolution characteristics. It has the ability to represent the local information of the signal in both the time and frequency domains. Although the wavelet analysis can perform decomposition, prediction and abnormal data point identification in different frequency bands of PV generation data, it is not able to predict the PV power. Thus the wavelet analysis often combines with other models to capture the relationship between variables and improve the forecasting accuracy. Random forest, which is one of the ensemble learning methods, has been utilized to forecast short-term PV power generation.

To summarize, the above algorithms establish the nonlinear relationship between input features and output power by using a large number of historical data. They change the dynamic time modeling problem into a static spatial modeling problem. In fact, as a typical time series, PV power data is not only non-linear but also time-relevant. It means that for a given PV power plant, the change in power generation is a continuous process, and the power at the current moment is relevant to the power at the previous moments. Powers in the same time-series are dependent on each other, which mean that they have a strong correlation among them. Therefore, the change of PV power at each moment depends not only on the input features at the current moment but also on the input features of the past moments. Thus traditional methods, which try to establish a nonlinear relationship between input features of an individual sample and the output power, lose the information between consecutive samples.

With the burst development of deep learning, [11], deep learning has achieved remarkable results in many areas, such as image analysis [12], speech recognition [13], and natural language processing [14]. In the field of power prediction, deep learning algorithms have also been initially applied [15]. The recurrent neural network is an excellent deep learning approach, which is suitable for sequential data. In order to explore the essential characteristics of the PV plant power generation sequence, this paper proposes a short-term PV power forecasting model based on bidirectional Long Short-Term Memory (LSTM). After analyzing the PC power generation daily curves, we find that the seasons and weather types have a great influence on the power generation of PV power plants, and the daily power curves of photovoltaic power generation under different weather types show different trends. Therefore, the first step is to cluster different types of weather by utilizing the irradiance index. And then, the bidirectional LSTM are employed to build forecasting models for different weather types.

The main contributions of this paper are as follows:

- Clustering different weather types with the irradiance index and verifying the effectiveness in experiments;
- Constructing PV power forecasting model using bidirectional LSTM not only models the nonlinear relationship between the input features of individual samples and output power but also captures the dependence in the time series, which effectively improves forecasting accuracy;
- A case study was conducted on the measured datasets of a PV power plant in North China and compared with the PV power prediction methods including Autoregressive Integrated Moving Average model (ARIMA), Extreme Learning Machine (ELM) and Multilayer Perceptron (MLP) to verify the effectiveness and superiority of this method.

The remaining parts of this paper are organized as follows: Sect. 2 describes the theoretical knowledge of LSTM. Section 3 presents the overall framework and workflow of short-term PV power forecasting based on the bidirectional LSTM. The experiments and analysis are provided in Sect. 4. Finally, some concluding remarks are given in Sect. 5.

2   Methodology

Recurrent neural networks (RNNs) are fundamentally different from traditional feed-forward neural network. They are sequence-based models, which are able to establish the temporal correlations between previous information and the current circumstances. For time series problem, this means that the decision an RNN made at time step t − 1 could affect the decision it will reach at time step later t. Such characteristics of RNN is ideal for power forecasting problems since it has been pointed out that the dependence in the power time series may be one of the most important factors to power generation at the later time intervals. RNNs are trained by back propagation through time (BPTT) [16]. However, learning long-range dependencies with RNNs is difficult due to the problems of gradient vanishing or exploding. Gradient vanishing in RNN refers to the problems that the norm of the gradient for long-term components decreasing exponentially fast to zero, limiting the model's ability to learn long-term temporal correlations, while the gradient exploding refers to the opposite event.

In order to overcome the issues, the long short-term memory (LSTM) [17] architecture was first introduced by Hochreiter et al. It has been the most successful RNN architecture and received huge popularity in many subsequent applications. To briefly introduce the concept of the LSTM, let $\{x_1, x_2, \cdots, x_T\}$ denote a typical input sequence for an LSTM, where $x_t \in R^k$ represents a k-dimensional vector for real values at the t th time step. In order to establish temporal connections, the LSTM defines and maintains an internal memory cell state throughout the whole life cycle, which is the most important element of the LSTM structure. The memory cell state c_{t-1} interacts with the intermediate output h_{t-1} and the subsequent input x_t to determine which elements of the internal state vector should be updated, maintained or erased based on the outputs of the previous time step and the inputs of the present time step. In addition to the internal state, the LSTM structure also defines candidate cell state $\widetilde{c}_t$, input gate i_t, forget gate f_t, and output gate o_t. The formulations of all gates in an LSTM cell are given by (1) to (6):

$$f_t = \sigma\left(W_f \cdot [h_{t-1}, x_t] + b_f\right) \tag{1}$$

$$i_t = \sigma(W_i \cdot [h_{t-1}, x_t] + b_i) \tag{2}$$

$$\widetilde{c}_t = tanh(W_c \cdot [h_{t-1}, x_t] + b_c) \tag{3}$$

$$c_t = f_t * c_{t-1} + i_t * \widetilde{c}_t \tag{4}$$

$$o_t = \sigma(W_0 \cdot [h_{t-1}, x_t] + b_0) \tag{5}$$

$$h_t = o_t * tanh(c_t) \tag{6}$$

where W_f, W_i, W_c, W_o are weight matrices for the corresponding inputs of the network activation functions, and b_f, b_i, b_c and b_o are the bias. $*$ stands for an element-wise multiplication; σ represents the sigmoid activation function, which $tanh$ represents the hyperbolic tangent function. The LSTM cell structure is illustrated in Fig. 1.

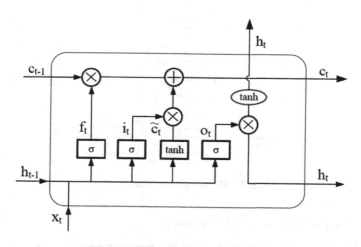

Fig. 1. The structure of a LSTM cell

3   The Forecasting Framework Based Bidirectional LSTM

3.1   Forecasting Framework

Figure 2 shows the forecasting framework based on irradiance index and bidirectional LSTM. Firstly, since PV power generation is greatly influenced by the seasons and weather types, the power data and measured weather data are divided according to the season. Then, clustering algorithm divides the dataset into three kinds of weather subsets (including sunny days, cloudy days, and rainy/snowy days) in the same season by using the irradiance index. A bidirectional LSTM is employed to train the prediction model in each subset.

In the testing phase, the corresponding seasonal model is selected according to the date of the day, and the similarity between the center of the clusters and the day is calculated to determine which weather type of the day belongs to. At last, the hourly power generation is forecasting by the corresponding bidirectional LSTM.

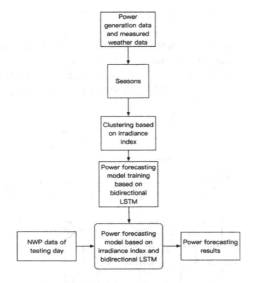

Fig. 2. The forecasting framework

3.2   Clustering Based on Irradiance Index

Since the short-term power forecasting is mainly used to predict the power in the future days. There is a strong periodicity for the daily power, which is described as follows. Firstly, the power curves of the same season have similar overall maximum output power. And secondly, the power curves of the same weather type have similar overall trends. Considering such strong periodicity of the daily power, we come up with establishing different prediction models for different weather types in different seasons to improve forecasting accuracy.

Therefore, it is very important to divide the weather types reasonably and accurately to improve forecasting accuracy and generalization of the prediction models. If the dataset is divided according to the weather types recorded in the weather forecast, there will be the following problems: Firstly, the weather types defined in the weather forecast are numerous, and the size of each subset is too small. That may cause overfitting in the training process. Secondly, similar descriptions, such as overcast to cloudy, light rain to sunny, and so on, cannot determine the type of the weather on that day.

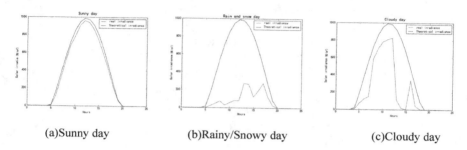

(a)Sunny day   (b)Rainy/Snowy day   (c)Cloudy day

Fig. 3. Theoretical and real irradiance comparison of three typical weather types

After the above analysis and observation of the data set, we get a large number of statistical findings that the areas enclosed by the daily curves of the measured irradiance and theoretical irradiance with the coordinate axes have obvious rules under different weather types. As shown in Fig. 3(a), the curves of measured irradiance and theoretical irradiance under sunny weather are relatively smooth and their amplitudes are close. Therefore, the area enclosed by the two curves and the coordinate axis is close to one another, and the ratio is larger. In Fig. 4(b), the measured amplitude of irradiance is low due to rain and snow weather, making the actual measured irradiance and theoretical irradiance greatly different from the area enclosed by the coordinate axis, and the ratio is small. In Fig. 4(c), due to the movement of clouds in cloudy weather, the PV power value fluctuates more violently. Therefore, in cloudy weather, the measured irradiance curve is between rainy/snowy days and sunny days, and the fluctuation is large. The area ratio of the measured irradiance and the theoretical irradiance curve is between sunny days and rainy days.

According to the above statistical findings, we propose a weather type clustering index and denote it as irradiance index K. The irradiance index is the ratio of the enclosed area between measured daily irradiance and the theoretical irradiance curve with the coordinate axis. $S\_theoretical$ is the area enclosed by the theoretical irradiance daily curve and the coordinate axis. And S_real is the area enclosed by the measured daily irradiance curve and the coordinate axis. The formula for calculating the irradiance index is as follows:

$$K = \frac{S\_real}{S\_theoretical} \tag{7}$$

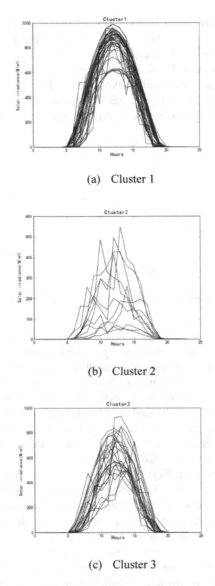

(a)   Cluster 1

(b)   Cluster 2

(c)   Cluster 3

Fig. 4. The cluster results of three types of irradiance cures in spring

K-means [18] is employed to cluster data into different weather types. We take spring dataset as an example for clustering analysis. Figure 4 is the clustering results of three types of irradiance cures in spring. From Fig. 4(a), (b) and (c), it can be seen that the daily irradiance curves of each type have distinct characteristics after clustering. The peaks of the irradiance curves in Fig. 4(a) are generally higher than those in Fig. 4(b) and (c), and the curves are relatively smooth, and the trend of most of the curves is the same. This is consistent with the fact that the physical state of the atmosphere on a sunny day is relatively stable and the sky is less cloudy, so the sample contained in Fig. 4(a) is classified as sunny days. The peak value of the irradiance curves in Fig. 4(b) is the lowest among the three types of curves, which is attenuated severely in rain and snow, and the difference between the theoretical irradiance and the measured irradiance curve is very large, so it belongs to the type of rainy/snowy days. In Fig. 4(c), the change of irradiance curve is more intense and the peak value is higher than in Fig. 4(b), which is related to the instantaneous decrease of irradiance caused by cloud cover. Thus they are classified as cloudy days.

Using the same method, the other three seasons are further divided into three types of weather: sunny days, cloudy days, and rainy/snowy days. When forecasting hourly power for a specific day, the seasonal model is determined according to the date, and then the irradiance index is calculated by the given NWP data of the day. After comparing with the cluster center, a prediction model is selected by the nearest cluster.

3.3   Bidirectional LSTM-Based Forecasting Model

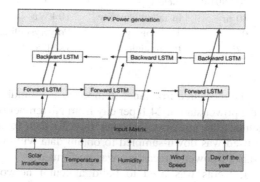

Fig. 5. Bidirectional LSTM-based forecasting model

The bidirectional LSTM-based [19] forecasting model is shown in Fig. 5. In the training phase, we combine the measured solar irradiance, temperature, humidity, wind speed and the day of the year as a feature vector x_t at a specific hour t, where x_t is denoted by $x_t = [x_{t,1}, x_{t,2}, x_{t,3}, x_{t,4}, x_{t,5}]^T$. Elements of the feature vector x_t are given as:

- $x_{t,1}$: the measured solar irradiance at the hour t;
- $x_{t,2}$: the temperature at the hour t;
- $x_{t,3}$: the humidity at the hour t;
- $x_{t,4}$: the wind speed at the hour t;
- $x_{t,5}$: the day of the year.

The bidirectional LSTM contains two directional LSTM: one is forward LSTM and the other is backward LSTM. They all use x_t as input but with opponent directions. The average of the output of corresponding two LSTM cells is the power prediction value.

Since the LSTM is sensitive to data scale, the five features are scaled to the range of [0, 1] according to the feature's nature.

4   Experiments and Analysis

4.1   Dataset and Computing Tools

The data used in this paper is from the PV testing platform of the State Key Laboratory of Alternate Electrical Power System with Renewable Energy Sources at North China Electric Power University in Changping District, Beijing, China, recorded with a sampling interval of 1 min. Table 1 shows the detailed information of the PV testing platform.

Table 1. PV power plant information

Item	Data	Item	Data
Longitude	116.3059°E	Mounting disposition	Flat roof
Latitude	40.08914°N	Field type	Fixed tilted plane
Altitude	80 m	Installed capacity	10 kWp
Azimuth	0°	Technology	Polycrystalline silicon
Tilt	37°	PV module	JKM245P

The data includes the measured irradiance, temperature, humidity, wind speed, and power generated by the power station 24 h per day from November 6, 2016, to October 28, 2017. It also includes the numerical weather forecast data for this period. In the experiment, the data used was down-sampled to obtain data with a time resolution of 1 h, and hourly day-ahead power forecasting was performed.

In the experiment, Keras was used to build a neural network model and all frameworks are built on a GPU server for high-performance computing [20].

4.2   Experiment Setting

In order to verify the performance of the LSTM prediction, the LSTM model is compared with three popular forecasting models: ARIMA, ELM, and MLP. In the experiment, MLP uses a single hidden layer network structure. The parameters of MLP are initialized randomly and trained by using BP algorithm. ELM is also a single hidden layer structure, and its parameters in the network are obtained by calculation. In the bidirectional LSTM network, 24 hidden units are set in each direction, and each hidden unit receives the feature input at the time of the day.

In order to verify the contribution of clustering in forecasting, a comparative experiment using weather type clustering and without using weather type clustering was also designed for the three models.

Ten-fold cross-validation was used during the experiment to evaluate the forecasting model.

4.3   Performance Evaluation

The performance of power forecasting is evaluated via different statistical indicators including the mean absolute error (MAE), root mean square error (RMSE) and mean absolute percentage error (MAPE). The nominated statistical indicators are reviewed briefly as followings.

The MAE represents the average quantity of total absolute error between the estimated and measured values:

$$MAE = \frac{1}{N} \times \sum_{i=1}^{N} \left| P_{fi} - P_{ri} \right| \tag{8}$$

where N is the total number of observations; P_{fi} is the estimated value calculated by different models; P_{ri} is the measured value.

The RMSE determines the precision of by comparing the deviation between the estimated and real data. The RMSE has always a non-negative value and is calculated by:

$$RMSE = \sqrt{\frac{1}{N} \times \sum_{i=1}^{N} \left(P_{fi} - P_{ri} \right)^2} \tag{9}$$

The MAPE is close to the MAE but each gap between estimated and measured data is divided by the measured data in order to consider the relative gap.

$$MAPE = \frac{1}{N} \times \sum_{i=1}^{N} \left| \frac{P_{fi} - P_{ri}}{P_{ri}} \right| \tag{10}$$

4.4   Experiment Results and Discussion

Performance Comparison of Different Models in Different Weather Types

Figure 6 shows the performance of bidirectional LSTM, ARIMA, MLP, and ELM in sunny days, rainy/snowy days and cloudy days. The green dotted lines stand for the actual output curves, the red ones are the bidirectional LSTM prediction curves. The blue, cyan and purple ones are the ELM, MLP and ARIMA prediction curves respectively. It can be seen from Fig. 6 that the prediction results of the bidirectional LSTM model are better than other three models under all kinds of weather, especially in cloudy and rainy days where the weather conditions are more complicated.

As shown in Fig. 6(a), when the weather type is sunny, all models obtain high accuracy, which can better reflect the output of the PV system on the testing date. In contrast, the overall prediction of the bidirectional LSTM model is closer to the true value. When the type of weather is rainy/snowy and cloudy, the prediction accuracy of the three models reduced. The reason is that in rainy/snowy days and cloudy days, the clouds in the sky may change dramatically. And there are other factors like aerosols. Thus, relying only on the limited data in numerical weather forecasting is not sufficient to accurately predict the changes in solar radiation.

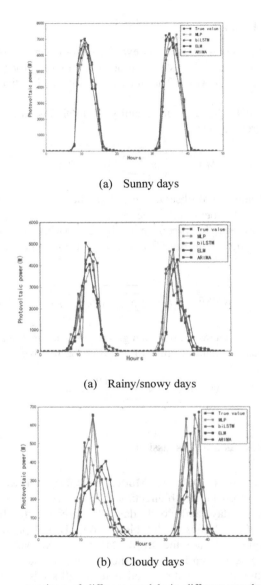

(a)   Sunny days

(a)   Rainy/snowy days

(b)   Cloudy days

Fig. 6. Performance comparison of different models in different weather types (Color figure online)

Table 2 shows the forecasting results of four models under different weather types in different seasons after clustering. It can be seen that most of the results of the bidirectional LSTM forecast model under various indicators are better than ARIMA, MLP, and ELM.

Table 2. Performance comparison of different models after clustering

Season	Model	Weather type	MAPE/%	RMSE/W	RAE/W
Spring	Bidirectional LSTM	Sunny	11.14	531.69	283.14
		Rainy/Snowy	26.97	365.20	162.41
		Cloudy	14.92	559.06	320.23
	ARIMA	Sunny	49.36	1049.88	682.13
		Rainy/Snowy	36.93	695.66	457.15
		Cloudy	50.72	1137.59	757.04
	MLP	Sunny	16.16	561.42	257.78
		Rainy/Snowy	26.89	579.47	198.72
		Cloudy	15.43	629.07	288.61
	ELM	Sunny	11.98	499.53	216.99
		Rainy/Snowy	39.03	386.30	172.25
		Cloudy	14.46	543.05	257.65
Summer	Bidirectional LSTM	Sunny	13.62	504.22	267.42
		Rainy/Snowy	39.81	554.64	287.25
		Cloudy	21.62	545.51	311.86
	ARIMA	Sunny	54.74	1700.95	1080.45
		Rainy/Snowy	64.28	831.97	443.22
		Cloudy	62.00	1636.79	1195.75
	MLP	Sunny	15.52	435.26	209.78
		Rainy/Snowy	42.75	545.84	242.98
		Cloudy	40.02	859.11	420.34
	ELM	Sunny	16.17	450.85	211.63
		Rainy/Snowy	44.06	663.37	285.37
		Cloudy	39.47	692.75	386.38
Autumn	Bidirectional LSTM	Sunny	8.68	487.86	244.17
		Rainy/Snowy	30.27	447.70	168.20
		Cloudy	22.67	513.79	284.60
	ARIMA	Sunny	26.91	1715.16	1208.88
		Rainy/Snowy	53.94	759.18	451.78
		Cloudy	34.36	1316.28	978.03
	MLP	Sunny	11.29	604.99	245.29
		Rainy/Snowy	50.84	389.47	145.56
		Cloudy	26.97	705.32	295.51
	ELM	Sunny	11.05	525.61	225.29
		Rainy/Snowy	44.39	598.20	217.87
		Cloudy	25.27	701.59	315.54

(continued)

Table 2. (*continued*)

Season	Model	Weather type	MAPE/%	RMSE/W	RAE/W
Winter	Bidirectional LSTM	Sunny	7.01	357.12	120.66
		Rainy/Snowy	18.64	371.81	169.65
		Cloudy	18.72	277.48	126.16
	ARIMA	Sunny	38.12	1477.19	952.99
		Rainy/Snowy	57.83	1520.16	893.37
		Cloudy	41.86	376.22	313.17
	MLP	Sunny	7.60	315.78	156.24
		Rainy/Snowy	19.36	338.62	133.84
		Cloudy	18.97	140.97	49.80
	ELM	Sunny	7.19	284.47	130.64
		Rainy/Snowy	19.59	430.83	177.22
		Cloudy	16.28	210.75	84.95

Performance Comparison of With/Without Clustering

Table 3 shows the forecasting results of the three models with/without clustering. It can be seen that the LSTM results are better than the other two according to each metrics. Comparing with Tables 2 and 3, we find that after using the clustering model, each error indicator has dropped significantly, which proves the effectiveness of the clustering model.

Table 3. Performance comparison of different models without clustering

Season	Model	MAPE/%	RMSE/W	RAE/W
Spring	Bidirectional LSTM	22.70	550.71	292.05
	ARIMA	39.39	1349.27	799.68
	MLP	31.90	874.03	422.58
	ELM	33.33	1050.95	497.00
Summer	Bidirectional LSTM	36.29	401.27	230.32
	ARIMA	63.45	1582.19	1051.36
	MLP	121.34	1318.74	693.25
	ELM	101.76	1187.93	651.77
Autumn	Bidirectional LSTM	34.36	588.00	283.69
	ARIMA	38.35	1215.53	829.90
	MLP	51.68	1065.28	474.85
	ELM	49.94	1064.95	473.88
Winter	Bidirectional LSTM	25.15	447.95	190.59
	ARIMA	49.82	1067.20	690.30
	MLP	35.24	728.27	319.04
	ELM	25.02	753.85	301.78

Discussion

From Table 2, it can be seen that the short-term PV power forecasting based on the irradiance index and bidirectional LSTM got the best results, which verifies the validity and effectiveness of the proposed method.

From the perspective of different seasons, each model has the best results in winter, followed by autumn and spring, and the worst in summer. This may be due to the fact that summer cloud movements are relatively fast and that prediction models relying on recent weather forecasts cannot accurately estimate changes in solar radiation. In the autumn and winter seasons, changes in the atmosphere are relatively slow and prediction results are better.

From the perspective whether the clustering or not, after adding the clustering model featured by the irradiance index, each error indicator decreased significantly. This shows that the irradiance index can better reflect the differences in weather types on an annual dataset, and at the same time the role of weather types in the prediction of PV power generation power cannot be ignored.

From the perspective of the forecasting models, ELM does have an advantage in terms of operating efficiency when the amount of data is small. However, when the amount of data is large, ELM requires huge computing resources, which limits its ability to learn. ARIMA, MLP and ELM models convert the dynamic time series regression problem into a static spatial modeling problem. They train only using one single sample and ignore the correlation between samples on the time series. The bidirectional LSTM builds models among two consecutive time sequences and capture the dependencies between the sequential samples. Therefore it has a stronger learning ability, which has been proved by the experimental results in Fig. 6 and Table 2.

5 Conclusions

In this paper, we propose an hourly day-ahead power forecasting approach for PV plant based on bidirectional LSTM. Clustering based on the irradiance index is used to classify the weather types in different seasons. After this, the bidirectional LSTM is employed to construct the PV power prediction model, which not only establishes a nonlinear relationship between input features of an individual sample and the output power but also captures the dependence between the sequential samples. Case studies show that the forecasting method proposed in this paper has good forecasting performance. This approach provides a new way for short-term PV plant power forecasting and other tasks with similar data forms [21].

Acknowledgements. The authors would like to thank the Fundamental Research Funds for the Central Universities (2017MS072, 2018ZD06), the National Natural Science Foundation of China (61503137) for financially supporting this work.

References

1. Voyant, C., et al.: Machine learning methods for solar radiation forecasting: a review. Renew. Energy **105**, 569–582 (2017)
2. Salcedo-Sanz, S., Casanova-Mateo, C., Pastor-Sánchez, A., Sánchez-Girón, M.: Daily global solar radiation prediction based on a hybrid Coral Reefs Optimization-Extreme Learning Machine approach. Sol. Energy **105**, 91–98 (2014)
3. Wang, F., Mi, Z., Su, S., Zhao, H.: Short-term solar irradiance forecasting model based on artificial neural network using statistical feature parameters. Energies **5**(5), 1355–1370 (2012)
4. Leva, S., Dolara, A., Grimaccia, F., Mussetta, M., Ogliari, E.: Analysis and validation of 24 hours ahead neural network forecasting of photovoltaic output power. Math. Comput. Simul. **131**, 88–100 (2017)
5. Deo, R.C., Wen, X., Qi, F.: A wavelet-coupled support vector machine model for forecasting global incident solar radiation using limited meteorological dataset. Appl. Energy **168**, 568–593 (2016)
6. Mohammadi, K., Shamshirband, S., Tong, C.W., Arif, M., Petković, D., Ch, S.: A new hybrid support vector machine–wavelet transform approach for estimation of horizontal global solar radiation. Energy Convers. Manag. **92**, 162–171 (2015)
7. Li, Y., Su, Y., Shu, L.: An ARMAX model for forecasting the power output of a grid connected photovoltaic system. Renew. Energy **66**, 78–89 (2014)
8. Yang, C., Thatte, A.A., Xie, L.: Multitime-scale data-driven spatio-temporal forecast of photovoltaic generation. IEEE Trans. Sustain. Energy **6**(1), 104–112 (2015)
9. Zhu, H., Li, X., Sun, Q., Nie, L., Yao, J., Zhao, G.: A power prediction method for photovoltaic power plant based on wavelet decomposition and artificial neural networks. Energies **9**(1), 11 (2015)
10. Sun, H., et al.: Assessing the potential of random forest method for estimating solar radiation using air pollution index. Energy Convers. Manag. **119**, 121–129 (2016)
11. LeCun, Y., Bengio, Y., Hinton, G.: Deep learning. Nature **521**(7553), 436–444 (2015)
12. Russakovsky, O., et al.: Imagenet large scale visual recognition challenge. Int. J. Comput. Vis. **115**(3), 211–252 (2015)
13. Hinton, G., et al.: Deep neural networks for acoustic modeling in speech recognition: the shared views of four research groups. IEEE Signal Process. Mag. **29**(6), 82–97 (2012)
14. Collobert, R., Weston, J., Bottou, L., Karlen, M., Kavukcuoglu, K., Kuksa, P.: Natural language processing (almost) from scratch. J. Mach. Learn. Res. **12**, 2493–2537 (2011)
15. Qing, X., Niu, Y.: Hourly day-ahead solar irradiance prediction using weather forecasts by LSTM. Energy **148**, 461–468 (2018)
16. Werbos, P.J.: Backpropagation through time: what it does and how to do it. Proc. IEEE **78**(10), 1550–1560 (1990)
17. Hochreiter, S., Schmidhuber, J.: Long short-term memory. Neural Comput. **9**(8), 1735–1780 (1997)
18. Kanungo, T., Mount, D.M., Netanyahu, N.S., Piatko, C.D., Silverman, R., Wu, A.Y.: An efficient k-means clustering algorithm: Analysis and implementation. IEEE Trans. Pattern Anal. Mach. Intell. **24**(7), 881–892 (2002)
19. Sutskever, I., Vinyals, O., Le, Q.V.: Sequence to sequence learning with neural networks. In: International Conference on Neural Information Processing Systems, pp. 3104–3112(2014)
20. Wang, J., Gao, F., Vazquez-Poletti, J., Li, J.: Preface of high performance computing or advanced modeling and simulation of materials. Comput. Phys. Commun. **211** (2017)
21. Wang, J., Liu, C., Huang, Y.: Auto tuning for new energy dispatch problem: a case study. Future Gener. Comput. Syst. **54**, 501–506 (2016)

A Reliability Task Scheduling for High-Throughput Computing Platform

Weipeng Jing[1,2], Chuanyu Zhao[2], Yaqiu Liu[1(✉)], and Chao Jiang[2]

[1] College of Information and Computer Engineering,
Northeast Forestry University, Harbin, China
weipeng.jing@outlook.com, yaqiuLiu@126.com
[2] Heilongjiang Computer Science Center, Harbin, China

Abstract. In order to meet the different quality of service (QoS), it is necessary to consider the performance of the system not only to consider the performance of the system, but also to consider the user's service quality requirements. Aiming at the existing problem of task scheduling algorithm with the goal of user service quality, in this paper we proposed a task scheduling algorithm which satisfies the service quality requirement of users, and carried on the three goals from the reliability, time and cost of service quality task scheduling research. We described the multi-objective constraint processing method used in this paper. For the target requirements of reliability, time and cost, the multi-objective optimization problem is transformed into a single objective optimization problem with constraints the time and cost are constrained by the deadline and the budget, and the reliability is used as the final goal of the task scheduling when the constraint is adopted. Finally, according to the task scheduling goal of this paper, the only solution with the highest reliability is obtained. The experimental results show that the RSL algorithm has better reliability than other algorithms, and it has better advantages in other performance indicators while satisfying the scheduling deadline.

Keywords: Performance · Reliability · Optimization · Algorithm

1 Introduction

First principles calculations have the potential to greatly accelerate the design and optimization of new materials, However, it also brings complicated computing tasks and leads to longer computing time. Computing has become an enabling paradigm for on demand provisioning of computing resources to dynamic applications workload [1]. Virtualization is commonly used in cloud, such as Amazon's elastic compute cloud (EC2), to render flexible and scalable system services, and thus creating a powerful computing environment that gives cloud users the illusion of infinite computing resources [2]. Running applications on virtual resources, notably virtual machines (VMs), has been an efficient solution for scalability, cost-efficiency, and high resource utilization [3]. There are an increasing number of scientific applications in the areas such as astronomy, bioinformatics, and physics [4]. The ever-growing data and complexity of those applications make them demand a high-performance computing

© Springer Nature Singapore Pte Ltd. 2019
C. Hu et al. (Eds.): HPCMS 2018/HiDEC 2018, CCIS 913, pp. 223–234, 2019.
https://doi.org/10.1007/978-981-32-9987-0_19

environment. Cloud as the latest distributed computing paradigm can offer an efficient solution. Many scientific applications are of the real-time nature where the correctness depends not only on the computational results, but also on the time instants at which these results become available [5]. In some cases, it is necessary to guarantee the timeliness of applications. For instance, the workflows of material simulations have strict deadlines which, once being violated, can make the result useless [6]. Therefore, it is critical for these kinds of deadline-constrained applications to obtain guaranteed computing services even in the presence of machine failures. It is reported in [7] that for a system consisting of 10 thousand super reliable servers (MTBF of 30 years), there will still be one failure per day. Moreover, each year, about 1–5% of disk drives die and servers crash at least twice for a 2–4% failure rate. Note that, it is even worse that largescale cloud providers such as Google, also use a large number of cheap commodity computers that may result in much more frequent failures [8]. As a consequence, delivering fault-tolerant capability in clouds, especially for real-time scientific workflows is critical and has become a hot research topic. Since occurrences of faults are often unpredictable in computer systems, fault tolerance must be taken into consideration when designing scheduling algorithms [9]. The replication approach makes multiple copies of a task and allocate each copy to a different resource to guarantee the successful completion of the task before its deadline, even in the presence of some resource failure. Basically, the more copies are allocated, the higher fault-tolerant capability of the system, which, nonetheless, may incur large resource consumption. Thereby, the two-copy replication (also known as the primary-backup model, or PB in short), has gained its popularity. With the PB model, a task gets only two copies: primary copy and backup copy [10]. In order to improve system schedule ability while providing fault tolerance with low overhead, many studies have concentrated on overlapping techniques when using the PB model. Currently, there are two overlapping schemes: backup-backup overlapping (BB overlapping in short, in which multiple distinct backup copies are allowed to overlap with each other on the same computational unit) and primary backup overlapping (PB overlapping in short, in which primary copies are allowed to overlap with other tasks' backup copies on the same computational unit). For example, Ghosh et al. employed a BB overlapping scheme allowing multiple backup copies overlap in the same time slot on a single processor; in their design, a deallocation scheme was used to release the resource reserved for backup copies after their corresponding primary copies finish successfully [11]. The work was extended for multiprocessor systems in [12], where processors are divided into groups to tolerate multiple simultaneous failures. Al-Omari et al. studied a PB overlapping policy for scheduling real time tasks to achieve high schedulability [13].

In this paper, we address this problem with the following contributions: We establish a real-time workflow fault-tolerant model on virtualized clouds, which extends the traditional PB fault-tolerant model by incorporating the cloud characteristics; we provide analytical strategies for task allocation and message transmission to support fault tolerant execution.

2 Model

2.1 Mathematical Model

Definition 1: cloud task mathematical model
The mathematical model of task in cloud computing environment shown by the following:

1. $T = \{t_1, t_2, \ldots, t_m\}$ represents a collection of n independent tasks, between each task which is independent of each other, no communication between tasks; and there is no interdependencies between all tasks, that means, the completion of any task has no effect on the execution of other tasks.
2. $L = \{l_1, l_2, \ldots, l_n\}$ represents a collection of n tasks lengths, where l_i represents the task length of the task t_i, the task length is represented by millions of instructions, the unit is MI.
3. $D = \{d_1, d_2, \ldots, d_n\}$ represents the set of n task deadlines, the user gives a deadline for each task, that is the latest maximum completion time, hope all the tasks can be completed within the deadline.
4. $C = \{c_1, c_2, \ldots, c_n\}$ represents a collection of n task scheduling budgets, the user gives the scheduling budget for each task, hoped that the scheduling overhead of all tasks on the computing nodes cannot exceed their own scheduling budget.

Definition 2: resource mathematical model
The mathematical model of cloud computing environment of resources that are as follows:

1. $R = \{r_1, r_2, \ldots, r_n\}$ represents a collection of cloud computing resources consisting of m heterogeneous computing nodes, each cloud resource is set up with only one processing unit, PE, and the computation speed of each processing unit is different.
2. $P = \{p_1, p_2, \ldots, p_m\}$ represents a collection of m resource unit time costs, where p_j represents the computing cost per second of the computing node r_j.
3. $MIPS = \{mips_1, mips_2, \ldots, mips_m\}$ represents a collection of computing speeds for m resources, where $mips_j$ represents the millions of machine language instructions processed by a computing node per second, the unit is MI/s.
4. $F = \{f_1, f_2, \ldots, f_m\}$ represents a collection of m resource failure rates, where f_j represents the probability that the computing node r_j will fail.

Definition 3: task scheduling mathematical model
The mathematical model of cloud computing environment of task scheduling to resources is represented as follows:

1. $S = \begin{bmatrix} s_{11} & s_{12} & \cdots & s_{1m} \\ s_{21} & s_{22} & \cdots & s_{2m} \\ \vdots & \vdots & \ddots & \vdots \\ s_{n1} & s_{n2} & \cdots & s_{nm} \end{bmatrix}$ represents the mapping relationship between a task and

a computing node, if the task t_i is assigned to the computing node r_j, the scheduler is executed, so the elements in a matrix $s_{ij} = 1$, or else $s_{ij} = 0$.

2. $E = \begin{bmatrix} e_{11} & e_{12} & \cdots & e_{1m} \\ e_{21} & e_{22} & \cdots & e_{2m} \\ \vdots & \vdots & \ddots & \vdots \\ e_{n1} & e_{n2} & \cdots & e_{nm} \end{bmatrix}$ represents the execution time of a task on a compu-

tational node, where e_{ij} represents the required time of task t_i is executed on the computing node r_j, the formula for execution time can be obtained by the definition above, as shown in (1):

$$e_{ij} = \frac{l_i}{mips_j} \tag{1}$$

2.2   Task Scheduling Objective

The algorithm proposed in this paper considers the three QoS requirements of deadline, scheduling, budget and reliability. Using the deadline and scheduling time and cost budget constrained task scheduling, task scheduling requires all task scheduling scheme to the resources of the execution time does not exceed the deadline of its own, and all the tasks to the resources execution does not exceed the cost of its own budget schedule. The goal of task scheduling is to maximize the reliability of task scheduling when the deadline and scheduling budget are satisfied.

In case of only hardware failure, the probability that a computing node r_j is in a reliable state within the task execution time τ_i is called the reliability of the calculated node r_j, denoted as $R_{res_j}(i)$. Assuming that the failure rate of the calculated node r_j obeys the exponential distribution of the parameter f_j, the reliability of the node r_j is calculated in the execution time τ_i of the task t_i, such as the formula (2):

$$R_{res_j}(i) = e^{-f_j \tau_i} \tag{2}$$

In order to maximize the reliability of task scheduling in task scheduling, we can obtain the objective function, such as formula (3):

$$R(x) = \max \sum_{i=1}^{n} \sum_{j=1}^{m} R_{res_j}(i) \tag{3}$$

Among them, the task $R_{res_j}(i)$ scheduling to the cloud computing resource t_i on the implementation of the reliability of the process, $R(x)$ indicates that n tasks have been scheduled to m computing resources, the highest reliability task scheduling scheme. In this study, $R(x)$ is used as the objective function of task scheduling, and the fitness function is redefined in later chapters, which is applied to the research of task scheduling algorithm.

3 Algorithm

3.1 Algorithm Flow

The algorithm is described in the following steps:

Step1. Initialization of particle population, including initialization parameters, such as population size NP, the maximum number of iterations I_{max} learning factors c_1 and c_2, inertia weight range, $[\omega_{min}, \omega_{max}]$, etc.;

Step2. In the constraints, the normal distribution of the way a feasible initialization particle, and randomly generated feasible particle position and velocity, calculate the feasible particle initial particle population in the fitness function value, thus determine the solution $pbest$ and the global optimal solution of $gbest$ local optimal current;

Step3. Update the velocity of each particle;

Step4. Update the positions of each particle;

Step5. The fitness function values of each feasible particle are calculated;

Step6. For each feasible particle, the fitness function value is compared with the local optimal solution $pbest$. If it is better than the local optimal solution $pbest$, it is used as the local optimal solution $pbest$;

Step7. For each feasible particle, the fitness function value is compared with the global optimal solution $gbest$. If it is better than the global optimal solution $gbest$, then it is used as the local optimal solution $gbest$;

Step8. Check if the termination condition is satisfied. If the number of iterations reaches the maximum value of I_{max}, then turn Step9, otherwise transfer Step3 to the next iteration;

Step9. Output local optimal solution $pbest$ and global optimal solution $gbest$.

4 Experimental Results and Analysis

4.1 Experimental Setup

In this study, the tasks submitted by users for the independent tasks, between the tasks submitted by users is not dependent on the task and no communication between each other, and the scheduling for static scheduling, namely after the tasks submitted by users no longer determine the dynamic change. In the simulation experiments of convergence analysis, the number of tasks is set at n 100. In the simulation experiment of performance analysis, set the number of tasks n in the interval [20160], each growth of 20, a total of eight different tasks. The length of the task l_i is randomly generated on [5010000], in units of millions of instructions MI.

4.2 Virtual Machine Resource Parameter Settings

In this paper, for the task of each physical host resources for heterogeneous forms, each virtual machine performs as index that simulation experiments, such as processing capacity, cost per unit time and bandwidth of different performance. In simulation, the number of nodes for setting virtual machine resources is 10. So on each virtual machine resource contains a PE which processing capacity and price as shown in Table 1. According to the definition of the failure rate of resources, the failure rate is defined and randomly generated in the range $[1 \times 10^{-4} - 1 \times 10^{-3}]$.

Table 1. Parameter settings for resources

VM	MIPS(MI/s)	P
1	100	0.7
2	200	1.3
3	300	2.8
4	400	5
5	500	9
6	600	10
7	700	12
8	800	14
9	900	15.8
10	1000	17.5

4.3 Algorithm Parameter Settings

In order to make the algorithm shows better convergence and avoid the local optimal solution cannot jump out into the search process, combined with previous research, according to the principle of parameter adjustment in reference [15]. The parameter in DPSO and PSO algorithm is set as shown in Table 2.

Table 2. Experimental parameter settings

Experimental parameters	Parameter values
NP	100
I-max	200
c1	2
c2	2
ωi	[0.4, 0.9]
vi	[-0.5 m, 0.5 m]

4.4 Task Completion Time

The task completion time is the total time to complete the task scheduling process, it refers to the first task scheduling has been to experience the total time of the last complete task scheduling Task completion time is an important index to evaluate the performance of the algorithm. The smaller the task completion time is, the faster the task is completed, and the better is the scheduling performance of the algorithm.

Simulation experiments are done for the algorithm, DPSO, PSO, EDF and DBC these five algorithms proposed in this paper, in the experiment with reference to the above parameters setting principle, setting parameters. α and β in the experiment is a random number in [0,1], said the tasks submitted by users in time and cost requirements, covering a variety of types of needs. For the general task, the performance of each task scheduling algorithm is verified by simulation experiments on the performance index of all task completion time.

Figure 1 shows how the tasks of each of the five scheduling algorithms compare with each other in the case of varying number of tasks. The analysis shows that the EDF algorithm has the least time to complete because of the principle of earliest deadline first. It takes more time to complete the PSO algorithm and the DPSO algorithm, because the PSO algorithm does not have any constraints on time, so all tasks have the largest completion time. Through the contrast can be seen in all the task completion time on the algorithm, DBC algorithm and EDF algorithm are relatively small and the value is close, QoS consider less, more excellent in time to complete all tasks on a single performance index. Therefore, for all task completion time values, the EDF algorithm is smaller than the DBC algorithm, and the DBC algorithm is smaller than the algorithm.

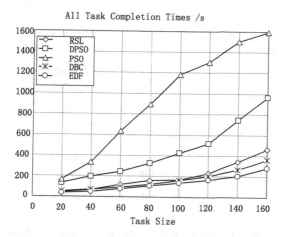

Fig. 1. Comparison of all task completion times

In this paper, the submitted user requirements have a direct impact for users on the scheduling results of task scheduling algorithms. The above experiments validate the user requirements in the general situation. The following tasks are analyzed for the task scheduling under the extreme situation, namely, task of urgency and overhead. For the two cases, the task scheduling algorithm is simulated, and the performance value of all tasks in the completion time is analyzed.

For user submitted tasks, each task has a requirement parameter cutoff time deadline, which is used to constrain the task scheduling to the execution time on the resource. Referring to the definition of the closing time Deadline and the dispatch budget above, the value of α and β is bound, and $\alpha = 0.1$, $\beta = 0.9$ is set. It shows that the tasks submitted by users require a short deadline, and the scheduling overhead is not high, that is, critical time tasks. The extreme environment required in the experiment is constructed. In the following experiments, the task completion time of each algorithm is compared for the critical time task.

From the analysis of Fig. 2, when the user submits tasks require smaller Deadline, for the two algorithm needs to consider the user Deadline, and DBC algorithms proposed in this paper has great influence in the completion time of all tasks. In order to meet the deadline user needs, the completion time of all the time to complete the task of these two algorithms have increased significantly, and with the increase of the number of users, more and more approaches do not consider the user needs of Deadline DPSO algorithm and PSO algorithm. Because the DPSO algorithm, the PSO algorithm and the EDF algorithm do not consider the user's Deadline, the $\alpha = 0.1$, $\beta = 0.9$ in this experiment has no influence on the task scheduling process of the three algorithms. However, although they have a slight advantage over all task completion times, they ignore the user's deadline requirements and reduce the quality of user services.

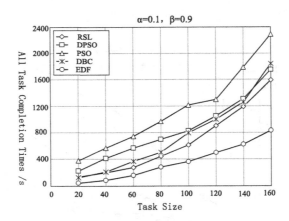

Fig. 2. All task completion time comparisons (when $\alpha = 0.1$, $\beta = 0.9$)

Task scheduling to resource execution, the higher the reliability, the greater the probability that the task can perform smoothly, reliability is an important indicator of service quality. In this paper, the calculation of reliability is related to the failure rate of virtual machine resources. The experiments in ibid, for average mission reliability, also need to be experimentally verified in three dimensions. In the first experiment, α and β are random numbers on the [0, 1], which represent the user's task to include various types of time and cost requirements.

Figure 3 shows the average task reliability contrast between the five scheduling algorithms in case of varying number of tasks involved in scheduling. As the number of tasks increases, the average task reliability of algorithm is obviously better than other algorithms, and the trend is more and more obvious. algorithm is in a reasonable range of acceptable performance of the two compared with other algorithms, all its task

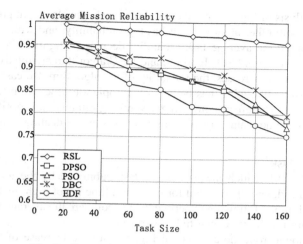

Fig. 3. Comparison of average mission reliability

completion time and the average task cost indicators, but the average task reliability, algorithm is superior to other algorithms. This shows that the algorithm has a prominent advantage in the reliability of the task. The above experiments verify the general user requirements, and the following analysis of the task scheduling in the extreme situation.

a. Critical time task

Set $\alpha = 0.1$, $\beta = 0.9$, which means that the tasks submitted by users require a short deadline, and the scheduling overhead is not high, that is, Critical time tasks. In the following experiments, we compare the average task reliability of each algorithm for Critical time tasks.

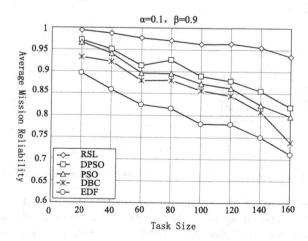

Fig. 4. Comparison of average mission reliability (when $\alpha = 0.1$, $\beta = 0.9$)

From the analysis of Fig. 4, for the critical time task, the algorithm proposed in this paper compared with other algorithms, it has high reliability, and with the increase of the number of tasks, the average task reliability decreased slightly. The average reliability of DPSO algorithm, PSO algorithm and DBC algorithm are relatively close, but as the number of tasks increases, the reliability of the algorithm decrease significantly. For EDF algorithm, although it has better task completion time, its average task reliability is the lowest. Therefore, comparing several algorithms, the algorithm presented in this paper has the advantage of obvious reliability when dealing with time critical tasks.

b. Tight budget task
Set $\alpha = 0.9$, $\beta = 0.1$, which means that the task submitted by the user is very low scheduling overhead, and the demand for execution time is not high, that is, the urgent task of overhead. In the following experiments, we compare the average task reliability of each algorithm for the task with tight overhead.

It can be known from the analysis of Fig. 5, with the increase of the number of tasks, the average task reliability algorithm always outperforms other algorithms. The overhead of urgent task, the constraint of Budget algorithm and DBC algorithm considered in the simulation experiments, the reliability was decreased, especially the DBC algorithm only considers the two constraints of time and cost, without considering the reliability demand of task. Therefore, the proposed in this paper is superior to the DBC algorithm in the average task reliability, and this is also the prominent advantage of the proposed algorithm over the DBC algorithm.

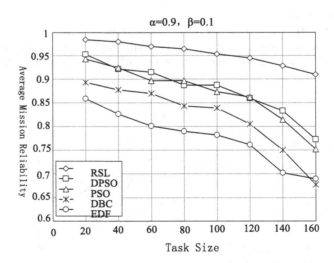

Fig. 5. Comparison of average mission reliability (when $\alpha = 0.9$, $\beta = 0.1$)

It can be seen from the above experiments, that the average task reliability of the performance, the proposed algorithm in general and extreme conditions are significantly better than the DBC algorithm, DPSO algorithm, PSO algorithm and EDF algorithm. Based on two experiments can be seen, although the proposed algorithm in all task completion time and the average task cost has little advantage compared with other algorithms, but from the average task reliability experiments show that the algorithm has obvious advantages than other algorithms. Therefore, this algorithm can realize the task scheduling time and cost, and in the acceptable range, it can provide highly reliable task scheduling, and realize the task scheduling goal in this paper.

5 Conclusions

The RSL algorithm proposed in this paper is slightly better than other algorithms in all task completion time and average task overhead compared with other algorithms and is in a relatively reasonable range. It is important that the RSL algorithm proposed in this paper is superior to other algorithms in terms of average task reliability, scheduling budget violation rate and deadline violation rate.

Acknowledgment. This work was supported by the China Postdoctoral Science Foundation by (2017M611407) and National Natural Science Foundation of China (31770768), the Natural Science Foundation of Heilongjiang Province of China (F2017001), the Fundamental Research Funds for the Central Universities (2572017CB32).

References

1. Duselis, J.U., Cauich, E.E., Wang, R.K., Scherson, I.D.: Resource selection and allocation for dynamic adaptive computing in heterogeneous clusters. In: IEEE International Conference on Cluster Computing & Network, pp. 1–9 (2009)
2. Schwertner, K.: Cloud computing as area of modern industry. J. Mod. Account. Audit. **8**, 907 (2012)
3. Ashraf, A.: Cost-efficient virtual machine provisioning for multi-tier web applications and video transcoding. In: IEEE/ACM International Symposium on Cluster, pp. 66–69 (2013)
4. Ebrahimi, M., Mohan, A., Kashlev, A., Lu, S.: BDAP: a big data placement strategy for cloud-based scientific workflows. In: IEEE First International Conference on Big Data, pp. 105–114 (2015)
5. Ramos, B., Farah, J.P.S., Teixeira, A.C.S.C.: Estimating reaction constants by ab initio molecular modeling: a study on the oxidation of phenol to catechol and hydroquinone in advanced oxidation processes. Braz. J. Chem. Eng. **29**(1), 113–120 (2012)
6. Calheiros, R.N., Buyya, R.: Meeting deadlines of scientific workflows in public clouds with tasks replication. IEEE Trans. Parallel Distrib. Syst. **25**(7), 1787–1796 (2014)
7. Hsu, C.-H., Slagter, K.D., Chen, S.-C., Chung, Y.-C.: Optimizing energy consumption with task consolidation in clouds. Inf. Sci. **258**, 452–462 (2014)
8. Liang, Q., Zhang, J., Zhang, Y.-H., Liang, J.-M.: The placement method of resources and applications based on request prediction in cloud data center. Inf. Sci. **279**, 735–745 (2014)
9. Convolbo, M.W., Chou, J.: Cost-aware DAG scheduling algorithms for minimizing execution cost on cloud resources. J. Supercomput. **72**(3), 985–1012 (2016)
10. Hu, Z., Wu, K., Huang, J.: An utility-based job scheduling algorithm for current computing cloud considering reliability factor. In: Proceedings of the 2012 IEEE 3rd International Conference on Software Engineering and Service Science, pp. 296–299 (2012)

11. Mandal, A., et al.: Scheduling strategies for mapping application workflows onto the grid. In: Proceedings of the 14th International Symposium on High Performance Distributed Computing (HPDC 2005), North Carolina, USA, pp. 125–134 (2005)
12. Iverson, M., Özgüner, F.: Hierarchical, competitive scheduling of multiple dags in a dynamic heterogeneous environment. Distrib. Syst. Eng. 3(6), 112–120 (1999)
13. Zhang, Y., Squillante, M.S., Sivasubramaniam, A., Sahoo, R.K.: Performance implications of failures in large-scale cluster scheduling. In: Feitelson, D.G., Rudolph, L., Schwiegelshohn, U. (eds.) JSSPP 2004. LNCS, vol. 3277, pp. 233–252. Springer, Heidelberg (2005). https://doi.org/10.1007/11407522_13
14. Zheng, Q., Veeravalli, B., Tham, C.-K.: On the design of fault-tolerant scheduling strategies using primary-backup approach for computational grids with low replication costs. IEEE Trans. Comput. 58(3), 380–393 (2009)

Topology Layout Technology of Energy Internet

Liandong Chen[1], Boyao Zhang[2,3], Fang Liu[2(✉)], Jingquan Li[1],
and Chenjun Sun[1]

[1] State Grid Hebei Electric Power Company, Shijiazhuang, China
[2] Department of High Performance Computing Technology
and Application Development, Computer Network Information Center,
Chinese Academy of Science, Beijing, China
liufang@sccas.cn
[3] University of Chinese Academy of Sciences, Beijing, China

Abstract. With the development of economy, the number of substations and the number of lines is continuously increasing, and the Energy Internet is becoming increasingly complex and changes frequently. It is more and more difficult to map the topology of energy grids used for large-scale dispatching by manpower. It is urgent to use computer-based collaborative systems and automated algorithms to solve the problem of Energy Internet topology layout.

The current general practice is to manually draw a one-line diagram and manually configure the real-time amount. Under normal circumstances, adjustments have been made on existing one-line diagrams; due to factors such as complex grid structure and the number of rows that are generally arranged by screen size, etc. In some complex areas, it will become more and more difficult to increase substations, increase or adjust lines to meet the basic requirements of energy Internet topology, which has exceeded the manpower.

The current Energy Internet expansion and transformation are more frequent, and the grid size is getting larger and larger, the corresponding automation transformation is also very frequent. It is determined that the topological layout of the energy Internet will also be updated frequently. At present, the wiring diagram production and maintenance of the Energy Internet are all completed manually. The pressure for manual production and adjustment of large-screen dispatches is increasing. It is eager to use computer-based collaborative systems and automated algorithms to solve the problem of frequent topology updates of energy Internet. This paper studies the topology theory of the Energy Internet, design and implementation of the topology algorithm of the Energy Internet.

Keywords: Layout problem · Energy Internet · Automatic layout · Simulated annealing algorithm

1 Introduction

This paper focuses on the issue of automatic layout of energy Internet topology. The layout theory has been widely studied and applied in the layout of irregular polygons such as integrated circuits and material cuttings and the layout of container components.

C. Hu et al. (Eds.): HPCMS 2018/HiDEC 2018, CCIS 913, pp. 235–245, 2019.
https://doi.org/10.1007/978-981-32-9987-0_20

In theory, the layout problem is a complex combinatorial optimization problem and NP complete problem, and its global optimal solution exists quite difficult. The problem of layout of energy internet topology is a professional layout problem with its own characteristics [1–4]. The main research content of this paper is as follows:

First introduced the automatic layout problem and the significance of the research on the automatic layout of the energy internet. Afterwards, the background knowledge involved in the research process of the subject was introduced, including the automatic routing rules, and several common random optimization algorithms were compared. Then, based on the study of the existing layout problems, the model of the layout problem and the corresponding solution method are studied and analyzed, which lays a theoretical foundation for solving the layout problem. The issue of automatic generation of single-line diagrams for large screen transmission networks has been proposed, fully considered the scheduling staff's habits of layout, and reduced the dimension of the solution to improve the efficiency of the solution. An automatic layout algorithm based on simulated annealing algorithm is proposed. It is calculated on the discretization of substation geographical coordinates or on any other initial solution, and a global optimization solution can be obtained, it calculates the substation geographical coordinates or other arbitrary initial solutions. The traditional method and the comparative method are used to choose the parameter, and taking the substation data model of a supply area as a case, the automatic layout algorithm was verified.

2 Energy Internet Topology

The application of graphics in Energy Internet topology systems has been very extensive, there are transmission network geographical wiring diagram, plant station wiring diagram and transmission network system wiring diagram etc. [5–8]. However, most current dispatch centers still use manual maintenance of these graphics. Therefore, the automatic generation of graphics has been widely and deeply researched. However, the automatic generation of complex and large-scale transmission grid diagrams has not made much progress. The automatic generation of the transmission grid pattern can be used to refer to the layout and wiring of the general network or circuit system, and is divided into two steps: layout and wiring.

The layout problem is given a layout space and a number of objects to be clothed, layout objects are reasonably distributed in a given space under certain constraints and achieve some optimal results. The layout and wiring theory and applications have been widely studied and applied, such as analog circuits, integrated circuits, machinery manufacturing, material cutting, transportation, medical physics applications, etc. Irregular polygon layouts and container component layouts are also included.

According to the space to be clothed and the shape of the object to be clothed, the layout problem is divided into: (1) The layout of two-dimensional regular objects or irregular objects; (2) The layout problem of 3D regular objects or irregular objects. The layout problem of the regular shapes such as circular or square objects to be clothed and objects to be clothed belongs to the layout problem of two-dimensional rules, such as the layout problem of Energy Internet topology. The space to be clothed and the objects to be clothed are at least one two-dimensional irregular object, which is a problem of two-dimensional irregular layout, such as the problem of cutting leather fabrics and cutting of steel plates.

So far, most of the theoretical research and practical application of layout problems have been limited to the regular objects. For such a layout, it has become an NP-complete problem in itself and can be abstracted as an expression of a purely mathematical model, which can be solved by using heuristic algorithms and other intelligent optimization algorithms. There are mainly two types of existing studies on the automatic layout of plant site wiring diagrams: gridless continuous layout algorithms and gridded discrete layout algorithms. In the former algorithm, the screen is divided into a number of equally-spaced grids, an algorithm is used to determine the grid in which each plant is located, and then the plant station graphics are plotted according to the size of the grid. In the latter algorithm, an algorithm is used to calculate the coordinates of the center position of the graphic of each station, and then the drawing of the station is plotted according to the coordinates.

Singaporean scholars have proposed wiring algorithms using large-scale circuit designs. The main principles are "The shortest connecting lines, the least crossings, and the even distribution of components". The force-directed method is used for layout. The wiring is divided into three processes: floor planning, placement, and routing. This method uses transmission networks as the main research object. This method uses transmission networks as the main research object, uses power plants to establish directed trees, elements (bars, circuit breakers) with the same series from roots are placed on the same ordinate.

The layout problem can be transformed into a combinatorial optimization problem. For example, when scheduling large-scale substation layouts, you can think of the power graph as a rectangular grid with M rows and N columns, each substation can be placed in the center of each grid. For N_sub substations, it is obviously required that N_sub is less than the product of M and N, and there is a connection between substations. It is required to arrange the positions of each substation in a rectangular grid so that the connection between them does not cross and the distance between the connections is as short as possible. Obviously, this problem cannot be expressed as a polynomial function of its size N_sub, that is, the layout problem belongs to the NP problem.

Here are some common layout algorithms [9–13]: Sugiyama proposed a good algorithm. The algorithm is divided into three phases: distribute vertices on each layer $O(|V| + |E|)$; minimize edge crossing (NP hard, but good heuristics); give the coordinates $O(|E|)$. Fruchteman and Reingold developed only two rules for graph layout:1. The connected edges must be close; 2. Different vertices cannot be close. This very simple algorithm produces very good results and its main point is the speed and stability, which is still one of the most commonly used graph layout algorithms.

3   Design and Implementation of Energy Internet Topology Layout Algorithm

The network topology is to graphically display the network topology information in the data file. It is an image between two different displays of data, from a text-based image to a graphical one in order to visually pass information to the user. By using automatic layout, Energy Internet topology can be achieved quickly and accurately. However, there are no accepted evaluation criteria for the automatic layout method. Therefore, most people designate the following aesthetic standards according to the layout effect [14–19]. The project mainly evaluates three aspects:

(a) Minimize the intersection of edges, and arrange the nearest nodes

Reducing the intersection of edges can make the layout look clearer. However, the intersection of edges in a two-dimensional figure that describes the topology of a Energy Internet is inevitable. The current automatic layout module arranges directly connected nodes according to the connection relationship of the nodes. For the same electrical equipment and subnet layout features, it highlights the physical connections and logical relationships between the nodes.

(b) Automatically determine the priority based on the node type and level

For a given data, the automatic layout module can clearly identify the central device and place it in a relatively central location; for other devices and sub-networks connected to the central device, the hierarchical layout is arranged on the concentric circle centered on the central device according to the different levels of the network. The radius of each level is automatically determined based on the number of nodes and the size of the layout. Nodes on the same level can be roughly evenly distributed on the circumference according to the connection relationship. Operators can easily distinguish the level of each network device, and the connection between devices and subnets at different levels.

(c) According to the characteristics of the Energy Internet, it is possible to clearly distinguish different node groups based on the degree of node correlation and highlight regional characteristics.

The automatic layout of Energy Internet topology and other automatic layout applications have obvious characteristics of the Energy Internet environment. Most devices and subnets appear in pairs and are in a similar position to ensure the robustness of the network. The automatic layout module focuses on the characteristics of the data itself and highlights this feature in the graphic display to make it more practical.

Nodes are divided into groups and meet the operator's layout habits and requirements to the greatest degree, while taking into account the physical connections between the actual devices. The automatic layout module enables the identification and division of equipment and power sub-networks at different voltage levels and their decentralized layout. For a compact layout of interconnected nodes in the same node group, the interleaving and overlap between different node groups is reduced. In short, the distances between connected nodes tend to be uniform, strive to evenly distribute, enhance the level of automatic layout effects, and the overall appearance of the graphics.

3.1   Automatic Layout Analysis

The method of automatic layout algorithm is roughly divided into three steps: First, the layout effect to be achieved is specified; second, the order in which the coordinates are assigned is determined; finally, a sequence that satisfies the conditions is designed and implemented in the preprocessing stage.

When the Energy Internet worker performs automatic layout of the network topology, the topology information to be laid out is first loaded, which may be obtained from a file, or may be obtained from topology auto-discovery. Then perform automatic layout, according to different levels of network nodes, different network topology, according to the automatic layout of the initial layout, choose the appropriate layout. Finally, save the layout result, and it can be directly rendered the next time it is applied, as shown in the following Fig. 1:

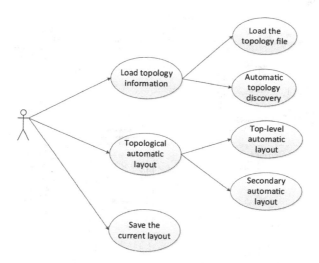

Fig. 1. A figure of automatic layout analysis.

(1) Load topology information: Collect topology information by loading topology files or using the topology auto-discovery function. Loading and parsing these data can be used for automatic layout. Loads the topology file, reads and parses all the information about the topology objects and connections saved in the specified file.

(2) Topology automatic layout: It can automatically select or manually specify the appropriate layout algorithm to automatically layout the current topology, construct clear and beautiful topological maps, realize the visualization of the physical or logical topology of the network, and facilitate the user to find, analyze and locate.

(3) Top-level automatic layout: The system automatically scans the topology files and automatically lays out the topological relationships between the highest voltage

nodes. Users adjust the layout of the automatic layout according to the geographic location. Finally, the purpose of rational arrangement of layout is reached.

(4) Secondary automatic layout: After the automatic layout system completes the layout of the top node, the layout of the secondary nodes is performed according to the results of the cluster analysis according to the top node association.

(5) Save the current layout: Write a satisfactory topology map to a file, save it to a local disk, and save the topology map that has been completely laid out and edited so that it can be directly loaded in the future and improve efficiency.

3.2 Algorithm Design

The process of automatic layout of network topology is mainly divided into three stages: data file analysis and conversion, data collection and processing, and finally data display (Fig. 2).

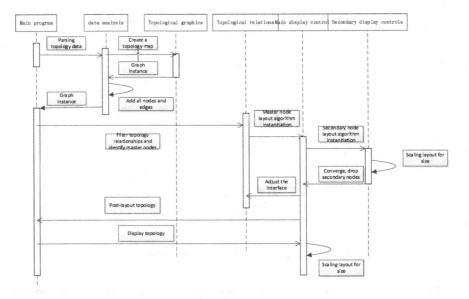

Fig. 2. A figure of automatic layout process.

In the data file analysis and conversion phase, the topology data file is obtained and analyzed accordingly. Extracting and transforming is the process of constructing the topology map data structure. The data collection and processing stage identifies and judges the previously obtained topology map. Performing preprocessing and automatic layout algorithms and transmitting them to the visual interface is the focus of algorithm research. The data display stage is based on different display requirements of users. The corresponding data is collected from the visual data interface, transmitted to the visualization engine for display, and the corresponding network topology elements are displayed according to the obtained data.

In order to adapt to the automatic layout of a variety of network conditions, only one layout algorithm is difficult to meet the needs, so through the integration of resources, research and development of a variety of automatic layout algorithms to build a strong practicality, a wide range of applications to meet a variety of needs. The independent topological auto layout component. For a specific meta-node such as bus, double-wrap, triple-wrap and other basic layout algorithms, encapsulate a unified call interface. The hybrid layout algorithm based on the secondary node model is fully studied and improved so that it can be applied to the topology layout of large-scale power networks.

3.2.1 Layout Algorithm Based on the Master Node

The nodes in the figure represent the objects to be laid out, and the edges between the nodes represent the determined connection relationships between the objects to be clothed. This translates the complex layout problem into the problem of finding the largest independent subset in a graph of known connection relationships. Then solve the problem by means of integer programming and dynamic programming.

3.2.2 Layout Algorithm Based on the Secondary Nodes

After the main node topology display layer layout is completed, a rectangular element is used as a layered model, and the position in the graph conforms to the relative geographical position. Manual assistant tools based on sub-windows can be used to manually adjust the relative position, space size, and intuition to judge whether there is an intersection, and to write partition parameters or layout parameters to the database. The basic idea of the simulated annealing algorithm is effectively used, and the distance between the number of crossover points and the distance between the lines is taken as an objective function. The effect of the subsequent wiring is also taken into consideration, and layout-wiring multiple loops can be avoided. Substation locations are randomly exchanged and the substation locations are automatically arranged. The proposed automatic layout algorithm based on simulated annealing algorithm, which is calculated on the initial solution to obtain a global optimization solution, which achieves effects that many local optimization methods cannot achieve.

3.2.3 Main Layout and Secondary Layout Fusion Algorithm

In order to be concise and beautiful, the routing uses direct, bi-fold, and quad-fold lines. The wiring categories are divided into the following four categories according to the positional relationship of the substations:

(1) Start and end substations on the same line: When two nodes are peers and neighbors, direct routes are used. When two nodes are peers but not adjacent, the four nodes are used.

(2) Start and end substations are in the same column: When two nodes are in the same column and adjacent, direct lines are used. When the two nodes are in the same column but not adjacent to each other, a four-fold line is used to route the two nodes.

(3) The terminal substation is at the bottom left of the starting substation: When two nodes are separated by one line, double fold line is used. When two nodes are separated by multiple lines, four fold line is used.

(4) The terminal substation is at the lower right of the starting substation: When two nodes are separated by one line, double fold line is used. When two nodes are separated by multiple lines, four fold line is used.

It should be noted that the trajectory of the route is determined by the coordinates of the point. For example, if the direct route is determined by two points, the bifurcation line is defined by four points, and the four-fold line is determined by the coordinates of the six points. And in the two coordinate values of the next point in the routing operation, one coordinate will hold one coordinate of the previous point at least. For example, if the horizontal direction, will keep the y-coordinate value of the previous point unchanged; the vertical direction will keep the x coordinate value of the previous point unchanged.

4   Results

The system draws a preliminary topology map based on the read topology connectivity of each node, according to the layout requirements, for example, no cross or other principles are allowed. Then through the interface operation, fix a few key points and continue to optimize. As shown in Fig. 3, a preliminary topology map is finally generated.

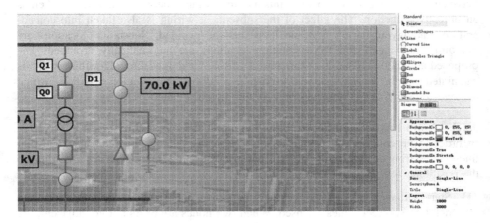

Fig. 3. A preliminary topology map

As shown in Figs. 4 and 5, then system-supplied tools are used to replace elements of different electrical types already laid out with specific types of graphics. Finally, the result generated in Fig. 3 are laid out on a new canvas, and the types of appliances are identified with different colors, and the user is allowed to make modifications on the basis thereof.

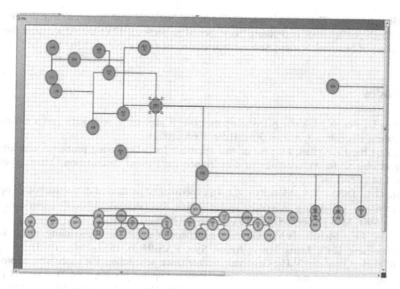

Fig. 4. Example of specific types of graphics.

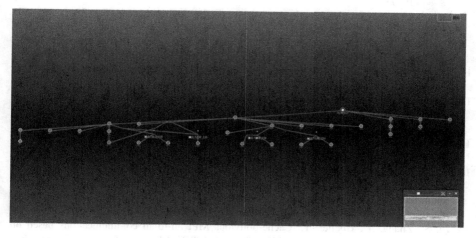

Fig. 5. Example of Energy Internet topology layout

5   Conclusion

This paper establishes a model for solving the problem of automatic layout of Energy Internet and the objective function of the optimization scheme, the automatic layout optimization program based on combination of hierarchical algorithm and core node layout algorithm, regional conflict adjustment layout algorithm and automatic routing algorithm. An automatic layout algorithm based on simulated annealing algorithm is proposed.

Acknowledgements. This work was supported by National key research and development program "high-performance computing" key special projects (2017YFB0202302) and the State Key Program of National Natural Science Foundation of China (No. 91530324).

References

1. Zhang, L., Pei, X., Ulrich, K.: Analog macro-cell placement with very fast simulated re-annealing algorithm. J. Softw. **3**(6), 1059–1068 (2002)
2. Dai, Z., Cha, J.Z., Yuan, J.L.: An oc-tree approach for 3-D packing problems with arbitrary shaped object. In: Proceedings of Conference on Design Automation, Minneapolis pp. 125–134 (1994)
3. Egan, G.T., Dillon, T.S., Morsztyn, K.: An experimental method of determination of optimal maintenance scheduling in power system using the branch-and-bound technique. IEEE Trans. Syst. Man Cybern. **SMC-6**(8), 538–547 (1976)
4. Dopazo, J.F., Merrill, H.M.: Optimal generator maintenance scheduling using integer programming. IEEE Trans. Power Appar. Syst. **PAS-94**(5), 1537–1545 (1975)
5. Zurn, H.H., Quintana, V.H.: Generator maintenance scheduling via successive approximations dynamic programming. IEEE Trans. Power Appar. Syst. **PAS-94**(2), 666–671 (1975)
6. Dowsland, K.A.: Efficient automated pallet loading. Eur. J. Oper. Res. **44**, 232–238 (1990)
7. Dowsland, K.A.: An exact algorithm for the pallet loading problem. Eur. J. Oper. Res. **31**, 78–84 (1987)
8. Leung, J.: A new graph-theoretic heuristic for facility layout. Manag. Sci. **38**(4), 594–605 (1992)
9. Dai, Z., Cha, J.Z.: A hybrid algorithm of heuristic and neural network for packing problems. In: Proceedings of Conference on Design Automation, Minneapolis, pp. 117–124 (1994)
10. Cao, Y.: Research on neural computational method for two-dimensional packing. Northern Jiao tong University, Beijing (1999). (in Chinese)
11. Klump, R., Schooley, D., Overbye, T.: Advanced visualization platform for real-time power system operation. In: Proceedings of 14th Power System Computation Conference, Sevilla, Spain, pp. 24–28 (2002)
12. Walker, J.Q.: A node-position algorithm for general tree. Softw. Pract. Exp. **20**(7), 685–705 (1990)
13. Wong, W.-C., Chan, P.C.H., Law, W.-O.: A technology-independent methodology of placement generation for analog circuit. In: Proceedings of the ASP-DAC 1999, Asia and South Pacific Design Automation Conference, 18–21 January 1999, vol. 1, Digital Object Identifier, pp. 141–144 (1999). https://doi.org/10.1109/ASPDAC.1999.759980
14. Li, S., Zhang, Y., Hoefler, T.: Cache-oblivious MPI all-to-all communications based on Morton order. IEEE Trans. Parallel Distrib. Syst. (TPDS'18) **29**(3), 542–555 (2018). (SCI, Impact factor: 4.181)
15. Zhang, Y., Li, S., Yan, S., Zhou, H.: A cross-platform SpMV framework on many-core architectures. ACM Trans. Archit. Code Optim. (TACO) **13**(4), 1–25 (2016). (Corresponding Author, SCI, Impact factor: 1.636)
16. Wu, B., Li, S., Zhang, Y., Nie, N.: Hybrid-optimization strategy for the communication of large-scale Kinetic Monte Carlo simulation. Comput. Phys. Commun. **211**, 113–123 (2017). (Corresponding Author, SCI, Impact factor: 3.635)
17. Li, S., Zhang, Y., Hoefler, T.: Cache-oblivious MPI all-to-all communications on many-core architectures. In: Proceedings of the 22nd ACM SIGPLAN Symposium on Principles and Practice of Parallel Programming (PPoPP 2017), Poster, pp. 445–446. ACM (2017)

18. Wang, J., Gao, F., Vazquez-Poletti, J.L., Li, J.: Preface of high performance computing or advanced modeling and simulation of materials. Comput. Phys. Commun. **211**, 1 (2017). (IF:3.653)
19. Wang, J., Liu, C., Huang, Y.: Auto tuning for new energy dispatch problem: a case study. Future Gener. Comput. Syst. **54**, 501–506 (2016). (IF: 2.430)

Author Index

Printed in the United States
By Bookmasters